The Good, the True and the Beautiful

Also available from Continuum:

What Philosophers Think, edited by Julian Baggini and
     Jeremy Stangroom
What More Philosophers Think, edited by Julian Baggini and
     Jeremy Stangroom
Philosophy for Life, Rupert Read
How to Win Every Argument, Madsen Pirie

The Good, the True and the Beautiful

A Quest for Meaning

Michael Boylan

continuum

Continuum International Publishing Group
The Tower Building, 11 York Road, London SE1 7NX
80 Maiden Lane, Suite 704, New York NY 10038

www.continuumbooks.com

British Library Cataloguing-in-Publication Data
A catalogue record for this book is available from the British Library.

ISBN-10: HB: 1-8470-6157-5
ISBN-13: HB: 978-1-8470-6157-7

Library of Congress Cataloguing-in-Publication Data
Boylan, Michael, 1952–
  The good, the true, and the beautiful : a quest for meaning / Michael Boylan.
    p. cm.
  Includes index.
  ISBN 978-1 -84706-157-7
1. Philosophy. 2. Ethics. 3. Truth. 4. Aesthetics. I. Title.
  BD21.B65 2008
  100--dc22
                                                                2007041473

Typeset by Kenneth Burnley, Wirral, Cheshire
Printed and bound in Great Britain by Cromwell Press Ltd, Trowbridge,
Wiltshire

Contents

Preface

Have you ever turned your head to your alarm clock (at whatever time that you are scheduled to wake up in the morning) and asked yourself the question: 'Why should I bother?' It is an important question. Why not close your eyes and sleep forever? Such a query is related to Albert Camus' famous speculation that the central question in philosophy is why we don't commit suicide. The most common response is about finding individual purpose. It's all about a *raison d'être*.

This book is about applying philosophy to one's own life profitably to make a positive difference and sharpen our own understanding of our life's purpose. Three popular candidates for our purpose in life are: (a) the good, (b) the true, and (c) the beautiful. These play out as follows.

Some say that the purpose in life – the object of our personal quest – should be becoming a good person. Of course, a lot depends upon what this means. 'Good' is often depicted prudentially as indicating 'good for my personal happiness'. If this is the case, then what constitutes the conditions that will satisfy this condition? Will money do it? Will power do it? Will sex do it? What does it really mean to be good? The first three chapters in Part 1 of the book address this problem in different ways.

Chapter 1 situates the quest within the realm of economics and the traditional theories of ethics and how these two concerns might be examined via a theory of rational choice called the personal worldview imperative. Readers are challenged through thought experiments to think about his or her own personal worldview and how it measures up to the evaluative criteria of good reasoning about individual purpose via the good. The tone of the presentation is evocative and meant to act as a stingray to focus the reader's mind to his or her own menagerie of facts and values that oftentimes veer in many contradictory directions. The admonition is to engage in a careful examination of who we are and who we wish to become. The criteria of the theory of rational choice via the personal worldview imperative give a structure for this process.

Chapter 2 discusses the possibility of altruism. It is the contention of this book that the possibility of altruism is essential to the possibility of ethics. Most of the major theories of ethics concur that unless it is possible to act contrary to one's egoistic advantage, that the project of morality is doomed. Thus, if altruism is false then maybe we should stop, throw in the towel, and look for purpose elsewhere.

Chapter 3 situates the discussion of finding purpose via structured analysis of the good in terms of a personal quest for self-fulfilment. Fulfilment is relative to some understanding of one's situation in the world and the nature of human beings in this process. Various possibilities are discussed and one approach is advocated that a major part of attaining self-fulfilment is tied up with becoming good.

Part 2 of the book highlights the quest for the true. Chapter 4 presents to the reader various traditional theories of truth and explores why we should be interested in examining them. With this vocabulary and set of concepts, the reader is ready to chart a course toward epistemology through the treacherous landscape of scepticism, illusion, and the sources of knowledge (Chapter 5).

Chapter 5 prompts the reader to explore what might count for an adequate grounding for knowledge. The problems addressed begin with the shoals of scepticism and appearance and reality. The groundwork for this standpoint rests upon the work done in Part 1 in deriving a proper personal standpoint that situates individual and social purpose. This standpoint allows the reader to ascertain which sources of knowledge are most reliable. Choosing between these options for a reliable source of knowledge requires one to recognize the external and internal approaches as well as how these are to be implemented and with what external constraints.

Chapter 6 situates the whole enterprise within the context of the tri-partite quest (the good, the true, and the beautiful). Just as the final chapter in Part 2 challenges the reader to consider the good in one's personal worldview and his place in the community worldview, so Chapter 6 asks the reader to ponder her personal theory of truth.

Finally, in Part 3 we approach the shores of the beautiful. Key figures in the history of philosophy and art criticism are brought forward with an eye to show how they also depend upon the good and the true in charting a purposeful course in life. Chapters 7 and 8 set out these thinkers in a critical context while Chapter 9 synthetically situates these myriad suggestions into four structured combinations that will stimulate the reader's own choice.

In the end, a process has been set out that strongly advocates that in order to arrive safely in the port of our personal and community purpose, we must have learned and mastered the tools of discovery and navigation: the good, the true, and the beautiful.

What is unique about this book is:

- A novel unifying approach to philosophy through philosophical worldview along with the personal worldview and community worldview imperatives.
- A conjecture that the relationship between the good, the true, and the beautiful is more than a relationship of minor resemblance. Rather, it is the case that one cannot explore any one of these three comprehensively without making reference to the other two.
- An original contention that the role of thought experiments is relevant only within a very specific range. Since this book is about applying philosophy to one's life profitably in order to make a positive difference, thought experiments need to be constrained so that they do not violate empirically based plausibility of what could possibly be the case. This is a novel restriction upon thought experiments.
- A bold contention that the process of self-reflection and discovery of meaning is analogous to the medieval European quest. Each reader is encouraged to follow along a positive path to personal self-improvement.

- A striking suggestion that art and the beautiful stand side-by-side with rationally based argumentation on the true and the good as a key component of our attaining authentic purpose. (Most often discussions of the beautiful are left out of philosophical discussions of the good and/or the true.)

It is my hope that readers will enjoy this journey and will accept the thrill of the quest. Such engagement in reflection and personal renewal are the most necessary and important of all human activities.

Acknowledgements

I have sought advice from quite a few people in the writing of this book. I would like to thank particularly: Annette Ames, Robert Paul Churchill, Bill Haines, Adam Kovach, and Wanda Teays for their comments. I would also like to thank the editorial team at Continuum: Sarah Campbell, Tom Crick and Neil Dowden. They helped make the book better. I also want to acknowledge my family – Rebecca (my wife), Arianne (my daughter), and Seán and Éamon (my sons). They put up with a lot and nurture me intellectually, emotionally, and spiritually. I dedicate this book to my family.

Part 1
The Good

1   Being Good

It is difficult to become a good person
Built flawlessly: foursquare in hands, feet, and mind.
Simonides of Ceos[1]

It's not that way, it's over here; it's not that way, it's over here . . .
From Eugène Ionesco, *The Bald Soprano*[2]

The Problem

How do we become good? Almost everyone that we meet presents us with a different prescription. Some claims tout becoming the 'material girl' (or boy): get the right clothes, the right cell phone, and the right set of wheels and you're there, baby! Having the right stuff makes you cool.

Other claims suggest that notoriety is what it's all about: find your 15 minutes of fame and you're set.[3] It doesn't matter whether your 15 minutes characterizes you as a hero or as a villain. There is no such thing as bad publicity.

A third popular way to become good is to become powerful: when you have the power you are invincible – just ask the fictional character Emperor Palpatine of *Star Wars* fame.[4] Getting power makes you awesome.

These first three ways are all about being good via the judgements and standards of others. Being good is based upon extrinsic criteria. Personally evaluating the criteria is rather senseless. They present themselves to you. Get on board or get off the train.

A fourth way takes a different track: being good is about fidelity to some norm or standard that is independently justified. Being good is about adjusting one's self to this standard. Sounds promising, but how does one discover the standard? Where is its authority?

This fourth approach is an instance where seeking the good requires thinking about the true. If one could justifiably discover such a standard, then surely one would be intrinsically compelled to follow it.

But how are we to know? How are we to choose?

Why Should We Bother About Being Good?

This is the million-dollar question. What would it be like if we didn't bother at all? We would be just like other animals that probably don't have such qualms.[5] These animals (many believe) just go about their tasks of foraging for food, avoiding predators, and mating (as often as possible). In this case there is no conscious aiming at anything good apart from the satisfaction of these basic biological needs. Some philosophers think humans are like this, too.[6] If that is the case, then how is it that we get such questions about being good into our heads? Why is it that we humans (across cultures and across time) seem to be interested in more than mere satisfaction of basic biological drives? One way to begin to answer the question is to start at our biological beginning as children.

For the most part, all of us when we are young want to be good. Our parents have their own message. They tell us to be good boys and girls. They mean different things by this. At the most practical level it amounts to: keep out of trouble and don't embarrass us. After all (the parents might assert) they work very hard to pay the bills so that the children might live a good life; therefore, the children should be compliant. In our youth, such an argument made sense to many of us.

Our society also sets before us a template of prescribed behaviour. No matter the version, the script is familiar to us all. If you do what they tell you to and don't make trouble, then there are some nice goodies that await you down the road. Be nice and Uncle Sam will give you a lollipop.

There are many senses of being good that are presented to us as we grow up, but what is most important are the *reasons* for being good, which may be quite a different matter. For example, your boyfriend might tell you that if you submerge your ego into *his* vision of life and if you are willing to sign on the bottom line, then you are good (and your parents might even agree!). However, you may not be so amenable to accepting the reasons that he proposes.

The first three of these prescriptions for living well or being good (above) begin *outside* of us. They have the society's imprimatur. As such, they form the basis of assumed group consciousness. Society and its institutions try to bring us all on board via intensive advertising. These are reasons, too. We all know that advertisers generally have a self-interested motive involved in trying to sell us on their own line of merchandise. These hawkers of wares include the commercial environment. The social inclination to be like others living near us is very great. It is so great that I have relegated this sort of good to a middle order of those things to which we all aspire.[7] For example, in the United States (at the writing of this book) roughly two-thirds of all adult citizens own a house or condominium of their own. Our entire tax code is skewed so that those who follow this road will be rewarded over those who do not or cannot. If you have a house in America you are good (economically) and if you do not own a house, you are probably not good (economically). When you add this onto the general social inclination to view the economic interpretation as primary, then these messages are powerful, indeed.

The economic interpretation reaches many levels. Children talk about the latest toys. Teenagers talk about electronic gadgets and clothes. Adults trot out houses, cars, and fancy vacations to show others that they are good.

Along these lines there are also the views of the good that require 15 minutes of fame. These are the folks at the cocktail party who are not shy about assuring you that you are quite lucky to be standing there at this very moment talking to *them*. This is because of their supreme importance. They tell you this even as their eyes scan the room for someone more important to whom they will sing their song of self-importance.

Then there are the devotees of power. At the writing of this book, I have spent the last 22 years in Washington, DC, magnet to those who hunger and thirst for power. Many of these Machiavellis in their power steel-blue tweed skirt-suits or in their navy blazers and Oxford grey trouers ooze alpha dominance. When you meet them, watch out. One untoward look and you are history. They are VIPs who do not bear fools lightly. Beware!

What these various *external* senses of good have in common is that they all require recognition from a real or perceived social group. Being good in this context means that people think well of us. When we were children this was signified by a kiss on the cheek, a pat on the head, or a large smile from our parents. When we received these external signs, then we knew we were being good. We might be confused about what prompted these smiles and rewards, but why quarrel with a positive thing?

As we grow up, our parents become less important in that way. We place ourselves inside other social groups and accept *their* judgements. What the members of those groups say to us is similar to being kissed by our parents. It takes the form of laudatory statements or signs of approval. These signs confirm to us that we are good.

Ah, but how transitory this can be! One day the teenager is admired for his new sweater and the next he is despised for his new pimples. This transitory nature of praise makes us look at our language a bit. The participle 'being' has the temporal emphasis of *now* attached to it. We may be good on Thursday afternoon, but that can change by Friday. The standard indicatives 'am', 'is', and 'are' connote a rather more permanent state. Saying, 'my father is good' seems to imply that he *possesses* something like a quality that won't ever change, viz., goodness. When I say that my father is good, it is as if it were set in stone. I could carve it as his epitaph.

So perhaps it is the case that we aspire to *be* good, but on a day-to-day assessment, the most we can hope for is *being* good for some transitory period of time. Our names are writ in water. This is especially true when the standards for goodness are external.

It is rather sad in a way to relegate one's self to being good only for a fleeting interval of time. There is within each of us an inclination towards the permanent. Hippocrates said in the first aphorism, 'Life is short and art is long.' This saying is very attractive to many of us –

especially to artists. Islam and Christianity offer the possibility of eternal life. This appeals to the same inclination. However the aphorism is reinterpreted, it means (at the very least) that we are all attracted to something good that will last longer than something that will be more fleeting. This is demonstrated by the fact that if we had to choose, most of us would rather be permanently good than temporarily good.

But, of course, many of us often pay little heed to the long term. Some even suggest that achieving some singular act (a short term good) is worth long-term pain.[8] For example, many athletes risk permanent injury in their quest for that one moment of glory in which their body is able to perform at its maximum. In these cases, the individual may accept long-term pain for short-term renown. From the point of view of the agent he is willing to accept physical debility over the long haul as the price of a moment of physical excellence.

Now some would say that this is not a counter-example at all. They would assert that the sportsman or sportswoman, who becomes permanently injured for one great act, has the memory of that achievement all his or her life. This *memory* is the long-term good that he or she uniquely possesses. The possession of this good (the memory and recognition of the achievement) is priceless.

THOUGHT EXPERIMENT 1.1[9]

You are on the Olympic team for your country. If you get a medal (gold, silver, or bronze), then your life in that country will be (at the very least) full of praise and material comforts until the next Olympics (an event that occurs every four years). Now it is not so very clear that you will get a medal. You are in a group of about twenty that could make it. If you take an illegal performance-enhancing drug, then your chances increase dramatically. Now a trainer, Julian, approaches you to offer you such a drug. He says that it won't be detected by any present testing. What do you do?

What if Julian said to you that he's positive that the drug couldn't be detected and that not only will you get a medal, but also it will be the gold medal. The only downside is that with this second drug

you have an almost certain chance of dying in five years. (But those
five years might be very pleasurable.) What do you do?

Thought Experiment 1.1 shows that it is hard to assess this sort of
claim unless we try to transform the possession of the good into a
pleasure quantity and compare it to the pain – using intensity and
time parameters. But this moves us away from being good. For the
time being, let us agree that the pursuit of the good is different from
the pursuit of pleasure (see Chapter 2).

All of these observations depend upon a model of receiving goods
from the outside – externally. The possession of these goods (be they
glory and renown as in Thought Experiment 1.1 or some other
source of social reinforcement) makes us believe that we are good.
We use norms outside of ourselves as the source of our own self-
assessment. The most popular exterior norm comes from society as a
whole. We use social norms to tell us what is good and how we might
become good. Since the social/economic 'outside' comes from a
variety of sources, shaping our judgement of good based upon these
criteria will result in a rather haphazard collection of standards for
goodness. These might include what sort of car to buy, how we
should look: fat, thin (or counterfeits of the same), hairstyle, fashion,
political opinions, religious opinions, artistic opinions, and who will
win the Super Bowl – all of these standards are carriers of normative
value. When they are chosen rather unreflectively à la carte and
piecemeal, they will not form any sort of coherent whole (but more
on that later).

Another worldview perspective is the internal standpoint. The
difference between the two can be illustrated by Plato's recitation of
the myth of Gyges. There once was a shepherd (an ancestor of
Gyges) who found a magical ring that would make the holder invisible. With such a ring, Gyges became invisible and killed the king and
married the queen.[10] The shepherd (now king) lived on external
standards only. When he could act in such a way that he was invisible
to man (the relevant external standard), then he reverted to *kraterism*. ('Kraterism' is a term I use to denote those who act on the sole
imperative of exercising their own power: 'to each according to his

ability to snatch it.' In the context of this chapter the term will be extended to all three of the externally based positions of money, fame, and power.) The goal of Plato in the rest of the *Republic* is to explore whether external grounds for morality are inevitable or whether there are also internal standards.

If external standards are *not* inevitable, then there is a possibility of being good that is grounded on intrinsic principles. How does one decide which is better? There are several possibilities that can be further tied to theories of knowledge (see Part II). The manner of the ethical/epistemological interaction requires us to make decisions about ethics and implied truth claims. One camp, the moral realists, believes there are moral facts in the world. Another camp, the moral anti-realists, denies this – more on this shortly. What is important here are the interdependence of the good and the true (since our understanding of this relation will colour how we understand the content of becoming good).

It is asserted in this volume that by nature we all desire to become good. It's human nature. We seek the state of being good. In that quest we employ various tools to guide us. These include the source and content of truth and of beauty. The question before us is how do we get there?

Economics and All That Jazz

In the first section of this chapter there were four prescriptions for being good: material acquisition, notoriety, power, and fidelity to some norm or standard that transcends social and historical contexts because it is based upon some internally accepted principle of human nature. The first three of these are about the human agent as an agent of power grasping and snatching what he will. We are good when we get a large quantity of material goods. Under this standard, Bill Gates (the founder of Microsoft) is the best man on earth. It's rather easy to measure: *Fortune* magazine publishes an annual list of the richest people on earth. Under this standard these are the best people in serial order from one to one hundred. Though this category is easy to measure, it is rather ambiguous whether the ability to amass money makes one good or merely makes one competent at a particular sort of game set in an historical time and place. In the early 1970s the world champion at chess was Bobby Fischer. Though most would cede to him supreme competence at chess, few would call him a good man.[11] This is because of his anti-social and bigoted positions against Jews and others.[12]

The second category of fame is a little more difficult to measure. Notoriety is a function of the public consciousness (what I call the shared community worldview). I suppose that the best way to ascertain who is foremost in our minds is to take a carefully constructed psychological poll.

THOUGHT EXPERIMENT 1.2

1. Write on a piece of paper the twenty names of individuals living or dead who come to mind.
2. Now cross out all people who are personal friends, relatives, teachers, etc.
3. Now re-arrange those who are left into three categories: the villains, the saints, and the competent.
4. Which of the three categories is greater? What does that tell you?

I have given this test to many of my classes over the years. For college-aged individuals the villains always won (by a large amount). What does this mean? That they'd rather laugh with the sinners than cry with the saints because the sinners have much more fun?[13] Perhaps villains place themselves highly in our collective consciousness because of various primitive factors of 'fight or flight'. I don't know.

Rarely do students cite people of the fourth category.[14] If the role of the villain is merely another instance of kraterism as fame, then such responses by my students also square with the popular press. In my home town of Washington, DC when Diana Spencer, the Princess of Wales, died in a car crash in Paris along with her lover, Dodi Al-Fayed on 31 August 1997, the story ran on the front pages of the newspapers and the top stories of the radio and television for weeks. Around the same time (5 September 1997) Mother Teresa of Calcutta also died. Now it is true that Lady Diana died first, but at least in the Washington, DC market and on national American television there was so much coverage of Lady Diana that Mother Teresa was relegated to interior pages of the newspaper.

Why is this?

The only way to answer this question is to examine the two characters as per thought experiment 1.2. Who was Lady Diana? She was the former Princess of Wales within one of the most prominent economic powers of the world, the United Kingdom. She was known for being flashy (never wearing the same dress in public twice – though each one was quite pricey – materialism), she made several charity photo-ops for causes she believed in, and she was once the potential Queen of England (a position of notoriety). On the kraterism index she scores a clear 2 of 3.

And then there is Mother Teresa of Calcutta. Her clothes were plain, she lived her oath of poverty, and her only power was in virtue of others trying to imitate her standard of service to others. On the kraterism index she barely ticks a fraction of a point.

It seems that most Americans are like my students in preferring to think about and revere the realm of renown (since by all accounts, in the realm of fidelity to an internal standard of abstract goodness, Mother Teresa far surpassed Diana Spencer – even though the latter did engage in some important charity work).

The inclination toward notoriety is not new, and it has always been controversial. For example, the fourteenth-century poet Petrarch said in his poem 'The Triumph of Fame':[15]

> What is renown? – a gleam of transient light
> That soon an envious cloud involves in night.
> While passing Time's malignant hands diffuse
> On many a noble name pernicious dews.

Petrarch speaks disparagingly about fame as a measure of being good. His criterion is permanence. (Fame is assumed to be transitory.)

When we think about a criterion for being good we must think both about the allure that we all feel toward fame versus these possible objectors.

The third category to measure under kraterism is power. There are various ways of measuring power. A popular way to measure it in the private sector is to determine the size of the budget you manage. (This assumes a direct connection between money and power.) The larger the budget you control, the more powerful a person you are. Again, in the United States, at the writing of this book, the winner is Bill Gates.

In the public sector it is essentially the same thing, but there may be other factors at stake – such as the ability to lead a country to war (i.e. to be able to marshal the entire country's resources toward a project of one's own design). At the writing of this book, George W. Bush is the most powerful man in the world. He brought his country to war using criteria that are now very controversial. Anyone can lead a country to war with clear, externalist criteria: such as the bombing of Pearl Harbor. But it takes a very powerful man to lead a country to war based upon data that his own intelligence agency presented to him as sketchy.[16] That's power!

But does that make George W. Bush good? Even though most people in the United States would not disagree that George W. Bush is powerful, would they also call him a good person in virtue of this exercise of power? I think not.

Those who admire Bush do so because they admire what they view as his piety or what they consider to be his moral purpose but it is *not* because of his ability to wage a war with a flimsy portfolio of evidence.

Be it the private or the public sector I would suggest that kraterism, as power, is not generally recognized as being synonymous with being good.

This leaves the kraterism (interpreted as money, fame, or power) as an insufficient description of what it means to be good. We need something more. Enter the traditional theories of ethics.

Traditional Theories of Ethics

There are many ways to parse the traditional ethical theories. I have set out ethical theories into four groups: ethical intuitionism, virtue ethics, utilitarianism, and deontology.[17] The traditional theories of ethics prescribe a way of being good that requires fidelity to some norm or standard that is independently justified. Let's briefly look at each of these theories.

First, there is *ethical intuitionism*. This theory of ethics is tagged by its epistemological origins (as opposed to being named via the operation of the theory) because its advocates claim that there are no natural foundations for being good. We look in vain to nature if we want to understand what it means to be good. Often, this amounts to two distinct standpoints. The first standpoint is that of a theist who believes that the source of good comes from God. Since God, by definition, is non-natural, it would be impossible to connect to God's will via natural means such as logic and empiricism. Enter ethical intuitionism.

The second standpoint is that of an agnostic or atheist who believes that there is no source of good in nature and that the meaning of good is rather arbitrary. The only way to give it rigor is to take human society as a given and look to the way good is described in society. This is a rather social-science approach. If we can understand the way the word 'good' is used in society as a reason, then we can construct a *description* of good's action-driving force.[18] But what are we really saying here? 'Good' is nothing more than some contemporary social fixing of word use.[19] Thus, if the social context of 'good' among the Latino gangs of Los Angeles (e.g. the Bloods and the Crips) is that 'good' means protecting your space (even if that means committing mayhem and murder), then so be it. Among the gang, to be good is to be forceful at protecting the gang's turf. Other social groups may use the word differently. Among the Lancaster County, Pennsylvania Amish being good may mean the abandonment of all material adornment – such as wearing buttons to close one's shirt (straight pins being the option). What a difference! The worldview conception of the LA gang member with its commotion and competition is quite distinct from that of the Amish who eschew motorized vehicles, violence, and all things modern in their quest for simplicity. If language usage mirrors community worldview, then each group fixes a sense of good that is relative to their sociological ethos.

For this *second sense* of ethical intuitionism, this is sufficient. Ethics is about *describing* various uses of *prescribing*. No single sense is correct, by itself. All are relative to their social origins. They reflect a context in which a person finds himself. Ethics, in this sense, is about understanding one's context and then acting appropriately within that context. The context itself cannot be examined because there are no criteria to do so. This is a source of criticism to objectors. They see 'immediate grasping' as allowing for all sorts of prejudice and discriminatory conduct because it may be in the social usage and a tipping point to what appears 'correct'. This is the lynchpin to this approach because intuition is about the 'immediate'. Any contrary candidates that objectors might put forward would become 'mediating agents'. This brings us into the realm of rational criteria (the most popular mediating agent). Enter candidate number two.

Virtue ethics or character ethics is the second claimant to the mantel of ethical theory that should guide our search for the good. In virtue ethics the focus is upon the agent's character. Its position is that in living, a person should try to cultivate excellence in all that she does and all that others do. These excellences or virtues are both moral and non-moral. Through conscious training, as a non-moral example, an athlete can achieve excellence in a sport. In the same way, a person can achieve moral excellence as well. The way these habits are developed and the community that nurtures them are all under the umbrella of virtue ethics.

Proponents of virtue ethics view the task of morality as attaining personal integrity (wholeness). The emphasis is not upon particular actions (as is the case with ethical intuitionism, utilitarianism, and deontology), but is upon the construction of a complete individual. This is achieved by isolating various important moral excellences, such as courage, self-control, wisdom, and justice. By education, training, and habit, the individual achieves the ability to become moderate in his approach to the world. The theory assumes that people of good character act ethically. They may stumble occasionally, but the window of examination is over a period of time and is not a microscopic examination of some particular decision.

The education, training, and habit are fostered by close and caring families and micro communities (schools, neighbourhoods, churches/synagogues/mosques, etc.). In this way character and a moderate approach to the world are fostered.

Critics of virtue ethics say that 'character' is a term that is inherently relative to the community that fosters its agents. It faces the same difficulties that ethical intuitionism experiences in the LA gangs v. Pennsylvania Amish cases cited above. If it all goes back to the social community as the source (of language in the case of ethical intuitionism or of community values in the case of virtue ethics), then is there an absolute benchmark? Surely virtue ethics gives a different emphasis: one that supports personal integrity (wholeness). But doesn't it matter *how* one is whole? Is it the same to be a killer who has wholeness – meaning that he has consistent criteria about when and where to murder – and someone who has wholeness about kindness to others? Most would say that it does. Is there some standard to which one can appeal that supersedes considerations of changing social mores? Are there real criteria that exist in the world to which we can appeal in order to form moral judgements? Those who concur to this thesis are called moral realists. Those who do not agree that there are any moral criteria but merely descriptive word usage about relative social communities are called moral anti-realists. Moral realism leads to moral absolutism while anti-realism leads to relativism (under the guise of ethical intuitionism).

The final two categories that we will examine in the traditional theories of ethics focus upon those theories that espouse moral realism: utilitarianism and deontology.

The third category of traditional theories is *utilitarianism*. Utilitarianism is a theory that suggests that an action is morally right when that action produces more total utility for the group as a consequence than any other alternative does. Sometimes this has been shortened to the slogan, 'the greatest good for the greatest number'.

This emphasis upon calculating quantitatively the general population's projected consequential utility among competing alternatives appeals to many of the same principles that underlie democracy and capitalism (which is why this theory has always been very popular in the United States and other Western capitalistic democracies).

There are two strong arguments for utilitarianism: (a) its clear connection to naturalistic principles of science and of social science and (b) its social orientation. Let's look at these in order. First, when one looks at the world of nature he finds that the principle of pleasure and pain is very good at explaining a large variety of animal behaviour. If homo sapiens are animals, too, then perhaps the pleasure principle is a good explanatory principle among us, as well. Certainly, many experimental psychologists think this way.[20] They believe that hard science will support the view that the pleasure principle is a fundamental component in human nature. Thus, since the nineteenth century, the British utilitarians Bentham, Mill, and Sidgwick used the pleasure principle as a foundational posit to justify utilitarianism, believing that they have provided a naturalistic grounding for ethics.

Social scientists come into the picture in order to measure what the general will actually is at any particular point in time. Utilitarianism requires such a measurement procedure since it is inherently quantitative.

The second drawing card for utilitarianism is its social orientation. For many (including this author) the moral turn occurs when one puts aside his or her own personal interests because of some other more compelling reason that is not based upon personal interest.[21] Thus, utilitarianism's embracing of the social standpoint puts the advocate into the theoretical realm of ethic's origins (often called metaethics).

This social feature that is strength is also a weakness. Sometimes the emphasis upon the group can disadvantage minority individuals. Let's examine this possibility in a thought experiment.

THOUGHT EXPERIMENT 1.3

You are a constable of a small, remote rural town in Northern Ireland. The town is divided into the Irish Catholics (20 per cent minority) and the Irish Protestants (80 per cent majority). All the Catholics live in one section of town that sits on a peninsula that juts out into the river just east of the main section of town.

One morning a young Protestant girl is found raped and murdered next to the town green. By general consensus it is concluded that a Catholic must have committed the crime. The Protestants form a citizens committee that makes the following demand upon the constable: 'We believe you to be a Catholic sympathizer. Therefore, we do not think you will press fast enough for this killer to be brought to justice. We know a Catholic did the crime. We have therefore sealed off the Catholic section of town. No one can go in or out. If you do not hand over the criminal by sundown, we will torch the entire Catholic section of town killing all 1,000 people. Don't try to call for help. We have disabled all communication devices.'

The constable worked hard all day in an effort to find out who 'did it'. It was of no use. He couldn't find out. It was now one hour before sundown. He didn't know what to do. His deputy said, 'Why don't we just pick a random Catholic and tell them he did it? At least we'd be saving 999 lives.'

'But then I'd be responsible for killing an innocent man', returned the constable.

'Better one innocent die and 999 be saved. After all, there's no way the two of us can stop the mob. You have to give them a scapegoat.'

Thought Experiment 1.3 focuses upon whether the interests of the individual or the minority should ever trump the happiness/pleasure of the group. This has always been the most challenging sort of example for utilitarianism advocates because it submerges the interests of the minority to that of the majority. The emphasis upon the group is both a strength and a weakness for utilitarianism.

The fourth and final category is *deontology*. Deontology is a moral theory that emphasizes one's duty to do a particular action because the action itself is inherently right and not due to any calculation about the consequences of the action. Because of this non-consequentialist bent, deontology is often contrasted with utilitarianism, which defines the right action in terms of its ability to bring about the greatest aggregate utility. In contradistinction to utilitarianism, deontology recommends an action based on principle. Principle is justified through an understanding of the structure of action, the nature of reason, and the operation of the will. The result is a moral command to act that does not justify itself by calculating consequences.

The pre-eminent advocate of deontology is Immanuel Kant. He sets forth categorical imperatives that define both positive and negative duties (those things we are required to do and those things we must refrain from doing). All other action choices fall under permissions – one may act according to how pleasing the alternative seems to him (prudentially).

What makes deontology attractive to some is its strict commands and the duties that they generate. The commands are few. Negative duties include not murdering, lying, or exploiting others. Positive duties revolve around the limited duty to rescue others and fulfilling one's natural talents (a positive duty to one's self). Though the list is small, the enforcement is absolute. For those seeking moral rigor, deontology offers a double helping.

In addition, the justification process in most deontological theories is logically very rigorous using the nature of human reason, human action, or human choice as its exterior foundational touchstone.[22] This logical rigour convinces adherents that they have connected to true, defensible criteria for being good. This standpoint (like utilitarianism) aspires to the naturalistic rigor of science. In the case of utilitarianism it was the pleasure principle, but in the case of deontology it is the examination of the nature of human reason, human action, or human choice (using the most current covering theories).

If the deontologists are correct, then so long as the grounds of human reason, human action, or human choice remain invariant, then the principles derived from them will also remain invariant. This lends universality to maxims generated. For proponents, the ability to generate a theory that says human exploitation *is* wrong, *was* wrong, and *always will be* wrong – no matter what the society or where it is located.

Detractors point to the touted strengths as weaknesses. First, there is the absolute nature of the generated duties. Detractors say that moral choice is far too complicated to subsume under universally binding rules. Particular circumstances are very important in defining just what is at stake. The action description is more accurate with all the details. Fewer details tend toward a caricature that *distorts* what is happening. Since deontology moves quickly to universal descriptions of duty, it is moving in the opposite direction of affirming the details. Those who take this approach point to ethical intuitionism or virtue ethics as offering better vehicles to accommodate the minutiae of particularity.[23]

A second objection concerns the absoluteness of moral judgements. According to these detractors the moral realm is not so black and white. There are many shades of grey that render absolute accounts almost always as inaccurate. Deontology, these critics assert, will always err because it is *event oriented*. These detractors suggest that a more generous and far-sighted standard is in order that views all an agent's actions that flow from her basic character. (This objection could apply to utilitarianism, as well.)

How is one to choose which theory of becoming good to adopt? This is a question that few address. This is because most invocations of assent only present one theory of ethics and press the advertising campaign forward to win over new customers. But is this the best way to proceed? This author thinks not.[24] For our purposes here, let us return to a way of addressing the problem. Finding a theory of ethics is only one part of the problem. Another part of the problem of becoming good is the way we approach the choice and the way that determines our lives. This experiential overview will make the choice easier because it is really more important than the particular moral theory that we select. This is because it describes the way we present ourselves to the world and the manner in which we deploy ourselves. What I am talking about is our personal worldview. This is the standpoint from which we confront everything and go forth from there. But are there any guidelines for developing, revising, and renewing such a global description of ourselves?

The Personal Worldview Imperative

Whether we adopt the external or the internal standpoint in our search for the Good, the True, and the Beautiful, one thing certain is that the way we evaluate anything begins in our personal consciousness. This consciousness is our personal identity. It defines who we are to ourselves and to others. Contained within this consciousness are our beliefs and attitudes about the world and ourselves. For the purposes of this discussion let us agree to call the content that structures and guides our consciousness 'personal worldview'.

We are reluctant to change our worldviews. For the most part, when we are confronted with a challenge to our worldviews we react by rejecting it out of hand. This is due to the dissonance of this new worldview to the one we already possess. Rather, what we prefer is to confront worldviews that coincide and amplify our own. However, on occasion we do change. This is when we confront a worldview that overlaps our own in certain critical respects and then veers in a different direction. An example of this sort of worldview change is found through the leadership of the Reverend Martin Luther King, Jr. Starting in the 1950s, King found an America – particularly the South – that was mired by Jim Crow laws that kept African Americans in a second form of slavery. The Thirteenth Amendment to the United States Constitution abolished slavery and the Fourteenth Amendment guaranteed equal protection under the law to everyone – not just to people of European descent. King took on the monumental task of challenging the shared community worldview that allowed Jim Crow laws to flourish and for segregation to seem natural. This was no easy project. As argued above, people are inclined to be conservative in changing their worldviews. But this does not mean that it is impossible.

Dr King was the perfect candidate for instigating worldview

change by overlap and modification. This is because Dr King over-lapped with much of the dominant white culture: (1) by being an ordained minister in the Baptist Church; (2) he was a man of intel-lect as evidenced by his doctorate from Boston University; (3) he led marchers non-violently singing religious hymns familiar to most Americans. In these ways, *his* worldview was like theirs.

On the other hand, what he was suggesting was racial equality and integration, which was not a part of the dominant culture's shared community worldview. But when mainstream America watched the scenes on their televisions of these non-violent protest-ers being savagely beaten by armed police, being bitten by vicious police dogs, and physically assaulted by fire hoses, then Americans began challenging their personal worldviews. In 1964 a major civil rights law was passed, while in 1965 the voting rights bill was passed. Both pieces of legislation would never have occurred had not there been a dramatic shift in the personal worldviews of most Americans. It took a crossover figure like Dr King to effect such a change through the overlapping worldview and modification approach.[25]

Obviously, the above example is a major shift in worldview. However, incremental modification also occurs all the time – but generally from trusted sources such as television advertising (why would they stretch the truth?).

For most people the management of personal worldview is based upon sentiment and intuition – often without any reflection. However, this need not be the case. If Socrates was correct in saying that the unexamined life is not worth living, then we should have a source by which we might take control of our worldview reflection. It is my contention that one of the most important components in becoming a *sincere* person is to accept the responsibility to critically reflect upon our lives. Being good requires sincerity – it is embedded in the concept of the word. We cannot imagine a good, insincere person. Thus, we should all actively engage in reflection in order to be sincere.

In addition to sincerity, *authenticity* is also needed. Authenticity will be taken to mean reflecting in a way that will lead to the best possible personal worldview. It is my contention that the formula most likely to lead one there is through the personal worldview imperative, 'All people must develop a single comprehensive and internally coherent worldview that is good and that we strive to act out in our daily lives.'

The reason that it is good to be a sincere and authentic agent is that only sincere and authentic agents fully actualize what it means to be a good human being. This is because only the sincere and authentic agent is truly autonomous, a self-law maker.[26] Only an autonomous agent can said to be fully responsible (both positively and negatively) for what he does. Our human nature dictates that before all else, we desire to be good. To be good we must act autonomously. Ergo, our human nature dictates that we strive to be autonomous. If the only way we can be fully autonomous is to be sincere and authentic agents, then on the pain of violating our human nature we should strive to be sincere and authentic agents.

But reflection, alone, is not enough. The sincere and authentic reflection advocated here is intended to lead the agent toward action that is in accord to her deepest ethical values. One must live out her worldview and not merely cogitate about it.

What lies behind all of this is the notion of normative worldview (a worldview that is, itself, good). It will be the purpose of this chapter to spell out in further detail what I mean by normative worldview and why this is such an important concept for creating an ethics that will be able to link with public philosophy.

The strategy of the rest of the chapter is to break down the personal worldview imperative into its component parts: goodness, coherence, completeness, and practical execution. Each of these elements will be examined in the context of the creation of moral theory. In this fashion the personal worldview imperative will act not as a moral theory, itself, but rather as a meta-ethical principle that may be applied to any moral theory in order to determine whether it ought to be accepted.

First, there is *goodness*. Our worldviews should be good. But what does this mean? It means that we connect our worldviews to some established authority about the good – such as the traditional ethical theories discussed above. For most, this requirement would be satisfied by internally accepting some established, respected body of knowledge, for example the normative theories of conduct from a major religion or from a philosophical theory of ethics. Since religions generally package their message better, probably most people take this option. The point is that the goodness of the worldview requires an operational moral or religious theory to independently set this standard in order to avoid circularity.

Second, there is *coherence*. I understand this formal requirement to mean two things: (a) deductive coherence and (b) inductive coherence. In deductive coherence the requirement is that we should not hold contradictory positions on the same issue. For example, if Sally meets with a group of work colleagues at lunch and ridicules and degrades Nicole (her team member on a current project) and then later cosies up to Nicole and tells her how much she respects her, then Sally is involved in deductive incoherence. Under deductive coherence one must act in such a way that there is consistency between what we are and how we act in various contexts. A worldview that morphs to whatever is expedient is not one to be trusted. It is intertwined with a personal identity that is not properly formed: one that is controlled by outside influences and circumstances. The ideal test of this would be if all of one's actions were broadcasted to everyone we knew, then would our friends and acquaintances be surprised at our behaviours in various contexts? Would they say, 'That's not Sally. She doesn't do/say/act in that way.' Would your actions in one context cause another to question your very personal identity? Would they say, 'I don't know that person; that's not Sally'?

Deductive coherence assumes that we should strive to become integrated in our worldview. Most of us when we were teenagers were deductively incoherent to some degree. When we were around our sports buddies, we were athletes and we thought and acted in that way. When we were around our drama and music buddies, we were music and drama aspirants. This is a natural part of development. But it is development *to* something else. And that something else is an adult with integrity. 'Integrity' comes from Latin and means a completed whole. Thus, the person who has deductive completeness is a completed whole who can be judged for his consistent composition.

Inductive completeness refers to the practical effects of various worldview strategies. The formal stipulation is that one does not embrace two or more strategies that end up in a 'sure loss contract'. The sure loss contract is a concept from inductive logic. It involves the choice of two action paths that will always fail according to probability theory. For example, if a person were to bet on who the next president of the United States would be, Mr B or Ms C, and I set my betting house to give 4–1 odds in favour of Mr B, then I would have to offer complementary odds on Ms C, 1–4.[27] The entire sum always has to equal 1. But if I offered positive odds on both Mr B and on Ms C, then I'm sure to go out of business because anyone with a bankroll could bet profitably on both at the same time! Poor me.

In real life this might equate to a person who wants to be, on the one hand, a good husband and family man and, on the other hand, wants to be a good philanderer. The very traits that it takes to be a good family man: sensitivity, honesty, willingness to put another's welfare above one's own, et al. are the opposite of what it takes to be a good philanderer: insensitivity, dishonesty, out for one's own personal pleasure. Devotion to one strategy will make one fail at the other, and vice versa. One cannot be a master at both. The result will be a disaster because it is inductively incoherent. It leads to a sure loss contract as surely as the betting house.

Thus, the second part of the personal worldview imperative, coherence, enjoins us to strive to be both deductively and inductively coherent in the worldviews that we fashion.

Third, there is *completeness*. Completeness is a formal property that generally requires a theory to be able to decide all possible cases within the formal universe. Thus a system would be incomplete if one plugged in allowable terms and no exact answer could be given. We all want systems to be complete because without this formal property they would not be serviceable.

In the realm of worldview evaluation, I take completeness to be satisfied by the creation of a good will. The good will can, in turn, be understood by two interpretations that I will call the Kantian interpretation and the Augustinian interpretation. The Kantian interpretation ensures that the good will is grounded in theoretical and practical reason in accordance with an established theory of ethics.

Because we are giving assent here to reason, it is requisite that we confine ourselves to the domain of reason: the natural world. The Kantian interpretation of the good will seeks rationally to understand its sphere of influence: prohibitions, obligations, and permissions. *Prohibitions* are what we cannot do. The Ten Commandments are a famous set of prohibitions. *Obligations* are actions we must perform whether we want to or not. The Good Samaritan Laws that exist in some locales in the United States are examples of legal obligations. Finally, what isn't prohibited or obliged is up to the agent to decide based upon his or her personal plan of life, permissions. Though there are multiple ways to create a good will on these terms, I will present my own version in Chapter 3.

The second version of the good will is the Augustinian interpretation. This understanding of the good will is driven by the emotions. Under this account a person is viewed more fully as being guided also by emotions that are situated in a social context. As such, this standard begins on the simplest level with two people, Jamal and Miko. When these two individuals interact they do so first at the level of emotional connection. It is commonly agreed that another facet of our human nature is that we are social animals. One aspect of our social nature is that when we encounter another there is an opportunity (however small sometimes) to emotionally interact. Now some (many?) do their best to squelch this inclination.

Be that as it may, our natural inclination toward emotional connection is strong. But we can connect in various ways. We can connect as equals. We can connect as the paternal/maternal to the child. We can connect as the child to the paternal/maternal. In different contexts each can have its place. For example, when we are children, our emotional connection is from the inferior to the superior and it is the opposite from the parents' point of view. But even here, there is a difference between the inferior-superior relationship and the master–slave relationship.[28] The master–slave relationship degrades both parties. It assumes that one party is, by nature, *better* than the other. I would argue that we are all fundamentally equal in a deep way as Homo sapiens. Some may be temporarily in a protection-needing-status (such as children) and thus are in a temporary paternal/maternal-to-child relationship. Others (such as the mentally handicapped) may be in a permanent protection-needing-status. Regardless, both parties are fundamentally equal in both relations such that neither is *better* than the other. Thus the relationship between parent and child is different from the master/slave relation.

Among people of equal status (normal adults-to-adults), the emotional connection must be equal. Neither party is above the other. The operational way that this is demonstrated is through *openness*. When we are candid with one another and don't hold things back or don't try to manipulate the other, then we are more likely to create an even emotional relationship. For the sake of clarity let us call this sort of relation: open sympathy.

There is some debate about what we should strive for in interpersonal emotional relations. Some say that *empathy* (the intellectual understanding of another) is to be preferred. But the problem with empathy is that one can *understand* but not *connect*. Sympathy is about emotional connection. Understanding, by itself, may be used for good and for evil devices. For example, the best torture master would probably be one who could empathize with his victim. In that way he could understand some individual's breakdown point and move right up to it.

Emotional connection is different. It is my conjecture that if we *connect* with another, then we *cannot* fail to take the other's best interests to heart. This solves the problem of moral motivation by proposing an affective understanding to the good will.

And isn't this what most of think, anyway? If you are confronted with someone who acts fairly to you but without feeling or emotion, don't you think something is missing? Some older readers may remember the original television series of *Star Trek* (which was also the subject of various movies). In the show the two protagonists, Captain Kirk and Mr Spock represented two individuals who both possessed the Kantian good will. Spock with his computer-like mind was, perhaps, more excellent here, but Kirk also excelled in this area to a high degree. However, it was only Captain Kirk who was able to emotionally connect with others in such a way that it was a major ingredient in his decision-making process. Thus, in the vocabulary of this section, it would be Captain Kirk who possessed the good will to a higher degree since he had both the two standpoints of good will (rational and affective).

Thus, we begin with open sympathy. This leads to an action response to another, *care*, and the whole amalgam would be philosophical *love*. Under the affective understanding of the good will, love is the final outcome. Love is a powerful motivator for being good. The affective part of the good will is no poor sister to the rational.[29] It can be an effective guide to good action.

The fourth and final criterion in the personal worldview imperative is that there is *practical execution*. It is not enough to *know* what it means to be good without trying to be good yourself. We call people hypocrites who profess one course of action and then do something else. Thus, one way to understand the fourth criterion of the personal worldview imperative is that we must 'walk the walk' and not be content with merely 'talking the talk'.

Further, the sort of action must be susceptible to practical execution. What is meant here by practical execution is that what is being demanded of agents is possible – albeit even if it is hard. This is to create a distinction between the *aspirational* (that which is possible even if it is hard) and the *utopian* (that which is impossible to fully achieve but which stands as a goal to mark one's direction in life). An example of a non-moral goal that is aspirational would be making it into the top income tax bracket. Only ten percent generally get there, but it is possible. Theoretically, it would be *possible* for everyone to be there. Improbable – yes. Impossible – no.

An example of a non-moral goal that is utopian would be to never make a mistake. Another example would be the Shaker ideal that everyone should be sexually chaste (in which case, all of humanity would cease to exist after one generation).

It is the contention of this essay that ethics should be about the possible, the aspirational. The reason for this is the 'ought implies can' dictum. One cannot command upon another that which is practically impossible for them to execute. It is the sort of command that is bound to fail, by definition.

But sometimes there are cases that are rather difficult. Take the social policy for combating AIDS by merely asking everyone to wait until marriage and to be faithful. Now this *is* possible (thus in one sense aspirational), but in another sense it is practically impossible (given the history of the world and the nature of biological desires). These situations will be termed grey areas. When one is confronted with a grey area, and if one wishes to effect a policy that will be beneficial, then it seems prudent to exhort only those public policies that are likely to succeed on some level. However, this strategy is also flawed in a world in which many seek to maximize individual gain and put on blinders to the fate of others. What is needed, instead, are realistic dreamers who can stretch us to what we might become – dreamers like the Reverend Martin Luther King, Jr.

This balance between the aspirational and the utopian is a fine distinction in many cases. It may also track on the boundaries of our personal worldviews. However, since the personal worldview imperative is not a one-time event but an ongoing process, it is important that we do not use the 'ought implies can' dictum to sell ourselves short on what we may become. In the end, we all want our vision to be realizable (otherwise we'll be forever frustrated), but if one had to err a bit, it would be better to be a bit more idealistic than a bit less.

If it is really correct that all of us naturally want to be good, and that when we fail it is because of an imperfect interface with truth or with beauty, then we will look at the world as containing various persons striving to fulfil their own vision of the good – so far as they are able. We begin our journey guided by our personal worldviews. Since this quest is so very important to us all (since it's part of who we are: our nature), it is important to have a way that our personal worldviews might check themselves. Such a check would be of invaluable importance to us all because it helps us to fulfil our autonomous search to determine our will. Because we all want to be good, the worldview we all desire is a good one. The personal worldview imperative is just such an imperative that will assist each of us in our lives to visit and re-visit the shape and constitution of the worldview that focuses the way we go about living in the world. It can be a source for hope and provides the most authentic reason to be.

2 The Self and Others

You shall love your neighbour as yourself.
Matthew 22:39/Leviticus 19:18

How do we regard others? If Chapter 1 concentrated on *us*, then the point of this chapter is to think about how other people fit into the picture. The first stage in this investigation is to discern whether we can act selflessly on behalf of others or whether this is some utopian fiction.

The Problem

Imagine this scenario: Mary Lou Sue promises Fred Football that she will meet him at the Bijoux Theater for a film at six. Six o'clock comes and Mary has not shown up. Fred waits until seven at which time he rips up the tickets he purchased, digs his hands deep into his pockets, slumps his shoulders forward, and shuffles home. The next day Fred sees Mary Lou Sue and he asks her, 'Where were you? I waited over an hour at the movie theater for you.'

Mary shrugs her shoulders and said, 'Hey, I found something more fun to do. I went dirt bike riding with Jamal.'

'But you promised – ', intoned Fred.

'Hey, don't try to lay a guilt trip on me. I found something better to do so I did it. You'd do the same and you know it.'

Mary pivoted on her right heel and walked away just as Fred said softly, 'No. I wouldn't have done that to you or to anyone else – including my worst enemy.'

Who's right? Fred or Mary? Why are they right? How much do we just act for our own perceived happiness? Is it possible to act merely on principle without any personal reward? This leads us to the question of altruism.

Altruism

It's pretty clear that each of us strives to secure what is in his or her own interest. It is also pretty clear that with a limited amount of desirables in the world that the satisfaction of *my* goal may come at *your* expense. This seems to most of us to be a fact of life that (though unfortunate) it is far better than the reverse, viz., *you* achieving your goal at *my* expense.

Thus, we begin our investigation with the realization that most of us strive to maximize our personal interests. This amounts to a general inclination toward the theory of psychological egoism. Some would go farther and say that it is more than a general inclination to accept a theory. These individuals claim that the theory of psychological egoism sets out an undeniable biological starting point for explaining all human action.[1] If this stronger position is correct, then it will foundationally affect the construction of personal worldview. Obviously, some clarity on this issue is needed.

The Psychological-Egoistic Worldview

The psychological-egoistic worldview believes that it is factually correct that we always act according to our perceived self-interest.[2] This is the way that the human mind is constructed. What would follow from this? It would be a calculus of cost/benefit considerations. Morality would morph into economics. The only motivation for action becomes maximizing one's self-interest. According to this worldview, people may construct models of action based upon the distribution and transfer of money (and other forms of wealth, such as real estate). Using money as our guide is very convenient because it always gives a definitive quantifiable outcome (unless one is involved in complicated accounting nightmares – the subject of much debate of late). If we could only view everything in terms of money, how much simpler everything would be! I could translate the time I spend helping my son with his homework into real opportunity costs of possible alternatives and compare the results. Thus, when junior asks for my help I could quickly go through the mental calculations and come up with my answer: yes or no. Or when my wife suggests we have lunch together I can calculate the cash value to me of the lunch versus the cost of the lunch plus the lost opportunity costs and balance this against any expected personal benefits. Once I make my calculations, I can turn on my smile and say, 'Happy Valentine's Day, dear! Let's go for lunch to celebrate.'

Obviously, one can be a psychological egoist in qualitative terms, too. Since there are no numbers involved, this will result in intuitive claims that will ultimately reduce to aesthetic assessments. So, for example, if I were to answer my son's request that I help him with his homework on the qualitative model of psychological egoism, I might imagine the scene of me helping him and his possible responses against other possible uses of my time. Which is the more beautiful vision for me: the more *kalon*? Notice, that the beauty here is defined in terms of my own pleasure. The same would be true about asking my wife to lunch for Valentine's Day. Thus, for the qualitative psychological egoist, the more pleasurable will be the fairest of the alternatives offered, by definition.

There is much to commend the theory of psychological egoism. It seems to comport with much of our everyday experience. Either quantitatively or qualitatively, for the most part, this is the way we all act. But this is not the proper question to ask. Rather, what we should be asking is whether it is *necessary* that it be this way. The psychological-egoist makes a scientific claim that all humans (unless they are pathologically abnormal) will act to their own perceived advantage. Period. The end.

Now this is a rather difficult claim to prove, scientifically. This is first because scientific tests on humans are bound by strong ethical guidelines, and second because the claim itself is rather difficult to put into a confirmation/falsification experimental situation. What would it mean to create a crucial experiment to prove this claim? Let's engage in a thought experiment on this very point.[3]

THOUGHT EXPERIMENT 2.1

You have been given the chance to interview for a potential con-
sulting contract that will greatly increase your professorial salary.
It's very competitive. You've got the first interview slot and it is a
position to be filled as soon as an appropriate person is inter-
viewed. You jump at the opportunity and travel to the metro to go
to the interview. On the way to the metro you see a man who is
seriously injured, and no one is helping him. You have a choice. You
can help the man or you can continue on to the interview. The man
is seriously injured. You choose to help the man. The man is un-
attractive and smells, but his life is in danger. You are able to get
him help that saves his life. As a result, you miss the interview. The
second person was chosen. You lose out for someone you don't
know, someone you don't care for, and someone whose body
smelled rancid. Why did you do it?

The psychological egoist would insist that you did it for your
own pleasure. But what if you were taken at the end of this experience to a hospital that hooked you up to the latest lie-detector
machines (assume that they are infallible). They ask you, 'Did you
help the man because it gave you pleasure?' You answer, 'Hell, no!
The man stank of his own urine. He was a derelict. Just being
around him repulsed me.'

The machine said you were telling the truth. Then the experi-
menter (a psychological egoist) said to you, 'Now it is perfectly
clear, you think you acted away from your own perceived self-
interest, but what really happened is that you suppressed your
pleasures and didn't even know them!' You are at a loss. How could
you respond?

At this juncture, the standpoint of the psychological egoist (that is
the dogma of many schools of traditional psychology)[4] is that the
stated doctrine is always correct: we *always* act for our own perceived
self-interest. When confronted with evidence to the contrary, the
adherent appeals to 'suppression' that is not scientifically testable.
Thus, it falls into the realm of belief or faith – not too dissimilar to

the realm of religion (though I'm sure that those practising psychology and psychiatry under these theories wouldn't care for the comparison).

Thus, here we are: a key tenet about human action (concerning the possibility of acting not in our own interest) cannot be determined empirically by any test. It thus falls into the realm of conjectures on human nature. It may be true and it may be false. What are we to do with these pesky conjectures?

Unfortunately, in philosophy there are a number of primitive statements about the truth of various states of affairs. These primitive statements constitute beginning points of theory construction. Once accepted, they can yield marvellous architectures of knowledge. The kicker is 'once accepted'. Virtually all of these primitives cannot be proven to everyone's satisfaction. For example, in the case of psychological egoism, it is just as rationally supportable to believe it as to doubt it. So what's a person to do?

First, let's identify this situation as *the rationality incompleteness conjecture* which states that rationality seeks demonstrably to prove all propositions – however, in cases in which there is no empirical, non-question begging, test for verifying a principle the best reason can do is to offer various plausible alternatives. The resolution can only come about through appeal to the personal worldview imperative and its application in the way we confront novel normative theories.

Personal worldview affords one the following: (a) general intuitions on life; (b) a collection of our presently held views of fact and value; (c) a general account of the nature of things; and (d) a procedure for reviewing and renewing itself (that includes changing itself). When I ask myself whether it is more plausible to believe in psychological egoism or not, I ask whether I always choose actions that I judge to be in my own benefit. My worldview directs me to look to my life experience in the world, and to how I understand it. I look to various actions that I voluntarily entered into and I ask myself whether at a base level I acted because it made me happy, pleased, or otherwise advanced my self-interest.

In the midst of such questioning, I also set up various parameters that allow me to ask the right question. Often, decision-making is really about asking the appropriate question at the right time. For example, in this instance I need to know whether I am asking (A-1) 'Whether whenever I perform a purposive action (that is completed the way I intended) I am pleased with execution of that action?' or (A-2) 'Whether whenever I perform a purposive action that I always choose the result I believe to advance my perceived self-interest?' A-1 is a trivially true statement about voluntary action. It says nothing about the content of the voluntary action. Thus A-1 is *not* the question to ask.

A-2 is a question that queries whether I act solely based upon a calculation about my perceived personal advantage. Thus, A-2 is the real question to decide the case and no one can tell me the answer save my introspection and personal worldview. There is no inter-subjectively definitive answer.

In my case, I can answer with a loud assent for the possibility of altruism (not acting solely for one's perceived self-interest in all cases). The burden of proof for the psychological egoists is rather heavy. They must prove we act for perceived self-interest in every instant (save for aberrant cases). This is because the basis of the primitive posit is a universal scientific (psychological) law. One solid counter-example would falsify the posit.

Intelligent people argue on both sides of this point. My personal worldview introspections suggest that I have (on a number of occasions) acted against my perceived self-interest in personally painful ways because I believed the proposed action to be the right thing to do. I enjoin the reader here and now to put down this narrative and do the same thing. Decide for yourself. Don't take *my* word for it. Can we act against our perceived self-interest because we think the proposed action is right? Stop right now and think about it – maybe create a thought experiment of your own!

What Follows from Altruism

Whatever your conclusion was to the conundrum of whether we can act contrary to our perceived self-interest, I will now show you what follows from accepting the possibility of altruism.

First, we may assume that it is possible that sometimes people act out their natural inclination to be good[5] by occasionally performing actions that they know will not enhance their well-being or self-interest. The actions are performed because the agent believes the action to be the right thing to do. This characterization of behavioural motivation highlights an individual's propensity to recognize and acknowledge the role of *duty* in one's life. What do we do when we confront duty?

The answer to this requires that we specify just what we mean by duty through inquiring as to its origins. Almost all duties confront us because of some rule or imperative that is outside of our worldview. When this call to action confronts us, we first inquire whether we ever accepted the authority of said rule or imperative. In other words, we ask whether we have internalized (via autonomy) the rule or imperative as our own. If we have, then we would have done it within our personal worldview. If we had done it *sincerely* and *authentically*, then we would have done it via the personal worldview imperative. If this were the case, then the response to the call to action would be assent because the exterior *exhortation* was one to which we had previously assented as part of a picture that we had created by ourselves of what it means to be a good person in the world (i.e. how we could sincerely and authentically fulfil our human nature).

According to this view, it is entirely plausible that a person might act in such a way that her actions were not advancing her perceived self-interest (except in the trivial sense of A-1), but instead were part of a recognized set of behaviours that she has previously agreed to herself to undertake, i.e. doing one's duty. One does it because one judged it to be the right thing to do (since it flowed from the personal worldview imperative and thus is representative of what the agent believes to be true) and because to fail to do it would be an ugly consequence (not-*kalon* = *eischron*).[6]

Again, the good bumps up against truth and beauty.

Rights

If you're still reading along, you've assented to the possibility of altruism as a way of describing human action (or perhaps the verdict is still open for you – read on!). In the last section it was asserted that the answer to the altruism question entailed recognition of what it means to personally accept a duty. When we commit to a reflective personal worldview, there are obligations we incur internally: it's our worldview and we have to obey what follows from it. Either we do or we have to change the worldview. To act otherwise would be inconsistent and a violation of the personal worldview imperative. Since our worldview reflects the structure of who we are, to violate the conditions of sincerity and authenticity would be tantamount to degrading ourselves to ourselves. This is serious business. It is no light thing to deny the duties that flow from our personal worldview.

There are some other duties that flow from our personal worldview. These come from the very autonomous process that we all go through if we accept the challenge of evaluating our worldviews. Now it is true that many do not step up to this challenge and thereby relegate themselves to accepting the worldview of another. These individuals are slaves to whoever foisted their worldview upon them. But for those who consider these matters (such as readers of this book), I would pose a second thought experiment.

THOUGHT EXPERIMENT 2.2

Consider a person thinking about the conditions that would allow him to realize being good (fulfilling his human nature). It would certainly involve the ability to act. Without action we couldn't realize anything – much less being good. Thus, the question becomes what goods are necessary for agency? Put these goods into a list of descending order beginning with the most necessary and ending with the least necessary. How should we think about this list?

Thought Experiment 2.2 enjoins us to do two things: (a) think about the descending conditions of agency and (b) think about what follows from the construction of such a list. This is a fundamental task not unlike the operation of the personal worldview imperative itself.

I've gone through Thought Experiment 2.2 and have created the requisite list that I will share with you now.

Table of Embeddedness

Basic Goods

Level One: *Most Deeply Embedded*[7] (that which is absolutely necessary for human action): food, water, clothing, shelter, and protection from unwarranted bodily harm (including health care)

Level Two: *Deeply Embedded* (that which is necessary for effective basic action within any given society)
- Literacy in the language of the country
- Basic mathematical skills
- Other fundamental skills necessary to be an effective agent in that country, e.g. in the United States some computer literacy is necessary
- Some familiarity with the culture and history of the country in which one lives
- The assurance that those you interact with are not lying to promote their own interests
- The assurance that those you interact with will recognize your human dignity (as per above) and not exploit you as a means only
- Basic human rights such as those listed in the US Bill of Rights and the United Nations Universal Declaration of Human Rights

Secondary Goods

Level One: *Life Enhancing,* Medium to High-Medium Embeddedness
- Basic societal respect
- Equal opportunity to compete for the prudential goods of society
- Ability to pursue a life plan according to the personal worldview imperative
- Ability to participate equally as an agent in the shared community worldview imperative

Level Two: *Useful,* Medium to Low-Medium Embeddedness

- Ability to utilize one's real and portable property in the manner one chooses
- Ability to gain from and exploit the consequences of one's labour regardless of starting point
- Ability to pursue goods that are generally owned by most citizens, e.g. in the United States today a telephone, television, and automobile would fit into this class

Level Three: *Luxurious,* Low Embeddedness

- Ability to pursue goods that are pleasant even though they are far removed from action and from the expectations of most citizens within a given country, e.g. in the United States today a European vacation would fit into this class
- Ability to exert one's will so that one might extract a disproportionate share of society's resources for one's own use

Now there is nothing sacrosanct about my list as opposed to other lists. Abraham Maslow, for example, undertook a similar project with some different results. Also, various philosophers have done the same with some overlap and some differences.[8] What is key here is that we all recognize that not all goods that are sought are at the same level respecting our ability to act in our quest to be good.

Now if you ask anyone what they'd like to possess, they'll tell you – level three secondary goods, baby! No doubt about it. Why not shoot for the top? So how do we get there? There are two trains: (a) the express train, and (b) the slow train.

THOUGHT EXPERIMENT 2.3

If you knew you needed to travel between London and Edinburgh and you had the power of making the train an express train or a regular train, which would you choose? Background conditions: there will only be one train this day. If you choose the express train, then you will get there faster and do your business more expediently, but then others waiting at intermediate stops (that are normally called upon) will be left waiting. Their business will not get

done. They will be suffering at the expense of your success. What
do you do: choose to alter the normal schedule or not?

Thought Experiment 2.3 focuses our attention upon others and
their needs. Those who do not care are those who emphasize themselves and their own personal needs above all else. Those who (given
the parameters of the problem) choose the regular train accept that
there is a context for all our choices. Many people may make an
equally valid claim for transport to Edinburgh without the chance
opportunity that I had. I began my journey at King's Cross Station
(the origin of the train), and I was given the role of choosing whether
the train would be an express or not. Others not beginning at King's
Cross or who weren't given the choices I had were not as fortunate.
What about *their* interests? What should my attitude be towards
them?

I think that the answer to Thought Experiment 2.3 will yield significant results in our understanding of our own paths towards being
good. It speaks to how we may proceed regarding our good fortune
and other's misfortune. The luck of life can be a powerful ingredient
in how we view our own successes and failures (and those of others).
Those of us who see our ability to act as being conditioned by factors
of nature and nurture (factors beyond our control) will put forth a
theory of personal liberty that is far from absolute. This is a controversial question.

On the one hand are writers such as Plato and Sartre who are
rather strong on the understanding of what we can do and our individual responsibility for failure. Is it the case that we should put
nature and nurture aside and just treat everyone on an equal footing?
This is a very appealing standpoint. It is clear and simple. It can be
easily transformed into a meritocracy in which we find single sorting
devices to discover desert. Give the person the test or whatever sorting device is chosen (such as college degree, rank in class, etc.) and
act without deviating from the outcome. Let us call this approach
the strong-liberty approach.[9]

The strong-liberty approach describes one version of distributive
justice. Distributive justice tells us just exactly how we should

allocate goods and services in a society. Thus, if we accept this assumption, then we would say that justice is creating clearly defined functional entry conditions for entry to college, graduate school, important jobs, government contracts, and all other desirable goods (as per the table of embeddedness). If there were a test of these functional entry conditions, then we should allocate all preferences according to the results of those tests.

The polar opposite approach is the hard determinism approach. This approach says that our biology and our culture completely determine who we are. Thus, the hard biologist might say to Mary Lou Sue (a young woman who does not want to sleep with her boyfriend, though she is fond of him): your actions are biologically determined. If we use group selection as our model,[10] we can say that as a member of some species (group) one's primary imperative in life is to transfer one's genes into the next filial generation. The best strategy for a male to do this is to inseminate as many females as possible. Hence, by nature, males are promiscuous. This is the do more, commit less approach.

The best strategy for a female (under the group selection hard determinist model) is to refrain from engaging in sex until she can acquire a commitment that the male partner will protect and defend her through pregnancy and into the early years of the offspring infancy. This is the do less; commit more approach.

The second hard determinist approach comes from nurture, the environment. Those who advocate this approach would address Mary Lou Sue's predicament as follows. All of us are determined by the events that happen to us. For example, if we are sexually abused as children we are more likely to sexually abuse our own children. Or if we come from homes where the Standard English dialect is spoken with precision, then the aptitude tests (that measure language usage more than anything else) will make us stars. Environment is everything. Thus, to answer whether Mary Lou Sue should sleep with her boyfriend, one merely has to refer to her background. How has she been programmed by her environment? If it is toward abstinence, then she will abstain. If not, then she won't. If she's been poorly programmed, then she may go opposite of her programmers' intent.

Still, the question is determined by environment. End of question.

The two poles of decision-making constitute the strong-liberty advocates versus the hard determinists. Which is better? This is one of those *pesky conundrums* that suggest the rationality incompleteness conjecture. There is no definitive answer to which all rational agents would agree. So what are we to do about it?

One approach would be to look at the scientific approach on its own terms and then to jump away to metaphysical positions. Under the scientific approach the nature versus nurture question can have some clarification from the writing of Barbara McClintock.[11] McClintock (who won the Nobel Prize for Physiology or Medicine in 1983) looked at the viability of corn (maize) cornels in various environments with a purpose of understanding how various strains would thrive in different environments. In the context of this discussion, this means a crucial experiment about nature versus nurture.

In McClintock's work the answer was that that some sub-species of corn were very hardy and could be planted most anywhere in the United States and produce fruit. Other species are very sensitive and can only thrive in very specific places.

What one can conclude from this empirical research (if it is correct) is that some individual maize individual types will thrive in almost any environment and that others are very particular and will only thrive in specific sunlight/rainfall/soil composition conditions. Thus to some sub-species of maize, environment is the driving factor of expression while in other sub-species it is not (leaving genetic habitability as the key factor). Under this account the answer to the nature v. nurture question is: *it depends*.

With free will as the third actor in the human calculus, it may be the case that one would have first to assess the power of the particular nature or nurture influence to determine whether in some individual – say Jamal – it is dominant. Jamal may be just the sort of person whose biology and environment have not overwhelmed his ability to act. But it is not always that way. It could be the case that in another individual, Sonia, some natural disposition is dominant with respect to some given set of action – say Sonia has a genetic predisposition to alcoholism.[12] With someone else it may be environment – say Juanita grew up without necessary calories, vitamins, and essential minerals. Her brain may be deformed as a result. In these latter cases, it may very well be the case that nature or nurture overwhelms the individual's choice of action – to a very large extent. For these people, their ability to act is circumscribed by these variables. They must not be considered to be fully capable agents.

But it will be the operating assumption of this book that though nature or nurture can overwhelm human choice, it is not definitive for most of us. For the most part, we are like Jamal who (though he may have difficult environmental events or may not be the perfect genetic model) can act effectively given the essential goods of agency (the table of embeddedness). If this assessment is correct, then for most of us it is still an active issue about the status of individual claims to the goods that enable agency and allow us to become good.

This moves us into the question about the moral status of the claim for basic goods of agency. If we use the table of embeddedness as our guide, then the question is what is the nature of anyone's claim to the basic goods: food, water, clothing, shelter, protection from unwarranted bodily harm (including health care), basic liberties, and education?

I would suggest that we address this question from the vantage point of the species Homo sapiens. If the basic goods of agency are requisite for action, wouldn't it be the claim of every person in society to possess these goods?

THOUGHT EXPERIMENT 2.4

The basic goods of agency are necessary for human action. Without them the person couldn't act at all (level one) or couldn't act effectively (level two). One's ability to realize her human nature is dependent upon the possession of these goods. Could you or anyone you can think of deny that they or anyone else would have a valid claim for the basic goods of agency? If not, then everyone should recognize a general human claim for these goods. They are necessary for us to fulfil our human nature (to act in the quest to become good). What would it be like to deny this attribution of a valid universal claim to the basic goods of agency? Could anyone sincerely or authentically make such a claim? Try to tease out possible scenarios that might make your case.

I have gone through this very thought experiment myself, and have come up with the following response in the form of a logical argument.

The Moral Statue of Basic Goods[13]

1. All people, by nature, desire to be good – Fundamental Assumption
2. In order to become good, one must be able to act – Fact
3. All people, by nature, desire to act – 1, 2
4. People value what is natural to them – Assertion
5. What people value they wish to protect – Assertion
6. All people wish to protect their ability to act – 3–5
7. Fundamental interpersonal 'oughts' are expressed via our highest value systems: morality, aesthetics, and religion – Assertion
8. All people must agree, upon pain of logical contradiction, that what is natural and desirable to them individually is natural and desirable to everyone collectively and individually – Assertion
9. Everyone must seek personal protection for her own ability to act via morality, aesthetics, and religion – 6, 7
10. Everyone, upon pain of logical contradiction, must admit that all other humans will seek personal protection of his or her ability to act via morality, aesthetics, and religion – 8, 9
11. All people must agree, upon pain of logical contradiction, that since the attribution of the basic goods of agency are predicated generally, that it is inconsistent to assert idiosyncratic preference – Fact
12. Goods that are claimed through generic predication apply equally to each agent and everyone has a stake in their protection – 10, 11
13. Rights and duties are correlative – Assertion
14. Everyone has at least a moral right to the basic goods of agency and others in the society have a duty to provide those goods to all – 12, 13

Now this reconstruction may seem a bit technical to many readers, but the point of it is to show that there is justified generic predication of the claims right to the basic goods of agency to all people. On the pain of violating the personal worldview imperative, everyone has to accept this. The consequence is recognition of a general duty to provide these goods to everyone who is lacking them – wherever they might live.

Our very humanity depends upon our fulfilling this duty. Notice carefully that the execution of this duty will entail giving up some of our money (if we already possess these goods and have more left over) so that others might possess the basic goods of agency. The result will be a society in which there are fewer people who will be enjoying luxury goods. This is because of the redistribution of wealth from *those who have* to *those who don't*. None of us wants to give up what we already have. But being good demands it of us. We have to share what we have with others who are impoverished. This is the first step of the journey from the way I complete these thought experiments. I enjoin each reader to think about these issues for him- or herself. What do you think?

3 Self-fulfilment

Nothing is better than a diligent life.
Ancient Roman adage

We all want to live lives with which we are satisfied (being good). But in which direction should we set out to create such a life, and what signs will mark our journey? These fundamental questions of life direct this last instalment in our examination of the good.

The Quest

When we think about what makes life worthwhile, we are often driven to metaphorical models (art bumping into ethics and truth). Most of us don't set out in our quest to be *fulfilled*. We seek immediate and long-term goals that are functionally defined. It is upon periodic reviews of our life we assess that we are more or less fulfilled. This is the sort of separate review suggested by the personal worldview imperative.

Thus, the first part of understanding self-fulfilment is to examine the short- and long-term goals that drive us forward. The best way to do this is to focus upon broad universal themes that characterize our understanding of the way we functionally fulfil who we are. These are best grasped via an examination of metaphorical models (the most general action-guiding stimuli to our imaginations). There are several very popular models that people use in the Occidental tradition, but perhaps the most popular is the hunting model. Let's explore this metaphor via a thought experiment.

THOUGHT EXPERIMENT 3.1

Your life is like a preliterate human hunting in the forest or
jungle. You are only a few meals away from starvation and there
are other hunters in the forest or jungle also trying to kill animals
in order to eat them. You must get to the prey first. In addition,
there are vicious animals who look at you as their next meal. It's kill
or be killed, baby. Everything's fair so long as it gets you to your
goal.

Does Thought Experiment 3.1 describe the essence of what life is all
about? Are we set in a stark survival situation that permits unlimited
action to attain the prize? When I have, on occasion, worked on
projects with business people or those involved in politics, it has
been my experience that the overwhelming number of individuals I
have talked to live within a worldview similar to the one suggested in
Thought Experiment 3.1. But what follows from this?

Certainly those who have the hunting-in-nature metaphor view
life as a continual struggle for survival. At any moment, you may lose
your hunting skills so that you will be forever lost. There is none to
help you. You are on your own to make it or fail. Success comes to
those who deploy themselves most effectively.

Those who hold this worldview metaphor will be suspicious of
those who are possible competitors. This is because they may take
from them their daily kill. As this metaphor is translated into its
modern referent, the animal carcasses become bank-account balances: everyone is after your money. The only way to protect yourself
is to accumulate and hoard large amounts of reserve cash to protect
you against a shortfall or an emergency (kind of like modern hunters
putting meat into the deep freezer). The vision of being penniless on
the street is constantly before the holder of this worldview as the
worst case – yet possible – scenario.

Sometimes the hunting metaphor is combined with a war
metaphor as in Thomas Hobbes' depiction of the state of nature:
'. . . there is no way for any man to secure himself, so reasonable, as
Anticipation; that is, by force, or wiles, to master the persons of all

men he can, so long, till he sees no other power great enough to endanger him.'[1] For Hobbes the metaphor is of a state of nature (forest, hill, and dale) in which all are equal – though not identical (e.g. you may be able run faster than I, but I'm stronger than you: in the end the sums are equal). Because of this summative equality, and the fact of scarcity of resources, the result is that there is fierce competition that will inevitably lead to continual strife (war). This is the human condition according to Hobbes and is depicted via his state of nature metaphor.

Another fellow traveller is Friedrich Nietzsche who seeks to describe the basic psychological nature of humankind in order to give a causal account from the agent's point of view.

> Suppose, finally, we succeeded in explaining our entire instinctive life as the development and ramification of *one* basic form of the will – namely, of the will to power, as *my* proposition has it . . . then one would have gained the right to determine *all* efficient force univocally as – *will to power*. The world viewed from inside . . . it would be 'will to power' and nothing else.[2]

For Nietzsche, the will to power is a psychological fact that finds metaphorical expression in *Beyond Good and Evil* and *On the Genealogy of Morals*. In some respects it is a deeper account than Hobbes' because it gives specification of *why* we are acquisitive. It is because, at base, we are psychological egoists whose quest in life is to exert whatever influence we can upon the world. There is a trust that those who can assert the most influence will also be driven by a love of nobility (beauty) that will keep them in check from being utter tyrants. Of course, sceptics of the regulative power of nobility (beauty) will see this depiction as one that devolves to mere *kraterism* (to each according to his ability to snatch it). Under this sparser interpretation, Nietzsche falls into the tradition of the hunting/war metaphor. (The more generous interpretation would put Nietzsche on the edges of the metaphor, given the tempering force of nobility (beauty).)

In either case 'the will to power', as metaphorical expression, is seen in the context of other writers who assert the same thing. Like Hobbes, Nietzsche can be connected to a vision of life on earth as a competitive contest. We are all engaged in seeking to extend ourselves over our environment and over others.

One practical consequence of the hunting metaphor of life is *laissez-faire* capitalism. We all strive to gain the goods, and the science of economics is created to describe (and not prescribe) the process. Since everything is all wrapped up tight in a theory of human nature, what could be more correct? *This metaphorical expression measures our goodness in terms of competitive acquisition of goods – money, status, and power. Thus, our primitive drive to be good is satisfied by the garnering of these goods in the highest amounts. The individual with the biggest heap at the end of the day is the winner!*

Ultimately, I believe that the end result of the hunting/war/will-to-power metaphor is that we cease to question (in our personal worldviews) the truth of the underlying metaphor.[3] This is unfortunate because, in the end, the influence of metaphor is so pervasive that it can guide our behaviour in very significant ways. It is important to confront the metaphors we live by so that we might assert our individual autonomy.

But what is an alternative?

I invite my readers to think about this. Since it is my contention that the hunting metaphor is the most commonly accepted metaphor in current Occidental culture, it is important to put forward at least one plausible contender.

THOUGHT EXPERIMENT 3.2

Imagine that each of us is on a quest to be good. We are seeking a means to be good that will make our world (and us) better through intellectual excellence (theoretical and practical reason) and emotional excellence (love), i.e. establishing the good will within ourselves. The quest may last a long time. The quest may end in failure. It is up to us to do our best to seek and obtain the object of the quest. In the process of our quest we may be required to undergo various ordeals and tests of our resolve and worthiness. It

is the nature of human existence to sally forth on this quest and do
our individual best at achieving the reward (though we may be
humbled, scorned, and ridiculed in the process).

Thought Experiment 3.2 differs significantly from Thought Experiment 3.1. In Thought Experiment 3.1, the metaphor was one of personal achievement through striving against various odds in order to survive. In this context becoming good means acquiring a stockpile of goods to ward off what calamities the future might bring. While in Thought Experiment 3.2 it is an idealistic journey to become good: to strive for intellectual and emotional excellence through creating the good will.

What would follow from this worldview perspective? The greatest difference is the outcomes measurement for success. Under the hunting-metaphor perspective, it is the acquisition of goods through victory in various competitive contests. We could judge whether John D. Rockefeller, Cornelius Vanderbilt, or Bill Gates was the best American based upon the inflation-adjusted value of their personal fortunes. Or we could judge whether Franklin D. Roosevelt, Lyndon Johnson, or Ronald Reagan was the most powerful manipulator of power by putting their greatest achievements side-by-side (how many laws were passed, how long did those laws stay on the books, and how much of the Federal Budget was dedicated to implementing those laws). Or we could judge whether Albert Einstein, Jonas Salk, or Robert Oppenheimer was the greatest scientist of the twentieth century by counting their awards and by conducting an influence survey of citations among other scientists. Obviously, the hunting model (by its Bell Curve definition) only allows a very small number to be judged as superior, and a larger (though still minuscule) group to be good.

Under the goodwill metaphor perspective it is the creation of a will in accordance with the personal worldview perspective also understood in community (what I will call the shared community worldview) that confers goodness. This second approach is measured by one's quest for truth (the intellectual standpoint) and by one's quest to be a loving person in community (the affective standpoint).

Thus, under the goodwill perspective, one would strive to develop her mind (according to one's talents as best she can), and to develop her loving disposition towards others. Together, these two perspectives constitute the good will. The measurement standard of the personal-worldview-imperative model must, by definition, be qualitative. The individual would report for herself and the community could assess the social perspective.

Unlike the competitive model that was driven by the Bell Curve to accommodate only a few at the top, this second model (based upon the personal worldview imperative), in principle, could accommodate *everyone*. We could all (in principle) commit ourselves to personal intellectual excellence and then try to make ourselves better lovers (as defined in chapter two). There are no arbitrary cut-off points. In the end, the second model allows us all to succeed. We all can become good: by achieving our human nature. This would also confer self-fulfilment.

So what would it mean if we adopted this second model? Well, for starters the metaphor that generates the quest is two-fold – it requires an individual commitment to himself through developing his intellectual talents regardless of job requirements (the imperative of avocation) and it requires one to connect to others in a loving way (sympathy, openness, and care). This standpoint answers a traditional chestnut in philosophy about whether one can be fully ethical without other people. Does ethics require a social setting?

Thought Experiment 3.2 suggests that the answer is 'yes'. Ethics (under this metaphorical description) is both involved with the solely personal (through the development of the rationally based good will) and with the clearly social (through the sympathy + openness + care = love ethic). The Robinson Crusoe scenario would mean that one could *only* fulfil one's duty to one's self (to become intellectually excellent according to one's personal aptitudes). Since there are no other people on your uninhabited island, one has no opportunity to realize his capacity for open sympathy that leads to care = >love.

We are a social species. We need to fulfil ourselves within a constraining context of living with others. The best way to evaluate Thought Experiment 3.2 would be to accept the probable consequences. The most adept at competition (probably most readers of this book) would not have as many material possessions under the good-will metaphor as they do under the hunter-metaphor world-view. This is because the *rational good will* would entail an accept-ance of the table of embeddedness that suggests a radical redistribution of wealth from the top to the bottom on the basis of rationally justified ethical rights claims (the argument for the moral status of basic goods). In addition, the *love-interpretation of the good will* would require the acceptance of the table of embeddedness on the basis of sympathy with others. No sincere and authentic individ-ual could deny the basic goods of agency to another human living in the world without breaking the emotional connection.

Thus, the consequence of adopting the metaphor suggested in Thought Experiment 3.2 is that each of the winners in the competi-tive game of making money would turn around their lives in such a way that they (personally) would not make the sorts of trade-offs that many make, viz., giving up on love simply in order to make more money. That is not where being good is located. Rather, it is located primarily in our personal intellectual development and in becoming better lovers of humankind.

Whenever there is a point of conflict, the intellectual personal talent fulfilment/lover of humankind side must win every time. It should be clear by my remarks where I stand. But there may be different key metaphorical models that others may want to explore. Though this book does take positions on these various issues, it is also interested in inspiring readers to consider these various options. What should be our life's quest?

The Community

Unless we are living on a desert island or away in the woods by ourselves, we all exist in a social environment. Some cultures – prin-cipally Occidental culture (particularly modern Britain and the United States) – want to put forth a metaphorical story that features *individual* accomplishment that is barely influenced by culture (except as a hindrance to be overcome: the difficult family, the narrow-minded village, the blind nation). Each person of worth (those who are not affected by their social environment) strides out on his own course to fulfil his individual mission (aka his quest). Pulp fiction depicts these individuals as Captain Horatio Hornblower, or Horatio Alger's Ragged Dick or Tattered Tom, et al. Literary fiction often follows suit with the strong-willed heroes of Ernest Hemingway or the freedom-asserting anti-heroes of William Faulkner, John Wain, Charles Johnson, Martin Amis and Roddy Doyle. These characters rise to the top and make culture almost irrelevant. These narrative depictions are akin to the hunter model of the last section. Revolution, independence, and supremacy are the favoured motifs that fashion this narrative structure.

In contrast, other cultures work to heighten the awareness of the community (such as Italy, many Hispanic countries, most Middle Eastern countries, most of Africa, and Asia). From this list it is apparent that explicit recognition of the community is the *norm* in the world rather than the exception. In these instances a person is seen in a *context*. The context dialectically interacts with the individual so that each informs upon the other. In its extreme form, this can be tyranny. The writings of Gao Xingjian, Gabriel García Márquez and Salman Rushdie explicitly play with the balance between being the individual and the power of a community's oppressive general will.[4]

There seem to be at least three alternatives in this classification: (a) extreme individualism, (b) extreme communitarianism, (c) something in between. Which is the best? As a way to evaluate this problem, let's create another thought experiment.

THOUGHT EXPERIMENT 3.3

You are Jamal, the big brother of Marcus Johnson. You began teaching your brother basketball when he was eight years old. You never made the teams in school yourself, but you always enjoyed playing the game and wanted to give your younger brother something to believe in. At first, Marcus was uninterested. He liked watching TV and snacking on peanuts, chips, and nacho cheese dip. But with some considerable nagging Marcus agreed to the regimen. Marcus became a good student of the game. He went from recreation-level team to select-level team in three years. Every day you would go over to the schoolyard and play an hour or so with your brother. Soon he became better than you and the number of days you played together became fewer and fewer until you stopped playing. Good thing, too, because you got a job that didn't give you very much free time. Soon everyone admitted that Marcus was good. He started on his high-school team and got a scholarship to college. On senior day (the last home game in high school) Marcus told everyone how he was an example of what it meant to be an American: even a kid from modest means could make it. You came to the game and never heard your name spoken. Was it true that Marcus did it by himself?

Contrast this with another thought experiment.

THOUGHT EXPERIMENT 3.4

Your name is Maria Alvarez. You are the first member of your family to make it into college (and on a full scholarship, too). Your father died when you were six and your mother supplemented the family's food stamps by working two full time jobs. You rarely saw your mother. Your two brothers are in jail for armed robbery. Your passion was always science. But in school your teachers told you that girls weren't cut out for science. You didn't listen to them. At first in college you realized that your math background wasn't up to the others. You took a few remedial classes, but eventually you graduated pre-med (in six years) and made it into the state university's medical school. When you graduated and began your residency, you thanked your mother and all the people behind you that made it possible.

What do you make of the difference between Thought Experiments 3.3 and 3.4? Let's examine a few comparisons and contrasts. First, in both cases, there is an interaction between individual achievement and community support. In the case of Marcus, there was a denial of his support (even though that support seems to have been crucial to his success). In the case of Maria there was perhaps an over-recognition of the support from others and self-effacement of her own contribution (in the face of considerable obstacles).

Second, the perceptions of the individuals were not conclusive about the balance of personal achievement and assistance from others. The standpoint of the so-called ideal observer (an independent individual, with full knowledge, who sits in the background to judge independently – the exterior perspective) would, in each case, be different from the agent's own, personal (internal) assessment. Thus, the ideal observer would probably judge that Marcus under appreciated the initial help his brother gave to him and Maria over-valued the community help she received.

In these simple examples, there is only a *family* v. *individual* contrast. But the community is much more than merely the family. For clarity let us create two large classes of communities: micro and macro communities. In the micro community one can personally engage with all the members of the community. Many neighbourhoods are micro communities, as are many schools, churches/synagogues/mosques, and some political organizations (such as small towns, or legislative wards/districts).[5] In a micro community our voices can be heard directly.

Macro communities are larger organizations in which our personal discussion with the community (as a whole) is impossible so that our social communication must become indirect. This is because there are just too many people for it to be practical that we are able personally to engage with all the members of the community. Larger cities, states, countries, companies, and many political organizations are examples of macro communities. The indirect influence we have is often through elected representatives with whom we can have personal contact, but who also must represent many others' perspectives, too.

Under the good-will standpoint our duty as community members can be summed up by the shared community worldview imperative: 'Each agent must contribute to a common body of knowledge that supports the creation of a shared community worldview (that is itself complete, coherent, and good) through which social institutions and their resulting policies might flourish within the constraints of the essential core commonly-held values (ethics, aesthetics, and religion).[6] To live in community is to contribute to and interact with (the creation of and the ongoing revision of) the mission of the community and how effectively that mission is being executed. This process requires speaking and listening. We must let others understand our deeply felt convictions about facts and values (oral presentation of our views). We must also open our ears and *listen* to what others have to say (listening and considered interaction). This doesn't mean always agreeing with them. This is especially true if the worldview (or metaphorical vision) is contrary to the personal worldview imperative. In those cases in which it is, the individual *must* work against any policies that might flow from such a vision. Racial discrimination would be an example of a worldview that some may hold in a community that generally results in repressive policies. Since racial discrimination is: (a) a violation of the intellectual goodwill because it suggests an unscientific connection between being the preferred race (whatever that might be) and the argument for the moral status of basic goods – because the argument for the moral status of basic goods never mentions race but only humanity, there would be a logical contradiction between a racist worldview and the intellectual good will (as per the personal worldview imperative's criterion of completeness); (b) a violation of the affective good will because no one could authentically deny connection with another based upon race – what would be the reason? If another is in need, our human sympathy connects to humanity – not to race. Thus, a racist worldview fails here, as well.

However, when others purport a worldview that is consistent with racism, it is our duty as members of a community to do whatever we can to fight these policies. The ground of this duty is the personal worldview imperative and the good will it entails.

In cases in which the individual encounters a difference that is jarring to him and the difference does not constitute a violation of the personal worldview imperative, then the disgruntled individual should seek to change his attitude and accept the difference. One example of this occurred in Hamtramck, a city of 23,000, surrounded by Detroit, a major US city.[7] In the incident there was a community that was once predominately Polish and in which there is still a 23 per cent Polish Catholic presence. There is also a rising Muslim population. The Christians were offended by the call to prayer five times a day. They based their complaint upon noise-control standards and circulated a petition to ban the call to prayer. The petition met the threshold to trigger a popular vote on the issue – what Americans call a 'popular initiative'. In the electioneering it was shown that the Muslim call to prayer was actually softer than the Christian church bells. The real cause of the petition was the anti-Islamic feeling in the post-9/11 era. The shared community worldview was being challenged. The shared-community worldview imperative dictates that as members of a community we also have the responsibility to *include* all others living within the community into the shared community worldview imperative (provided that their worldview does not violate the personal worldview imperative). In these situations, toleration is not some sort of charitable gift, but it is demanded of all. The town of Hamtramck responded according to the shared-community worldview imperative and voted to allow the call to prayer during the normal times for public noise: 6 a.m.–10 p.m. This community faced a critical division and overcame it.

THOUGHT EXPERIMENT 3.5

Imagine that you learn (by some fluke) that your neighbourhood is really your extended family. Variations in race occurred because Uncle Elmer married someone of a different race. Variations in religion occurred because Aunt Amelia converted. Variations in sexual preference occurred because of evolutionary diversity. So how would you act to others in your neighbourhood if you learned that you were related to all of them?

Now, imagine that you had lots of relatives who had 30 kids each (polygamy?). The result is a small community in which everyone is related to everyone else. Even if someone is different, s/he is still your relation. Does this change anything? Should it?

The issue is connectedness. The argument for the moral status of basic goods suggests that because of the generic predication of rights claims, the rational good will must (on the pain of logical contradiction) accept that we have a duty to provide to all who lack it the basic goods of agency. The act of accepting this implies an awareness and agreeability to being socially situated in this way. When we accept our rationally based duties to others, we have acceded to being members of a community and to being under the purview of the shared-community worldview imperative.

The issue is connectedness. The loving good will puts us into an even-handed emotional connection with others that will cause us to recognize that we are not alone but that we must accept our community responsibilities.

Thus, the fully understood goodwill requires that we accept our community connectedness just *as if* we were biologically related to all of them (Thought Experiment 3.5).

What follows from this? First, our life plan, hopes, and aspirations must include others. The non-social standpoint is not viable. It is a false metaphorical construction that does not take into account 'life as it actually is'. All individually biased metaphors must be revised so that they include complex social connections. For example, the recent movie *Brokeback Mountain* takes one traditional icon of the individualist metaphor (the rough-and-tumble straight-arrow cowboy – who only strays when it's necessary to kill someone) and deconstructs it in such a way that it is no longer about a single man's individual quest in a non-social environment (with only the cowboy and his horse), but is a socially-connected love story that intertwines homosexual feelings with other social relationships of family. The complicated ménage that results is really the revelation of the social dimension of *Homo sapiens*. This controversial movie takes one of the most sacrosanct icons of the individualist metaphorical narrative and moulds it in such a way that the metaphor is transformed.

Another form of false metaphor construction concerns the 'man as an economic animal' metaphor. The nature of this metaphor can be revealed in another thought experiment.

THOUGHT EXPERIMENT 3.6

You have an important decision to make in your life. You are
unsure whether you want to marry Fred Football. You've decided
that the best way to assess the question is through a cost/benefit
analysis. Fred's family has loads of connections and they are
wealthy so that you'll never want for material possessions or
important dinner invitations. On a 1–100 scale give Fred a 92 here.
Fred is handsome and deports himself well. On a 1–100 scale give
Fred a 95 here. Fred does have a roving eye for other women so
deduct 50 points. But Fred is very discreet so give him back those 50
points. Fred will also let you have your own way (unless it's an issue
of importance to Fred) – give him 80 points. Averaged out, Fred
gets an 89! That's a B+ or an A– (depending upon the scale). For a
man these days, that rates pretty well. You decide to marry Fred.

There is much social-science-oriented research that will describe
human problems in much this way. For example, in economic game
theory, there is often posited a rationally self-interested party who is
driven by such cost calculations. All factors affecting the choice are
given some value (positive or negative) and the result describes what
is a rational choice for some individual.[8] (There are group models of
choice, as well, but the groups end up being substitution instances
for individuals – in the interests of calculation parameters.)

The principal problem with this approach is that it suggests that
everything from the affective side (with its irreducible qualitative
character) is translatable into quantifiable terms. This assumes that
such translations are possible. When Fred Football says he loves
Mary Lou Sue and wants to marry her, does he put the act of marrying Mary Lou Sue into an indifference curve and say, 'Well, how
much do I love Mary Lou Sue? If someone gave me a thousand
dollars to leave her, would I? What about a million?'

There may be some interest in such questions, but they do not
capture the essence of human love and commitment. This is because
the categories do not reduce to one another. Paradoxes of romantic
love can only be evaluated in qualitative terms. The fundamental

basis is emotion via its most reliable interpersonal form, open sympathy. Most people readily accept this two-tiered nature of the will.

The reason that the good will is bifurcated between reason and open sympathy (love) is that neither realm is sufficient to describe the realm of what it means to be human.

The result of Thought Experiment 3.6 is that: (a) metaphors that blur or obscure our social dimension should be revised so that they are more accurate to the way we are; (b) metaphors that obscure both sides of the good will (either rationality or love) should also be revised. It is important to create metaphorical descriptions that do not distort who we are. Distorted models of life are false and will lead us astray. These false metaphors will increase the probability of inductive incoherence (contrary to the personal worldview imperative).

The Good Life

In the end, what we all want is to be good. We want our lives to be good. At the moment of our death (if we even consider such things) we want to be able say that we have lived a good life.

In the course of Part I we have considered various interpretations of what 'being good' means. If we (upon retrospection) feel that, in the end, the choices we have made have been good and that we have done what we could to develop ourselves intellectually (to possess the rational good will) and that we have nurtured our capacities for open sympathy (to possess the affective good will), then we have done what is within our power to lead the good life. But is this retroactive standpoint productive? Let us examine another thought experiment.

THOUGHT EXPERIMENT 3.7

Think about theses lines of poetry:

> How vainly seek
> The selfish for that happiness denied
> To aught but virtue! Blind and hardened, they

> Who hope for peace amid the storms of care,
> Who covet power they know not how to use,
> And sigh for pleasure they refuse to give –
> Madly they frustrate still their own designs;
> And, where they hope that quiet to enjoy
> Which virtue pictures, bitterness of soul,
> Pining regrets, and vain repentances,
> Disease, disgust, and lassitude, pervade
> Their valueless and miserable lives.
>
> (Percy Bysshe Shelley,
> Queen Mab, ll. 237–248)

What is the poet saying about the retrospective vantage point? What would you feel if at the end of your own life if it were apparent to you that you merely frustrated your own designs? Would this make you judge your life as valueless and miserable? What a prospect! It's not one I would willingly choose. This is because it strips me of my humanity: the volitional striving to be good.

What drives us forward? Is it the possibility that in the end we will say that we led a worthless life? Does it motivate us to think about the moment of regret for a life poorly lived? Most of us believe we don't get a second chance. How does the finality of this possibility affect the choices we make now?

One philosopher with a potentially correct answer is Aristotle. He thinks that we are driven (rationally) to fulfil our human nature. Thus, he comes up with what some have termed the 'Aristotelian Principle'.[9] Under this idea we must always strive to actualize our rational capabilities (Aristotle's idea of human nature) above all else. This has often been characterized as choosing the most rationally engaging venue for living.

THOUGHT EXPERIMENT 3.8

Let us assume that there is a principle called the Aristotelian Principle that dictates that (all things considered) when given a choice between playing checkers and chess (assuming equal facility at

each) that all human agents, for the most part, will choose chess
over checkers to play and to do otherwise would be to degrade
one's human nature.

So what do you think? Is the Aristotelian Principle true? I'll tell you
flat out that when I was a college-aged person I resented this proposition. I thought that often I could be authentic while with my girl-
friend, or playing basketball, or running indoor track. These weren't
the most intellectual things I could do. I also sang in the chapel choir
and loved liturgical choir music. This wasn't intellectual either. So
what is the status of this critique of Aristotle?

There are several ways to approach the thought experiment. Some
would begin by describing romantic love, athletics and music as
rational spaces. This is similar to the economist who says that all we
do can be translated into a quantified game situation. No. It is not
reducible to that. Rather, the Aristotelian Principle must be evaluated in its own terms as a descriptive or prescriptive principle. Let's
start with these.

Is it descriptively correct that we all (for the most part) seek the
most intellectually stimulating over the less? Here we are involved in
a choice between two activities. It will be very hard to evaluate the
choices when two different kinds of activities are compared: such as
playing basketball against reading Plato. Multiple complications
arise when we add an additional variable to the question: besides
mere intellectual complexity let us include *the way* that complexity is
expressed via some medium. This increased complexity raises the real
possibility of unfair weighing of alternatives. Therefore, to make the
choice simpler (and therefore fairer), we should concentrate upon
the same sort of activity in two forms. For example, if we are watching television, will most of us (say 80 per cent or more) watch the
more intellectually engaging show over the less intellectually engaging? I have asked my college students this question for years and
I've never gotten anything close to a 50 per cent 'yes' response. What
does this mean about the way we phrase the question? Many
students when probed about this say that they often watch television
for affective reasons and not intellectual reasons. Therefore, for

them, the Aristotelian Principle does not apply since when they watch television they are not entering the realm of truth but rather the realm of beauty (albeit a low level of beauty). For these students, television offers an emotional escape of sorts. It makes emotional sense to them concerning their affective good will. For this reason, the television question is not a fair test of the Aristotelian Principle.

The best test is when we are clearly in the intellectual realm to begin with – such as the choice suggested in Thought Experiment 3.9: checkers or chess. Again, we must clear away all extraneous factors such as whether we are playing against one of our young children or whether we are keen on not hurting the feelings of our companion as a result of the competition. These must be excluded. So, after excluding so much, does it turn out to be true? And even if it does, have we excluded so much about what makes us human (namely that there is never such a pure choice before us). This smacks of the 'thought experiment fallacy' discussed in the notes to Chapter 2.

My personal conjecture on this question is that there is *something* true about the Aristotelian Principle, but that it is not the all-encompassing *raison d'être* that some would have it be.[10] What is true about the principle is that a very important part of who we are is rational. It is a connecting factor between genders, races, and cultures. We all connect to the same canon of reason. The principle of non-contradiction is true for all of us despite time and place. Each of us honours our powers of reason to a high degree. No one I know (save for those committing suicide) would choose to lessen their powers of reason; therefore, the development of and maintenance of our powers of reason is of utmost importance to us all. The Aristotelian Principle is one expression of this side of who we are.

But we are more than thinking machines. We are also emotional creatures capable of love and care. So what follows from this? Before we can answer this question, we must determine our metaphysical standpoint. This is one aspect of the truth question. So let's have it: what are we meant to do? There are at least two general answers to this question. In the first place, it may be the case that we are only accidental representations of a long process of events that (due to the laws of nature) have in all the universe presented rational creatures that are basically about surviving and continuing the species (most especially perhaps their kin in ever increasing circles of class inclusion).[11]

Of course, the other possibility (one that this author endorses) is that there exists something that *is*. The '*is*' possesses properties such as: creativity, truth, and goodness. In this way, whatever *is* (in this sense) acts as a background condition for this entire discussion.

If we have more than just the Kantian regulative principle of reason,[12] then one must determine what exactly is the nature of this principle. One possibility is that the principle is a set of mechanical laws that do not exist, as such. They are only constructions in people's minds. They do not have their own separate existence. Under this worldview, scientific laws do not really exist. They are only Bayesian modelling of what is. But what of the status of Bayes Theorm? Is it just a useful device within a probability method (or even the result of a more systematic scientific method)?[13] Could be. There is no conclusive proof that all would accept one way or the other.

Another possibility is that the rules of nature actually *are* – apart from the phenomena they describe. This would, of course, be a ground for theism. Since this author is a theist, such a possibility does not sound bad. But some are not so sure.

When we consider what we should be doing with our lives, the answer is rather different if we believe that the various principles to which we devote our lives, viz., the Good, the True, and the Beautiful, really *are* or whether they are merely temporally constrained fantasies that we create to keep us mellow.

Readers of this book: I enjoin all of you to think about this. The answer that you arrive at will condition your understanding of what it means to live the good life. This is because thinking about what is true affects what you think about the good. If there are propositions that exist apart from us and if their metaphysical reality does not depend upon us, then the answer to question of what it means to live the good life must also include this standpoint (theist or non-theist).

There are many questions that can have common answers regardless of whether one is a theist or not, but in the end one's personal worldview will be balanced differently depending upon the outcome of this question.

And so we conclude this exploration of being good through self-fulfilment by setting out the directions ahead. If self-fulfilment means developing the two parts of our good will (the rational and the affective), then we must discover whether and how the rational good will connects to truth and beauty. The first part of the conjunction seems simple. Truth and reason traditionally align themselves. But what about truth and beauty? This is more difficult.

And what of love? It seems rather commonplace to assert that love and beauty connect, but what of love and truth?

It is these further questions that we must pursue further. It will be my contention that we cannot fully understand being good without exploring these other questions as well. And so let's begin the next phase of our quest.

Part 2
The True

4 Finding Out What is True

'There are more things in heaven and earth, Horatio,
Than are dreamt of in your philosophy.'
William Shakespeare, *Hamlet*

The Problem

Contemporary humans find themselves bombarded by claims that present themselves as being true: the best auto value for your money, the new skirt that everyone is wearing, the best candidate for office, the perfect vacation spot, et al. In the *information age* we are bombarded constantly throughout the day. Suddenly, at your computer up pops a claim of some sort. On your telephone an unsolicited phone call rings demanding your attention. In your mailbox are countless claims upon your pocketbook. What's a person to do?

One solution is to ignore the claims all together. Just go forward. Stay the course. Full speed ahead!

The problem with this strategy is that it violates the dictum of the Good that one pursues the personal worldview imperative that enjoins us all to engage in periodic self-reflection about who we are in order to fulfil the requirements of: consistency (deductive and inductive), completeness (the two forms of the good will), goodness (connection to a major theory of ethics or a major religion), and live-ability (the ability to actually strive for something possible).

Instead of ignoring everything and staying the course, one should confront the claims that are presented to us (at least by category) in order to determine whether they say anything true and whether we wish to act on these claims.

This is a multi-faceted problem that will require a careful examination of what is at stake. First, we must determine why we should be so concerned about truth. Second, it might be nice to explore just what truth might be. Third, we need to explore the ways we can come to know truth and its sometime companion: scepticism. And finally, we need to examine the ways that we might integrate these concerns into the lives we intend to live.

These will be the driving questions behind the next three chapters. It will not be an easy journey and we can expect some minor collisions with the good and the beautiful along the way.

Why Should We Bother about Truth?

William Kingdom Clifford, a British mathematician and philosopher who lived and wrote in the latter part of the nineteenth century, told a story that will be the subject matter of Thought Experiment 4.1.

THOUGHT EXPERIMENT 4.1

There was once a ship owner who sent a ship to sea full of people to be exiled from Britain. It was an old ship and was rather cheaply built to begin with. It was suggested to him that the ship might not be seaworthy. But the ship had been on many voyages and had always come back so the ship owner decided to trust in the sincerity of his conviction that all was well with the ship full of exiles. He waved at the ship when it set sail. Later, when the ship went down in the middle of the ocean with all people lost, the ship owner received his insurance money and no one was the wiser.[1]

What should we think about the ship owner? At the very least the man was negligent in the care of his ship. This negligence was criminal because it resulted in the death of all the exiles (people being shipped from Britain). Most of us would say that the ship owner should be sent to jail for his failure to have the ship inspected and kept in proper repair. But what if the ship owner said that he had a *sincere conviction* that the ship was seaworthy? Does this make any difference? Sincerity is a good attribute (as we've seen in connection with the personal worldview imperative). But sincerity is not enough. In the case of the personal worldview imperative, *authenticity* (basing judgements upon the personal worldview imperative) is also required. In Thought Experiment 4.1, authenticity would be connected to doing empirical tests on the boat by a contractor qualified to judge whether it was seaworthy. These empirical tests would be intersubjective and thus from the external standpoint. The failure to augment sincerity with authenticity (intersubjective empirical tests) makes the boat owner criminally negligent: normatively he is a scoundrel. In this case truth bumps into ethics.

Our judgment of negligence would not be altered if somehow the boat had made it to its destination. This would constitute a lucky occurrence. It would not be deserved. The ship owner would still be a scoundrel (albeit a lucky scoundrel).

In the end, Thought Experiment 4.1 suggests that we have a moral duty to question our beliefs in order to assure ourselves that we do not believe falsely. To fail this command is to be negligent as humans. For simplicity let's call this maxim the *careful scrutiny maxim*. Before we act, according to the *careful scrutiny maxim*, we must question and examine all the relevant beliefs that ground that action.

But is the *careful scrutiny maxim* too strict? Certainly in one respect it sounds something like the personal worldview imperative that enjoins periodic personal examination of the worldview that guides us personally and also structures community norms. But the *careful scrutiny maxim* goes farther than this. It suggests that in every case we must not act upon any belief *until* it has been thoroughly examined according to the highest standards as set by external criteria. However, there may be some beliefs that are not amenable to such scrutiny (in principle). What happens to the *careful scrutiny maxim* then?

THOUGHT EXPERIMENT 4.2

Kenshasa was a mathematics student who believed in the careful
scrutiny maxim. She became upset one day because it occurred to
her that the number line, which grounds number theory, was
rather arbitrary. The number line she had been taught looked like
this:

. . . −1_____0_____1_____2 . . . , all the intervals
were equal. Thus, each number would be related successively in the
same way. However, a terrible thought occurred to Kenshasa: what
if the number line really looked this way:

. . . −1___0_____1_____2 . . . , all the
intervals being randomly spaced. If this conjecture were correct,
then all number theory that she had been taught would be false.
Kenshasa was in a tizzy.

In Thought Experiment 4.2 there is no external intersubjective test
for Kenshasa's quandary. It is rather like the rationality incompleteness conjecture that attaches itself to some of the fundamental
conundrums described in Part One (such as the possibility of altruism). Though there may be some external input to the question
(such as talking to others, or studying nature, et al.), there is no
definitive, intersubjective answer. Since number theory underlies all
our mathematical operations, and since mathematical operations are
of crucial importance in our modern lives (because they are the foundation of quantitative description, the language of science, economics, business, and much of our everyday lives), the answer to this
question would hold considerable weight.

One sort of response might be that there is no empirical test, but
it is not important since the truths of mathematics are not empirical.
They are abstract concepts that are true if they exhibit internal
consistency or that they are true if they allow us to do useful things –
such as guide our monetary system. (More on this later in the
chapter.) However, Thought Experiment 4.2 poses the possibility

that empirical sources of knowledge may be incomplete. Fundamental postulates may be unverifiable according to the careful scrutiny maxim. Since the careful scrutiny maxim advises that we do not act unless we have sound, empirically based reasons to do so, dilemmas such as Kenshasa's are more than mere exercises in trivial pursuits. I believe that Thought Experiment 4.2 poses a limiting case upon the careful scrutiny maxim.

Another sort of response might be that there is a fairly large class of beliefs that cannot be verified according to the careful scrutiny maxim due to their connection to action. Life requires action. Systems of knowledge in order to work must dispel uncertainty about the future. Thus systems of knowledge must support us as we live in the world. There are many propositions that cannot be verified (for the purposes of action) by the careful scrutiny maxim. A short survey of the history of philosophy supports this view. We are still talking about the same problems that Plato and Aristotle discussed. There are no universally agreed upon solutions to these issues. This is because of the rationality incompleteness conjecture. But action has a short time span. The alternative to the careful scrutiny maxim is *the selective faith maxim* that enjoins us to make our best stab at critical answers and go forth from there.

THOUGHT EXPERIMENT 4.3

Suppose you are a mountain climber in the Alps and you have accidentally put yourself in a dangerous situation. Your only escape route seems to require you to perform a dangerous leap. You have never done this before. You very well could die as a result. Should you act on the careful scrutiny maxim and do nothing since you have no body of empirical evidence to fully support your decision? Or should you execute your escape plan knowing that you may fail (and die)?[2]

Thought Experiment 4.3 creates an unusual situation.[3] The urgency of action makes it impossible to call in a consultant. We are thrust into a situation that will impose its own solution unless we do something. This suggests acting according to the selective faith maxim.

However, the objector might claim that this is not a choice situation at all. If one is thrust into a life or death possibility in which you will die unless you do x, then you will do x (assuming you want to live). You will do x even if you know that x, itself, poses risks. But if the probability of dying by doing nothing is 1, then anything less than 1 will be an improvement. Perhaps one might think about various ways of executing x: call them x_1, x_2, x_3. How does one choose between these various options? For example, x1 pushing off with your left foot so that you might grab with your right hand (assuming you are right handed) versus x_2 twisting so that you can repel with both feet and grab with both arms versus x_3 climbing higher to improve the trajectory of your leap. One's choice of strategy might be conditioned by one's assessment (based upon recent empirical evidence) of one's physical talents. Thus, it is possible that the novel situation does not entirely divorce itself from one's empirical past. Thus (perhaps) the careful scrutiny maxim is really at play, after all. Perhaps one should return to one's past climbing experience and choose the option that fits one's proven skills best in this particular situation. In the end, this prescription suggests that empirical history (albeit incomplete) should guide our action as much as possible.

However, others might contend that the previous paragraph misses the point that the necessity to act can put us into situations in which novel approaches must be undertaken that are empirically unproven. That in these instances the careful scrutiny maxim is to be replaced by the selective faith maxim. This is a question that each reader must answer for herself. But this author believes that as much as possible in a *daily context* one ought to employ the careful scrutiny maxim (the personal worldview imperative seems to demand it), but that in novel situations or when one is personally in a state of transition, it may be necessary to employ selective faith.

What do Thought Experiments 4.1–4.3 tell us about general worldview stances in our quest for truth? If we accept that sometimes both are required, then should we lead with the careful scrutiny maxim or should we lead with the selective faith maxim? When we undergo the kind of periodic personal assessment that the personal worldview imperative suggests, which approach will carry the day in difficult cases? The result of this strategy for finding truth will make global differences in the way we live our lives. It is not an issue to be taken lightly. It is connected to our human nature as rational animals. To simplify this, let us call this the quest for knowledge. Each of us, as people living in the world, quests for knowledge. This means that we all (a) want to embrace all that is true and (b) reject all that is false. To deviate from this quest is to degrade our human nature.

One way to think about the difference between the careful scrutiny maxim and the selective faith maxim is to focus upon possible outcomes. If one were to lead one's life based upon the careful scrutiny maxim what would be the result? Well, for a start the individual would be very careful. Each maxim would have to be verified (as much as was prudently possible) before proceeding. Thus, this individual would seek to minimize his or her mistakes and seek a life with as few errors as possible.

On the other hand, the person who advocated the selective faith maxim would be very open to exploring possible avenues even if they seemed rather risky. This second individual is more interested in embracing a potentially fruitful direction even if that direction is not well supported. They are the venture capitalists of Truth. Such an individual will trade-off a certain number of failures in the search for one fruitful success.

Here we are no longer talking about a *daily context*. In the daily context we pursue choices that will lead us to truth in the midst of day-to-day decision-making. This sort of thinking (this author believes) should be dominated by the careful scrutiny maxim with occasional intervention by the selective faith maxim whenever there is an inadequate empirical context for choice – either because this is the case, in principle, or because a novel situation (requiring action) necessitates, at best, a sketchy empirical foundation for action.

Instead, we are engaging in *strategic context thinking*: pursuing rules that will frame our daily context thinking. Strategic context thinking underlies the standpoint with which we face the world (our personal worldview). The personal worldview imperative is a regulative boundary condition upon strategic context thinking, but it does not tell us how we should go about creatively composing it. To answer this, we must return to the two competing maxims: careful scrutiny v. selective faith. Which disposition should guide our strategic design?

Two thought experiments can further stimulate contemplation about this problem.

THOUGHT EXPERIMENT 4.4

There was a fisherman who was passing his fishing business over to his son. The old fisherman was keenly concerned not to bother himself with catching fish that he did not want. This fisherman was after tuna (a rather large fish) and didn't want to pick up anything else. He sewed his nets to 50 per cent of the target-tuna head size so that he would not be bothered by smaller fish. The worst thing you could do, the older fisherman would say, would be to have to clean up your nets – discarding lots of fish you don't want – the mistakes. Better to seek for exactly what you want. But his son said that he would create nets with a finer grid. This was because the younger son was interested in expanding his catch selection and wanted to see what might come in. He knew he'd get more trash fish, but he was willing to take that chance for the opportunity of success.[4]

THOUGHT EXPERIMENT 4.5

You are an athletic director for a prestigious division-one college men's basketball programme. You must hire a coach who will go to the national tournament or you will lose your job. Now there are two finalists for the job: Mr A believes in very careful defence. He wants to win games by making the fewest number of mistakes. The scores of games he wins are generally 46–42. Then there is Mr Z. He believes that you have to risk making a lot of mistakes to get the fast break going. He says, 'Hit the boards, make the outlet pass to mid-court – if there is no one there, then the pass goes into the stands, but if there is, we've got two points for sure.' Mr Z is willing to allow a lot of turnovers so that he can have an up tempo game that maximizes the positive potentialities of his team. The scores of games he wins are generally 101–90. Both coaches win by 8 per cent. Which general strategy do you trust most? Who do you hire?

Thought Experiments 4.4 and 4.5 are meant to explore whether one should feature the selective faith maxim or the careful scrutiny maxim in strategic thinking. I've never been a commercial fisherman, but I did play basketball in school. I played for different coaches who emphasized one or the other strategy successfully. Thus, personally, I can see how each can work in Thought Experiment 4.5. But this begs the question of which is to be preferred – especially if we wish to make the thought experiment relevant to life, in general.

In Thought Experiment 4.4, the metaphor is less concrete and so better (and worse). It is worse because it requires more interpretation, but it is better because the range of application is more suggestive. The metaphorical suggestion is that it might be best to construct nets that are more inclusive on the off chance that something rather extraordinary might turn up. The down side is that one *knows* that he will also capture a lot of trash fish (defined as catching something that the fisherman considers worthless). Does the higher upside possibility validate the downside certainty?

Let's translate this metaphorical description to the problem at hand. Two ways to perform strategic thinking are suggested: (a) the careful scrutiny maxim, and (b) the selective faith maxim. In 4.5 the careful scrutiny maxim would be the defensive-minded basketball coach. He doesn't want to make a mistake (here understood as embracing falsehoods). He wants to win by not making mistakes. The selective faith coach wants to stretch the envelope. He is willing to allow mistakes in order to maximize the opportunity of scoring baskets (here understood as embracing truth).

If we take it as a given that all of us (a) want to embrace all that is true and (b) reject all that is false, then it seems that each strategy tries to get there by giving priority to one or the other alternatively.[5] If it is impossible to give priority to both at the same time, then which is to be preferred in strategic thinking? This is an impossible question to answer to everyone's satisfaction – another instance of the rationality incompleteness conjecture. I guess that readers will split on their choice on this. For my part, I would suggest that the selective faith maxim has a larger role to play in strategic thinking than it does in daily thinking. The reason for this involves the imagination. The imagination is very active in strategic thinking. This is because it is able to present novel suggestions to the worldview for consideration. Imagination is also involved in the way we chose novel normative theories. If we allow that imagination is beyond total rational control, then any activity that requires considerable imaginative input will automatically fail the careful scrutiny test. Rather, it is more like the selective faith approach. It seems to this author that in each of our lives there is at least one moment, which must imaginatively be considered strategically in order for us to fulfil our quest. As Brutus said in Shakespeare's *Julius Caesar*:

> There is a tide in the affairs of men
> Which, taken at the flood, leads on to fortune;
> Omitted, all the voyage of their life
> Is bound in shallows and in miseries.

The way one can strategically assess one's personal tide is via imagination. This is because reason here will come up short. The recognition of broad patterns and their possible significance is the role of the imagination. Of course the patterns and their significance can later turn out wrong. On the other hand, they can turn out right!

Imagination guides novelty in science, art and social affairs (the shared community worldview). In this way it connects the good, the true and the beautiful as nothing else can. Imagination is also behind the limited faith maxim. It is what gives it plausibility. An outcome is pictured that is appealing because it seems beautiful or because it seems good or because it seems true. But the operative word here is 'seems'. Since we have left the external standpoint of intersubjective verification and have entered the internal standpoint of imagination, the agent can only claim a single, personal vision.

As Wallace Stevens describes in his poem 'The Man with the Blue Guitar', the musician (after the Picasso painting) is told to play things as they are. But he demurs saying that the artist changes things when he plays. Nonetheless he is enjoined to play 'Of things exactly as they are'. Though bound to the internal, subjective standpoint, imagination seeks to sketch the outlines of a universal truth without other grounding. As such, it fits into the selective faith epistemological mode.

In strategic thinking, imagination can give rise to selective faith by presenting to us our time of choice. It can be our moment of discovering personal meaning. It can impel a dialectical process that leads us to change our lives (or at least some important tenets therein). All of this falls under the selective faith maxim.

However, this cannot be a regular occurrence. One cannot experience *satori* daily! For the most part, our strategic thinking will also follow the careful scrutiny maxim because most strategic planning does not question mission or critical objectives. These are taken as posits. In these situations – just like daily context thinking – the careful scrutiny maxim is our most dependable guide. But in those singular moments in which the posits, themselves, come into question – in which one's most general assumptions are up for review – then the selective faith maxim via the imagination is the mechanism for moving us forward.

Thus, we have two sorts of strategies to guide our quest for truth: the careful scrutiny maxim and the selective faith maxim. Each can claim a legitimate realm of sovereignty. Together, used within their selective domains, they will allow us all to fulfil our epistemological and moral duty to (a) embrace all that is true and (b) reject all that is false.

Theories of Truth

The last section discussed *ways of coming to know*. But the follow-up question is: 'Knowing what?' The object of our quest for knowing is truth. Now some have said that we can make far too much of this. They want to *deflate* the concentration on the nature of truth and rather concentrate on the processes we undergo and the checks on the same. I have some sympathy with this critique, but since the history of philosophy has put forth depictions of truth, and since this essay is an exploration of the good, the true, and the beautiful, it seems rather straightforward to enter into some analysis of what the true might be.

Correspondence Theory

Correspondence theory states that a proposition is true when it accords with the actual state of affairs. In this case the proposition is in fidelity with the way things *are*. This definition presupposes a number of things. First, and foremost, it suggests that 'true' is an ascription based upon resemblance, but it does not offer criteria for evaluating how resemblance is to be evaluated. Second, it finesses what constitutes the actual state of affairs. Let us begin with the first hurdle.

Gottfried Leibniz (1646–1716) suggested a principle of identity that said if two entities x and y had all and the same properties, then they were identical.[6] This seems quite reasonable, but it finesses the question of how various properties are identified and described. From the externalist, intersubjective perspective, asking questions of the community could solve this. The general agreement (based upon empirical data) would constitute grounds for acceding to a claim of identity (resemblance). Thus, we would posit the natural thing (say my aunt Mollie). Then we would posit the representation of Mollie (say in the form of a photograph). Resemblance in this way is principally understood empirically. One might look at the photograph and declare that it is flawed because it depicts Mollie as having red eyes when everyone knows she has brown eyes. In this respect, the photograph does not resemble what *is* and so is false to some degree (according to the correspondence theory). Most would probably say that the photograph is *almost* correct – except for the eyes. But what if Mollie's most distinguishing feature is her eyes? She is known for those chocolate irises. And now they are red!

Does the case with Mollie get any worse if she also looks fatter in the photograph than she does in face-to-face confrontation? Is it enough that when you show someone the photograph, that they recognize the figure as Mollie? Under this view, when the community agrees that the picture is of Mollie, then there is a social acceptance of resemblance and a subsequent social acceptance of its truth. From the external standpoint this may be enough. It is a separate question to determine the *degree* of resemblance (comparing various other pictures of Mollie, for example). For now, let us accept that this, too, might be brought to a panel of judges (acquaintances of Mollie) to socially determine. In principle, since the question involves two empirical experiences, there can be agreement. Agreement, in this context, will confer truth.

Figure 4.1 Square

A more difficult situation occurs when we ask whether Figure 4.1 resembles a square. One way to answer the question is to take out a ruler and protractor and measure each side and angle. By definition, a square is a quadrilateral with four equal sides that meet at right angles. So let's pretend we have done this and the sides are equal (according to my ruler) and the angles are all right angles (according to my protractor). Is this the end of the story? In other words, is it true that Figure 4.1 is a square? What if there were a geometric fanatic in the crowd who said that my ruler and protractor were sorry examples of geometric measuring. And what if I replied that if the fanatic had a better pair of measuring devices that he was welcome to step forward and enlighten us all. But the fanatic demurs and says that there are no perfect measuring devices since lines exist in only one dimension and plane figures (such as quadrilaterals and squares) exist in two dimensions while all measuring devices (including our own eyes) require three dimensions. By definition, there is no way to compare the original to the resemblance as there was with Mollie and her picture. Rather, what we have is a rational definition that the imagination must picture and then the line drawing before us is compared to each according to some notion of 'artistic rendering error'.

But a problem with this approach is that it conflates the purely empirical social agreement of Mollie and her photo with some particular person (the *external standpoint*) and the observer's personal imagination along with his own notion of rendering error. This latter effort is more akin to the *internal standpoint*. Now, it can be the case that we can get a group of people to all do their measurements, to all employ their personal imaginations, and to all reckon on rendering error – and the result is that they all agree! What has happened? This is still not the same case as we had with Mollie. For this coven of internal standpoints do not socially experience the same phenomena. Instead, each has a personal experience that is then shared with the community. If there were an objector, it would be different from the Mollie case. We could not bring out the picture and Mollie and hold them side-by-side for some sort of reconciliation. This is because (though the square would be available to all) the imagination of the objector (as well as the imaginations of each of the other participants) is inscrutable. No one can view this experience. It is private. As such it is impossible to evaluate. This sort of case seems difficult for the 'picture resemblance position' to accommodate.[7] This situation is not improved if we try to substitute some linear account of resemblance. The deductive truths of one set of criteria are matched logically against another. If the logical truth squares, then a state of synonymy exists. That is to say when two or more propositions (one or more of which may be logical interpretations of an empirical entity that claims to be accurate of that entity) commit themselves to logical tautologies,[8] then the two propositions are synonymous.

This sounds all very high and mighty, but if you read closely enough, you may have noticed the nasty word 'interpretation'. This means that the observer, who is making the judgement, says that the figure presented is such and such. Obviously, this means that we are subject to a wide variety of interpretations. The farm worker in Arkansas might say of figure one that it is a basketball hoop (since on the farm they used an old fruit crate). Another might say it is a Rubik's cube, while a third might say that it is the video-game system that loads his latest *Grand Theft Auto* game. Thus, this solution may be no better than its progenitor.

A still more difficult case for correspondence theory is set out in the following thought experiment.

THOUGHT EXPERIMENT 4.6

Frederic was reading Kant's Critique of Pure Reason on the four general categories that present data to the understanding. These categories are: quantity, quality, relation, and modality.[9] Frederic is intrigued by these and thinks that Kant's depiction of mind is the way it actually works. Frederic is also a believer in the correspondence theory of truth. But in this case Frederic is unsure about the way correspondence theory works between two abstract entities. How should Frederic think about this?

Now many readers of this book who aren't philosophers are probably saying, '*Whoa there*! I've never read this book or if I did, I sure don't remember any of *that*.' A note of assurance: this doesn't matter in this context. The point of the thought experiment is to speculate on resemblance between two abstract entities. Once we have jettisoned our empirical touchstone, what do words like 'resemblance' mean anyway? Aren't they grounded in metaphor theory that begins in experience? Don't we need a different term once we totally discard experience?

This is the problem of abstraction. In abstraction, one does not totally discard experience since all language communication depends upon an acceptance of experience at some level – albeit through analogy *however extended*. Thus, some might say that the non-empirical to the non-empirical is extended and fuzzy at best. Others might say that the fuzziness exists in the realm of the empirical since it is so complicated. Once we jettison the empirical and can compare the truth claims of two propositions or compare the plausibility claims of two metaphorical descriptions, then everything is clearer. This is because the boundary conditions of these non-empirical are specified very exactly. They are true if they meet our worldview expectations of what *is*. But what are these expectations based upon? They are part of the fundamental assumptions about the world. For some, this may include theological understandings. For others, this may include pure materialism. Since the rationality incompleteness conjecture suggests that many fundamental starting points cannot be conclusively proven, only plausibility is left. Thus, at the level of the abstract-to-abstract resemblance there is on the one hand, 'seeming ease of execution' since the abstract is so much clearer than fuzzy empirical experience, but on the other hand, there is 'greater difficulty in execution' since the process of comparing requires the implementation of non-empirically based posits that cannot be thoroughly defended. They can only be plausibly presented.

The second hurdle correspondence must surmount is to identify what exactly constitutes the actual state of affairs. This ambiguity between empirical and non-empirical groundings created most of the problems with the first hurdle. In this instance, we must address these issues head on. The answer to this issue requires that we retreat to a question and answer test in metaphysics.

The Official Question and Answer Test

Part One: Ontology

Check off the number of entities that exist:

(a) material things

(b) non-material things

(c) both material and non-material things

(d) write-in candidates: _____

Part Two: Cosmology

If you answered (a), skip to part three

If you answered (b), skip to part three

If you answered (c), then

    Which is greater the material or the non-material?

If you answered (d), then

    Which is greatest, the material, the non-material, or the write-in candidate?

Part Three: Answer time

Part One (a) – you are a monist materialist. You think that there is only one sort of thing that exists and that it is material. For you cosmology is a snap.

Part One (b) – you are a monist non-materialist. You think that there is only one sort of thing that exists and that is non-material. For you cosmology is a snap.

Part One (c) – you are a dualist. For you, the metaphysical realm is populated by more than one thing. For you, cosmology is nuanced. Whatever is noted first is your guiding principle. You must also be sensitive to level interaction problems.

Part One (d) – you are a pluralist. Yours is the most complicated cosmology because you need to rank each item against the other and then all together.[10]

The result of taking The Official Question and Answer Test is that each contestant declares what will count for 'the actual state of affairs'. Since the actual state of affairs is given content by answering the question of *what is*, and since The Official Question and Answer Test determines this, then these answers will give specification to what will count (in your worldview) as the entity against which all things are measured (vis-à-vis their verisimilitude).

However, the external and the internal perspectives are different when one chooses (a), (b), (c), or (d) on The Official Question and Answer Test. Those who choose (a) can always claim to offer (at least 'in principle') an externalist perspective that is capable of intersubjective verification.[11] Those who choose (b) are bound to an internalist perspective or a naïve empiricist perspective that refuses to assign substance to empirical perceptions or (c) rely upon the subject and her reliable procedures for picking out just what is true for acceptance and what is false for rejection. The 'reliable procedure' may be open for public scrutiny, but the data inputs are not. Thus, the mechanical operation of the process remains intersubjectively inscrutable. In the case of correspondence theory, the truth of the object is given and only our ability to fashion replicas is in question. Such is a quick take on correspondence theory.[12]

Coherence Theory

Coherence theory stipulates that a given body of knowledge is true if and only if there are no internal deductive contradictions. (Sometimes people also add the stipulation that the body of knowledge is also complete – meaning that one cannot pose a problem from the covered universe and not generate an answer.) *Truth* here means that everything works smoothly together so that an artificial whole is produced that has boundaries and symmetry. Proponents of the coherence theory of truth often point to symmetry and elegance as properties attaching to true bodies of knowledge. This sort of language is obviously evocative of Beauty. One views an elegant system as one that *must* be true because it is elegant. The beauty of a coherent system stirs the student's aesthetic sensibilities. This collision of beauty and truth also has ethical ramifications. When we think of coherent accounts of nature by scientists I have observed that there is not only an overlap with beauty but there is an action-guiding response. When I was doing research on my co-authored text *Genetic Engineering: Science and Ethics on the New Frontier*, I observed this very behaviour that I term *The Value-Duty Doctrine*: Whenever agent

X studies P and discovers various properties about it (seen in light of his personal worldview), then if X decides that P is elegant, then X values P (where P is an artifact, a natural object, an agent, or a human institution). As a result of this process of observing and classifying that leads to the judgement of elegance and its resultant valuing, X takes on a corresponding duty to protect and defend P subject to the constraints of the principle of human survival[13] and the 'ought implies can' doctrine.[14]

What this argument sets out is that when an account of nature (in this case) is seen to cohere, then the meaning that is conferred upon the entire context is normatively assented to. This confirmation implies that the sincere and authentic scientist will strive to protect the natural phenomenon and the context in which it is understood.

This argument completes the triple play: (Truth <=> Beauty) => Good. The scientist working within her coherent system of Evolution/genome expression/PCR to demonstrate the same is often confronted with failure. Conjectures that form the basis of hypotheses and their protocols most often fail. Then the researcher modifies and fiddles around. Then sometimes it happens: the expected results occur. The paradigm is verified (in this small instance). As the researcher reflects on what has happened she is astounded at the beauty of the coherent theoretical construct. The beauty is situated within the coherent system that guides the scientist. When experimental results and expansion of the *explanans* come together, the result is experientially significant to the researcher – and not because of an expected publication or promotion – but because the co-recognition of Truth and Beauty has made an impact. The result is an ethical duty.

What lies behind the coherence theory of truth is an internalist perspective that suggests that the *agent's* judgment about the consistency is definitive. Certainly, the person making the judgement could confront and defend his or her judgement to an objector who thought there was a contradiction, but that is not what makes coherentism attractive. One may be able to refute all external challenges to the coherence of the system – or better yet provide a theorem that proves it, but the assessment apparatus suggests that one's judgement about *truth* is a separate and private exercise. Whenever the driving force behind a theory of truth is *internal*, then it is immune from any telling falsification from the outside. As was the case in correspondence theory, there is an intersubjective scrutable part and a personal inscrutable part. The external part is connected to grounds of coherence and completeness evaluation. One may set out the rules of system evaluation for all to see. One may also propose various proofs for completeness or consistency (or both) for all to evaluate. But in the end, the inclination for one to accept this as being true (in a strong sense) will be internal. This is the case in two senses. In the first case, the origins of any artificial system are random. They come from the subject's own intellectual/imaginative vision. Thus, the genesis of the system comes about from the internal perspective of an individual.[15] Some of these dynamics can be teased out in the following thought experiment.

THOUGHT EXPERIMENT 4.7

Your name is Johannes. You live in Europe at the beginning of the seventeenth century. You have just read a bootleg summary of *De revolutionibus orbium caelestium* by Copernicus. The first book is a general overview trying to lay foundations based in ancient Greek philosophy. What interests you are some of the tables that present a different approach to standard problems. Now the Ptolemaic tables that your teacher, Tycho, taught you are tried and true. These star tables can get you from Marseilles to Naples without a problem. In fact, you detect a number of factual errors in these new Copernican tables that would probably mean that under these new tables you might end up near Lucca instead of Naples. However, something captivates you about Copernicus' account. It is simpler, more elegant, and employs no ad hoc additions (unlike the Ptolemaic system that uses ad hoc additions all the time – such as epicycles to explain retrograde motion and equants to account for variations in angular velocity). Because Copernicus is simpler and more elegant, you feel that the Copernican account is more coherent and therefore probably true. You pledge yourself to promote Copernicus' theory.[16]

Thought Experiment 4.7 demonstrates some of the internal–external tension that was evident in correspondence theory. On the one hand, the star tables at the time (externalist/intersubjective criteria) favoured Ptolemy and his geocentric hypothesis. Because Ptolemy had been in practice so long, various corrections to the way the phenomena were depicted (epicycles, equants, et al.) had made the Ptolemaic star tables more than adequate for travel in the Mediterranean. Thus, the externalist perspective would side for Ptolemy.

However, in the spirit of the personal worldview imperative, there is also an internalist perspective that trumps the swaggering externalist claims. In this case, coherence is understood in tandem with beauty. What I mean by this is that what was *wrong* with the Ptolemaic theory was that whenever there was a problem, the theory was adjusted with *ad hoc* modifications. This was under the doctrine of 'save the phenomena' which dominated ancient and medieval science.[17] Under this doctrine, the practitioner of science didn't actually believe in the literal truth of the purported theory (such as epicycles and equants) but valued the fact that Ptolemaic star tables worked (cf. pragmatism). The emphasis was upon creating a coherent account that squared with observation or utility (such as travelling to Naples). Whatever modifications had to be made to the theory were OK so long as coherence (even coherence purchased at the price of obvious non-realism) was maintained. This was the sense of coherence that Tycho (Johannes' teacher) advocated.

Now Johannes (Thought Experiment 4.7) thought of coherence in a rather different way. For him, coherence meant *no ad hoc additions*. A theory must work purely – without addition (for the most part). This is a doctrine of simplicity. But simplicity is essentially an aesthetic, normative judgement.[18] Therefore, Johannes understands coherence rather differently than Tycho. For Johannes, it is *not* enough to save the phenomena. It is not enough to fiddle with essential parts of the explanatory apparatus so that everything fits together. These are not enough.

Instead, one must consider coherence in a broader sense: conceptual coherence. This would suggest that a system is coherent only if its broad conceptual commitments fit together without artificial gerrymandering. When one achieves coherence in an artificial fashion he has created a technical coherence that does not resonate fully within the system. In contrast to mere technical coherence (that *may* satisfy some externalists), a holistic conceptual coherence is advocated. This conceptual coherence is judged by the individual from an internalist perspective. It involves judgements about system-wide elegance, also known as beauty.

From a purely externalist standpoint, Ptolemy wins the day: all the inconsistencies have been worked out via *ad hoc* additions and there is positive confirmation since boats can reliably use these charts to go from Marseilles to Naples. But other coherentism advocates would demur due to their internalist judgements based upon aesthetic and holistic considerations that they personally judge as decisive. This is a decision that is made via the personal worldview imperative.

Thus, Thought Experiment 4.7 acts as a watershed in coherentism thinking. It causes us to set out of a *thin* and a *thick* sense of what coherence means. The thin sense emphasizes only getting rid of contradictions. This means that if a contradiction occurs in the thin sense, then we must act to eliminate it in the easiest way possible – generally through *ad hoc* additions (however ludicrous they may appear).

The thick sense requires a holistic overview of the situation such that the system's general flavour is maintained. This may require wholesale changes (as opposed to tinkering and gerrymandering). The added criterion is something like *elegance*. 'Elegance' can include simplicity and presentation (much as we judge fine food at restaurants!). Obviously, this added criterion comes from *outside* the functional outcomes of coherence itself. Thus, coherence transforms from a simple 'interior check' that, in principle, could be performed by a computer, to a reliable, thoughtful examination that requires an internalist perspective via the personal worldview imperative in order authentically to assent to its truth.

One should note when examining the coherence theory of truth (unlike the correspondence theory), there is no ontological commitment that propositions and theories necessarily *are*. This means that there is no affirmation of separate and independent existence. The reason for this is that the truth claim is dependent upon an observer making a judgement about the claim. The observer judges the claim to be coherent or not (thin or thick). That's as far as it goes. If the observer is confident in her judgement, she may declare that her judgement (if made by reliable means) may be sufficient to assert truth as separate and independent. But that is only a conjecture. There is no attaching necessity to some ontological claim. Whereas, in the case of correspondence theory, the truth of the object was given necessarily and only *our* ability to fashion replicas was in question. In the case of coherence theory, the ability to fashion sound, error-free accounts is given and only the account's ultimate mode of existence is in question – just the opposite!

Pragmatic Theory

The pragmatic theory of truth asserts that a theory is confirmed to be true relative to the work it can perform. There are two distinct ways to understand this: 1) relating to mere personal expediency (the internalist perspective), and 2) relating to intersubjective scientific confirmation in the experimental method (the externalist perspective). Let's examine these in order.

The first interpretation of pragmatic theory follows from William James who said, 'The true is only the expedient in the way of our behaving, expedient in almost any fashion, and expedient in the long run and on the whole course.'[19] This means that a success standard arises to justify what is or is not true. When related to personal expediency from the internalist standpoint, this amounts to the criteria for justifying some belief as true. Plato, in the *Theatetus*, floats the claim that if someone believes something, and is justified in that belief, then the belief is knowledge. However, Plato is careful to suggest various pitfalls in what would count as a justification (Plato was a correspondence theory advocate). In the twentieth century the problem of what counts as adequate justification for belief from the internalist perspective has led to arguments concerning adequate conceptual grounds for justification.[20] From the internalist perspective it all returns to some belief being good for us. This may be understood as holding a belief that it is better for us to hold than some other belief. Richard Rorty has taken this position:

> The aim of all such explanations is to make truth more than what Dewey calls 'warranted assertibility': more than what our peers will, *ceteris paribus*, let us get away with saying. Such explanation, when ontological, usually takes the form of a redescription of the object of knowledge so as to bridge the gap between it and the knowing subject. To choose between the approaches is to choose between truth as 'what is good for us to believe' and truth as 'contact with reality'.[21]

Thus, according to Rorty, one would espouse positions based on personal utility. States of affairs or propositions are true *to us*. This position, of course, bumps up against the good. The true equals *the good for us*. For example, at the writing of this book, in the United States the Congress is being asked to make permanent a series of tax breaks that greatly increase the wealth of the richest 2 per cent of the population at the expense of middle and lower middle classes (whose social-welfare support programmes are being cut to support this initiative). If you are one of the 2 per cent, the tax programme is good for you and therefore represents true/correct tax policy. If you are one of the 98 per cent, then you take the opposite opinion. (Unless, perhaps, you are *near* the 2 per cent and think that you might get there soon.) The problem with this (and any other perspective that is largely *pro se* internalist) is that it has a great potential to be very eccentric. Thus, if Baron von Frankenstein believes that eugenics is beneficial to him because of his research programme, and if his programme is successful, then eugenics is true. If Hitler believes that creating a national scapegoat (the Jews) and murdering them along with an ambition of global conquest is beneficial to him and to Germany, and if he is successful (or so long as he *was* successful), then it was true. When he was defeated, it became false. But what of Joseph Stalin, who died on top? Was his murderous regime of empire building *true*? Under these criteria, it would be true *to him*.

The point of these three examples is to demonstrate how the true dialectically interacts with the good. I argue that the subjectively based criteria of this first interpretation of pragmaticism make it less a theory of truth and more a theory of egoistic hedonism (a contender of sorts among ethical claims). I think this is a very dangerous stance because it violates the balance between the subject and society, which is embodied within the personal worldview imperative and the shared community worldview imperative. Donald Davidson has echoed my apprehension to relativism: 'Conceptual relativism is a heady and exotic doctrine, or would be if we could make good sense of it. The trouble is, as so often in philosophy, it is hard to improve intelligibility while retaining the excitement.'[22] The excitement is often generated at the expense of the logical argument. In Rorty's case, the two statements of the good (that his argument imply) demand (if we wish to heed to Davidson's admonition) that we never engage solely in either the internal or the external perspective but rather hold each in dialectical tension so that each might inform upon the other. Thus, this first understanding of pragmatism must be constrained by these criteria.

The second interpretation of pragmatic theory states the work performed refers to scientific confirmation in the experimental method. A hypothesis is proved whenever its predicted results come about under controlled conditions. In this way, the pragmatic theory (under the second interpretation) is the most externalist of all of the three theories. It emphasizes a test that is, by definition, open to public scrutiny.

Since we live in an age that worships the scientific method and the technological advances that it has brought to us, pragmatism is the default theory of truth for most people in the developed industrial world. Thus, it is a theory to be reckoned with.

Some of the difficulties associated with the theory track closely to the alleged problems with the scientific method of theory confirmation. The first of these can be illustrated in the following thought experiment concerning what can be understood as confirming evidence.

THOUGHT EXPERIMENT 4.8.[23]

Suppose we wish to confirm the following proposition, 'All ravens are black.' One way to confirm this is to go out into the world and look at as many ravens as possible. When you find black ravens, this confirms the hypothesis. When you have observed what you feel is an adequate sample, then you claim confirmation. Another way to think about this is to alter the proposition into logically equivalent forms. One legitimate logical transformation is via contraposition[24] that alters the generating proposition into an equivalent one: 'All non-black things are non-ravens.' The first form (call it X) is logically equivalent to the second (call it Y). Thus, if they are logically equivalent, then anything confirming X also confirms Y and vice versa. But this creates a strange situation in which the Washington Monument (a tall white building) confirms X because it confirms Y! But things can get even worse. Consider Z (logically equivalent to X and Y), 'If anything is (a raven or not a raven), then if it is a raven, then it is black.' Z makes the comedy complete since now non-ravens and black objects – as well as ravens – confirm that all ravens are black. We can now do science in the comfort of our office study without having to go out into the field!

On first glance many readers might think that we have committed the thought-experiment fallacy via the back door because the conditions seem rather artificial. However, I would contend that there is something to be learned here. It is that propositional language (that philosophers employ for clarity) is not benign, as many believe. For example, the proposition 'All ravens are black' seems to be about the subject, ravens. But it is really about the way we predicate essential properties to ravens – such as their blackness. If we choose logical expression as our *only* vehicle of expression, then we severely limit ourselves. Hempel thought that one key problem in the logical expression of the proposition was moving between the class description (of ravens as a species) and particular ravens (confirmation instances). Since individuals and class descriptions are different logical types, there are many possibilities for error in the transfer. Further, when we are thinking about confirming X we must not be deluded that we are only thinking about ravens! Overly analytical thinking (by itself) can create narrow viewpoints that often give rise to false results (such as thinking that the Washington Monument or random black things can help us with a problem in ornithology). A more contextual approach is needed that better takes into account background information.

This leads to the next thought experiment:

THOUGHT EXPERIMENT 4.9[25]

Perhaps a way to introduce relevant background conditions is by focusing upon which phenomena are causally connected to the explanandum. In science, the experimental method is one way to do this. If one can create a crucial experiment that identifies white or other coloured ravens, then it would seem that we have falsified the generating hypothesis that all ravens are black. Thus, perhaps what we should emphasize in our examination of how a proposition works are the conditions that might demonstrate its falsification.

Thought Experiment 4.9 seeks to solve our problem concerning background conditions by offering an operational procedure that would determine whether the generating hypothesis is true or false. If the experiment fails to falsify (a work performed and therefore a pragmatic device), then it is either assumed that the hypothesis is correct or that the wrong sort of experiment was created. One's confidence in the experimental design will correlate into one's confidence in the experimental outcome. This whole process rests upon a truth test based upon pragmatism.

The falsification test has been influential and useful. For example, the claim that Freudian psychological theory was scientific has been criticized on the basis that it couldn't be falsified – particularly the tenet concerning suppressed feelings and Oedipal development. Freud contended that part of normal development was to undergo the Oedipal or Electra developmental stages in which (as children) we imagine killing our father/mother and marrying our mother/ father. This tenet was then used to explain certain adult behaviour. However, when confronted with evidence to the contrary (i.e. statements by individuals that they did not experience these feelings), the theory responded that the individuals were mistaken and were merely suppressing these feelings. Thus, the theory was 'in principle' non-falsifiable.[26] This caused some to re-classify the Freudian doctrine from science to religion (a belief category not amenable to empirical falsification).

However, there are problems in paradise. Though falsification seems to work very well in some cases at singling out cogent background conditions (based upon a scientific, externalist standpoint), it does not do well at identifying whether that background condition is conclusive. Going back to our raven example, what if finding a white raven were trotted out as a falsifying instance against the hypothesis that 'All ravens are black'? It *could be the case* that it isn't a falsifying condition at all. This is because it could be due to environmental contamination (such as dioxins or other pollutants). Thus, without further examination it is unclear what to make of a falsification instance. One true example in the history of science concerns the orbit of Uranus. Newton's calculations of Kepler's laws seemed to be falsified by empirical data obtained by astronomers. If we were to jump to conclusions, then we would discard Newton's laws. But nineteenth-century astronomers were not so quick to do this. They searched further and discovered the planet, Neptune that then confirmed the observed orbit of Uranus.[27]

Thus, though falsification can do much to highlight critical background conditions, it isn't a perfect tool. We are still searching for a principle of relevancy. One way to proceed in our quest is to consider another thought experiment.

THOUGHT EXPERIMENT 4.10[28]

Imagine that we are thinking about the proposition M: 'All ravens are black' in the context of time. At the first time (t$_1$) we will say is

M (all times before 2020) and at the subsequent time (t2) we will
say N: 'All ravens are brue' (all times after 1 January 2020).

At t_1 – All ravens are black

At t_2 – All ravens are brue (where brue applies to all things examined before t_1 just in case they are black but to others at t_2 just in
case they are brue).

What are we to think about this?

First, it is the case that confirmation or falsification instances of M
are also confirmation or falsification instances of N. But this is
strange because brue is an arbitrary predicate. It is not projectible
causally into any known scientific theory.[29] If such transformations
as M-to-N were possible, then all extrapolators on graphs would be
subject to question. We assume a constant in time – yet, this is just
one more background condition that we need to consider.

The point of Thought Experiments 4.8–4.10 is to emphasize that
though the promise of pragmatic science as a springboard to truth is
immense, just *what* is known is rather ambiguous. There are so many
variables that those who depend solely upon these tests for truth may
be disappointed.

Conclusion

This is the longest, most difficult chapter in the book. I hope most of
you are still here. This is tough stuff, but it is crucial to our quest. I
believe it is important to try to wrestle with these questions. It is my
contention that, like ethics, we should choose a dominant worldview
position on truth – whether it is correspondence theory, coherence
theory or pragmatic theory. The other theories may offer key
insights, but they are rather seasoning on the main course and not
the main course itself.

Of course, there are those who demur such as Donald Davidson
who said: '"My skin is warm" if and only if my skin is warm. Here
there is no reference to a fact, a world, an experience, or a piece of
evidence.'[30] These are the deflationists who will discount the

import of much of this chapter – except as a propadeutic for later rejection.

In the spirit of this book, I end the chapter with this alternative perspective (though it is not one with which I agree), in order to stimulate readers' thinking on what should constitute the grounds of truth.

5 Scepticism, Illusion and the Sources of Knowledge

And if he left off dreaming about you . . .
  Lewis Carroll, *Through the Looking Glass*

This chapter will first confront the problem of scepticism and its role in our quest for truth. This investigation will cause us to consider how appearance and reality follow as a consequence and the subsequent turning to various sources upon which to ground knowledge.

Scepticism

I doubt it! Is this really the title of this chapter sub-section? Maybe not? How can I know – oh, let's get over it. We've had enough of this. How many things should we doubt? Is the President of the United States an honest fellow? (I don't suppose it matters too much the year that you ask this question.) Is the British Parliament honest? Should we believe that we can continue driving Hummer SUVs that get seven miles a gallon of gas and have a BTU construction coefficient that is many times that of the Toyota Prius or Honda Civic and not turn the world into an oven of death? In life we are presented with many rather dubious claims. It seems that a degree of scepticism is in order. But what is scepticism and how much is too much? To answer this question we must hit the rewind button and review the history of philosophy.

The ancient Greeks coined the cognate for 'scepticism' in the Greek word *'skepsis'* that means to consider something on the basis of the senses. The ancient Greeks such as physician Sextus Empiricus (c. 160–210 CE) and the medical 'empiric' and 'methodist' schools distrusted rational coherentists.[1] The reason for this is that they felt that the physician could only help his patient if he had so much concrete detail that it defied any general rules. Some writers in modern theories of the good (called particularists) echo this caveat.[2] They believe that theories of the good ignore particular circumstances and thus distort any proposed solution. Each case had to be considered on its own terms. On this approach, one would resist (as much as possible) forcing any general accounts upon the phenomena at hand.

I had first-hand experience of proponents of this position when I used to work at the philosophy registration desk at Marquette University where I once taught. In those pre-personal-computer-registration days, we handed out a limited number of IBM punch cards for students wishing to take a particular class. We also had a not-so-secret group of cards that we could give that would allow the number of students to exceed the declared class size. The department chair admonished us only to give these out in the direst situations. Thus, the contest was engaged: students found out about the supplementary cards and set out their creative skills to get into the classes they wanted (that were already closed). They would say things like, "I know that there is a rule . . .' or 'If only you knew my circumstances . . .' or 'My situation is special because . . .' and so forth. The point of these petitioners was to let me know that the general covering rule was designed to apply to certain situations, e.g. A: $\{s_1, s_2, s_3, \ldots s_n\}$. Despite the intention of the covering rule, the petitioning student wanted to convince me that their situation did not fall into A because it is $s_n + 1$. Instead, it belongs into the set of anomalies, B, that contain none of the same members as A. All the rules that apply to A do not apply to B. Since the student before me is asserting that she is in B, then I should not use A-rules to adjudicate her case. In other words, the rules don't apply to her because her situation is different. She wants me to give her one of the special cards that the department chair has told us not to do except in extreme duress. To consider this claim let us consider a thought experiment.

THOUGHT EXPERIMENT 5.1

What if everyone were different, and we couldn't classify anyone because all the rules of class inclusion would fail to recognize those

properties that were different? And what if all general rules were
based upon people being included into classes? Wouldn't that
mean that there would be no general rules (except the self-referential rule just enumerated)? What would be the consequence?

Thought Experiment 5.1 points us to problems posed by the ancient
sceptic and their modern counterpart, particularism. The 'anti-class
=> anti-rule' folk believe that one should somehow immerse himself
into the rich empirical detail, and that this belies all but individual
recognition.

Now I *am* a proponent of contextualized individual recognition.
We live in a world of particulars so that to ignore this would be
anti-empirical. When it comes to people, we all possess individual
dignity, and individual dignity recognition must always be maintained. (Again Truth bumps up against the Good.) But it does seem
rather implausible to me to rid ourselves of rules and set-inclusion
procedures. The very formulation of our thoughts through vocabulary, syntax, and grammar seems to demand that we bounce back
and forth between the general and the particular. Thus, I take the
ancient sceptics to offer a cautionary tale: don't forget individuals
and particularity in your quest for the truth. These sceptics are
saying that particularity is much more plausible than a rationally
abstract prescription for finding out what *is*.

A more contemporary usage of 'sceptic' came about in the
medieval times in the person of the African philosopher, Augustine
of Hippo (354–430 BCE), in his work *Against the Academicians*.[3] In
this work Augustine makes the following two arguments:

ARGUMENT 5.1
'Either p or ~p is true'

1. 'P or ~p' cannot be denied – Fact[4]
2. That which cannot be denied is true – A

---

3. Either p or ~p is true – 1, 2

ARGUMENT 5.2
'Senses do not err in what they report'

1. When you report seeing something you either are using your senses or not – F

2. Senses acquire appearances and present them to the mind – A

3. What appears truly is apprehended – A

4. Senses do not lie – 2, 3

5. Appearances not from senses (like madness or sleep) cannot be blamed on the senses – F

6. The falsity of non-sensed appearances is not the fault of the senses – 5

7. Senses do not err in what they report – 1, 4, 6

These two arguments set a stance against the ancient understanding of scepticism (based upon *skepsis*). There is no legitimate reason to deny argument one. This is often called the law of the excluded middle. When considering mutually exclusive complementary sets, it is always the case that if one is a member of one set, then one is not a member of the other. One cannot be in both at the same time in the same respect. An example of this would be pregnancy. At any given time, Mary Lou Sue is either pregnant or she isn't. There is no in-between.

It would be impossible to refute this. This is because the very use of language requires the acceptance of this law of thought along with its sister: the law of non-contradiction that says that we cannot conjoin a proposition and its contradictory opposite: $\sim (p + \sim p)$. Along with propositional identity $(p = p)$ these primitive statements seem beyond scepticism. To doubt them would be to deny one's entire rational consciousness. However, by the same measure, we can't prove them. Once again, we fall prey to the rationality incompleteness conjecture. One must shift to the selective faith maxim and adopt it the most plausible hypothesis.[5] It seems more intuitively plausible to accept a principle upon which all rationality seems to depend than to reject it – even if there is not a conclusive positive proof to that effect.[6] Given these foundational conditions, it seems reasonable to accept Argument 5.1.

In Argument 5.2 the most controversial premise is number 3: What appears truly is apprehended. This amounts to an affirmation of the veracity of sense impressions from the internal perspective of the agent. Let's examine this further through another thought experiment.

THOUGHT EXPERIMENT 5.2

Fred Football is the quarterback of his team. On a crucial play of the final minute of the game Fred threw an interception (a pass intended for his own player that was caught by the opposite team). Let's assume that Fred Football threw a pass to an individual waving his hands and appearing to Fred to be his receiver. Let us also assume that that player was not Fred's teammate (he wore a different coloured jersey), but because Fred focused upon the waving hands and physique of the player, who resembled in this way his teammate, he thought it was his teammate. Therefore, Fred threw the errant pass that cost his team the game. What happened?

If Argument 5.2, premise 3 is correct, then what appears is truly apprehended. Yet a mistake was made. How are we to understand this? There are at least two answers: (a) the judgement made by Fred (inside his brain) was flawed, or (b) the senses *did* err and thus Augustine's refutation of ancient scepticism is flawed. Under this first account, one might say that the processing procedure of interpreting the sense impression was hurried or otherwise impaired (perhaps also because a 250-pound linebacker was about to crush Fred). As a result, a flawed outcome (at the processing end) resulted.

Which hypothesis is correct: (a) or (b)? This is a difficult problem to solve. Augustine chose (a) because he felt that there must be some foundational acceptance of sensory data input. Without such a commitment, much of the raw material upon which we construct our personal worldview would be in such disarray that a holistic worldview would be impossible to construct.

However, on the other side, René Descartes (1596–650) chose (b).[7] He believed that sometimes the senses might betray us. Ultimately, they couldn't be relied upon for the foundation of all knowledge. Only reason could perform such a task. Eventually, Descartes comes to a provisional acceptance (for the most part) of empirical input on the basis of a rationally based set of arguments for the existence of God and the further assertion that a good God (an unexamined posit) would not create illusions of what seemed like truly perceived experience when, in *fact*, it was false. This would amount to a trickster God (and being a trickster is not to be good), thus God would not make the senses unreliable. Thus, at the end of the day, Descartes agrees with Augustine, but not for the same *reasons why*. In philosophy, the reasons why are very important. Thus, though Descartes ends up agreeing with Augustine, he cannot be said to be an advocate of (a). This is because the *verification* of the senses came through an extended rational defence that *began* with the assumption that the senses were faulty.

This discussion initiates the modern understanding of scepticism. In the modern realm (defined by philosophers as beginning with Descartes in the seventeenth century), scepticism began to be associated with "critical inquiry". But Descartes, in the first meditation of his *Meditations on First Philosophy*, suggests that he will engage in a radical doubt (not unlike Sextus but without Sextus' empirical foundationalism). In practice, Descartes is more reasonable. He doesn't (and couldn't) doubt *everything* – who could doubt the laws of identity, excluded middle, or non-contradiction? But Descartes does make a rhetorical point that leads subsequent philosophers to ponder the place of scepticism in creating a personal theory of knowledge.

The role of scepticism as critical understanding is advanced by David Hume (1711–1776) in the following arguments:[8]

ARGUMENT 5.3

1. Action requires the mind operate on various principles – F
2. Acting on various principles implies accepting various principles – F
3. A radical sceptic cannot accept any principles – F
4. A radical sceptic cannot act – 1–3
5. Action is necessary for common life – A

6. Radical scepticism is refuted by action in common life – 4, 5
7. Mitigated scepticism eliminates false beliefs – A
8. Getting rid of false beliefs is good – F

9. Only limited and mitigated scepticism can be useful – 6–8

ARGUMENT 5.4

1. There are two types of reasoning: (a) (analytical) arguments about relations of ideas, and (b) (synthetic/empirical) matters of fact – A
2. Science is properly about matters of fact – A
3. Mathematical reasoning (quantity and number) is properly about relation of ideas – A
4. (There is no proper third form of thinking) – A
5. Science and maths should be based upon their proper form of reasoning – 1–4
6. Sometimes people mistake one form of reasoning for the other – F
7. When people mistake one form of reasoning for another, they create a new (third) form of reasoning – F
8. Creating a third form of reasoning leads to error – 4, 6, 7
9. Intellectual belief should not be based upon error – A

10. Intellectual belief that is not based upon reasoning about quantity and number or experimental fact is not justifiable – 5, 8, 9

In Argument 5.3 Hume argues against radical scepticism – the kind that Descartes seems to imply in his first meditation. Argument 5.4 combines aspects of Augustine's Arguments of 5.1 and 5.2 as offering the foundations for knowing as fundamental logic and math along with empiricism. Let's look at Hume's arguments a little more carefully in order.

First, let's examine Argument 5.3. This argument puts forth the claim that radical scepticism should be abandoned and mitigated scepticism adopted. Radical scepticism is the revolutionary position that many have attributed to Descartes. In the *Meditations on First*

Philosophy Descartes employs construction metaphors in describing how one might build an edifice of knowledge that begins with a single point of absolute certainty (a sound foundation). According to the ancient Greek philosopher Archimedes, if one could find a single absolute point, he could use it as a fulcrum to move the world.[9] Thus, Descartes gives the impression that he almost doubts everything in search of this point. This is the backdrop of his famous 'cogito ergo sum/je pense donc je suis' argument.[10] This argument (though an imprecise popularization) was extremely influential. Set in the revolutionary era of the seventeenth century, it was part of the shared community worldview of advancement and progress in thinking. Imagine the freedom: everything could be doubted! You could doubt the authority of Charles I of England and chop off his head. You could imagine challenging the Roman Catholic Church. You could imagine many things – but they all equalled freedom.

THOUGHT EXPERIMENT 5.3

Find a safe place. Find a spotter who will protect you in case things get hairy. Now sit down in a comfortable position, shut your eyes, and try to doubt everything you ever believed. This is all provisional, but try it. Assume that everything can be doubted. What happens to you? How did it happen? Were you systematic in your doubt? Did you begin imagining music? Did you imagine painting? Poetry? Total blankness? Anxiety? Pain? A swollen scream from the centre of your being? Stop! It's getting a little dangerous. Write this all down and talk about it with a friend.

Thought Experiment 5.3 is an attempt to experience radical doubt. Many people who have tried this thought experiment end up unable to empty their mind. Others relate an experience of focused meditation. Most fall asleep. No one seems to be able to talk about it except in the most general terms. Virtually everyone ends up disappointed.

Many contemporaries of Hume attributed radical scepticism to Descartes. But careful readers of Descartes know that he did no such thing. Descartes knew he couldn't doubt everything since the mind required certain clear starting points for its very operation.[11] This is why people are disappointed with Thought Experiment 5.3. It is because radical scepticism is an impossible project. The reason for this is that (like Thought Experiment 5.1) radical scepticism involves a self-referential paradox:

ARGUMENT 5.5
The Impossibility of Radical Scepticism

1. Proposition M: 'We must doubt everything' – A
2. Proposition M is true – A
3. Radical scepticism is true if and only if proposition M is true – A
4. Radical scepticism is true – 1–3
5. To doubt something is to assume it is false – F
6. Proposition M is something – F
7. We must doubt proposition M – 1, 6
8. We must assume proposition M is false – 5, 7
9. Radical scepticism is true and assumed false – 4, 8
10. Premise 9 states an impossibility – A
---
11. Radical scepticism is impossible – 9, 10

Hume (Argument 5.3) and others properly reject radical scepticism. Instead, another form of questioning, mitigated scepticism, is proposed. Mitigated scepticism is very much like the careful scrutiny maxim. One ought to be very careful about what she embraces as true. We do not act unless we have sound, empirically based reasons to do so.

The grounds overcoming mitigated scepticism are found in Argument 5.4. Here, Hume is a bit more specific than Augustine was in Arguments 5.1 and 5.2. Relations of ideas are true in virtue of their internal criteria (coherentism). Matters of fact are verified at once through empirical correspondence between the subject's idea and the physical object. They are understood by the subject to be fundamentally true. This cannot be questioned. This certainty of our brute sensory experience is so strong that it can be called *the dogma of empirical rectitude*. All of us assume that our senses properly report to us facts about the world. This means that we assume in a dogmatic way that our sense experience is correct unless we are given very strong reasons (rational and empirical) to the contrary. However, such counter-examples will not work unless at least one sense is operating correctly. This is called a *dogma* since there is a natural tendency to disregard counter-examples. It is only when one sensory power in the individual is pitted against another (along with a rational argument) that we will accede to sensory defect.

Hume here has it right that though we must discard radical scepticism, we should not discard scepticism as an attitude within our personal worldview. This is because it permits us to execute the careful scrutiny maxim in our daily context thinking. A certain amount of scepticism is essential if we want to fulfil the quest for knowledge that requires that we all (a) want to embrace all that is true and (b) reject all that is false. To deviate from this quest is to degrade our human nature.

Appearance and Reality

The juxtaposition of appearance and reality confronts us all the time. Fred Football tells Mary Lou Sue that he will be true to her and yet he is found stepping out with Sally Mae! Or Jamal tells Rashid that the thousand-dollar name-brand notebook computer can be his for only three hundred dollars. It fell off a truck! Who will know? Maria wants to confide in Mercedes the secrets of her job ambitions on the understanding that it is confidential. Then Maria finds out that Mercedes used the information to get herself the job instead. And there are so many more.

What are we to think about the question of what appears to be true versus what is actually true? Well, for starters, the question assumes that there is a 'true'. The discussions in Chapter 4 discuss three ways to understand this sort of claim: correspondence theory, coherence theory, and pragmatic theory. But this does not address the real possibility that lots of people may never really possess the true (however it is described).

To address this possibility, we must turn to Plato's cave.[12] In the allegory, Plato depicts the general populace as ignorant folk (based upon the correspondence theory of truth). These cave dwellers use vision as the basis for their knowledge claims. What they see against the cave wall are only shadows of puppets. If the puppets have any connection to what *is* (and this need not be the case), then they are watching an image third-hand.[13] If we assume that each level of imitation infers a loss of fidelity, then a third-hand rendition isn't very good. (Of course, it must be remembered that this allegory assumes a correspondence theory of truth in order to work.)

The key moment in the cave allegory is when the rare individual breaks free from the constrictions of the cave (perhaps because he has engaged in the process of the personal worldview imperative?). This person goes outside the cave and discovers that things are really different than they appeared to be in the cave. In the light of the sun the newly freed individual sees the world as it is.[14]

This is heady stuff. What you previously saw third-hand, you now see directly *as it is*. Now what are you going to do? Option (a) would be to lie on your back and just bask in the truth; option (b) would be to go back into the cave and share your insights with others. What would you do?

Plato suggests that option (b) carries great risks – even death as per his teacher, Socrates. (We can all think of other victims, such as Jesus, Gandhi, Malcolm X, Martin Luther King, Jr., Yitzhak Rabin, and others who presented a vision of truth that so disturbed some in the populace that they killed these messengers.)

Since the presentation of an alternate worldview is extremely threatening to those content with the one they already have, it is quite reasonable from their point of view to move to the *dissonance and rejection* response. This very well might inspire those with the threatened worldview to take any action they can – including murder – to contain this alternate vision of truth.

This truth business is dangerous. It can kill you from without and from within.

But where is the origin of this discontent? It implies a seeker who is overcome by his inability to find his Archimedean point. To quote from Matthew Arnold's poem 'Dover Beach':

> The sea is calm to-night.
> The tide is full, the moon lies fair
> Upon the straits; on the French coast the light
> Gleams and is gone; the cliffs of England stand;
> Glimmering and vast, out in the tranquil bay.
> Come to the window, sweet is the night-air!
> Only, from the long line of spray
> Where the sea meets the moon-blanched land,
> Listen! you hear the grating roar
> Of pebbles which the waves draw back, and fling,
> At their return, up the high strand,
> Begin, and cease, and then again begin,
> With tremulous cadence slow, and bring
> The eternal note of sadness in.

The poet's narrator here is indulging in the so-called pathetic fallacy as he imputes his own sadness and anxiety about life and love in the context of ancient history and military warfare. The metaphor of the changeable sea as a touchstone of immutable truth creates a dramatic tension. Arnold's narrator is asking what can we really believe in now that Victorian modernity has thrown much up in the air.

The stakes are high: death and madness possibly rest in the balance. So where is the source of this difficulty? It lies in those who engage the quest. Plato suggests that the number of those who are content in their personal and community worldviews and do not want to be bothered is rather large. He never tells us how many, but it is assumed to be an overwhelming majority of people.[15] If this is the case, then most people live in a sort of delusion. They are just not up to the task of undergoing the quest demanded by the personal worldview imperative.

Friedrich Nietzsche concurs with Plato on this point. Nietzsche makes Plato's allegory more concrete with the connection of this journey to the ascension to nobility and power. It becomes an empirical truism that only a few can be at the top.[16] In this case, knowledge is equated with power. Power confers nobility, and thus the überman (the excellent achiever) by seeing the truth can use it to his own advantage – in a noble way.[17] These will be (as a matter of fact) the rulers of society. (Thus, there is a pragmatic test dropped in: if you aren't a ruler or powerful individual, then you aren't an überman.)

It is interesting that both Plato and Nietzsche depict a populace that is largely under a herd mentality. The general populace doesn't recognize or respond to Truth (in any of its actual forms). So what do we do about this? In Plato's case there is recognition of some sort of demographic power on the part of the *hoi polloi* (ergo, they will put the seer to death). In Nietzsche's case the überman will triumph. If he doesn't, then he was never an überman.[18]

A final note in this section on the nature of the appearance-and-reality conflict comes from George Berkeley (1685–1753). In his seminal work *Of the Principles of Human Knowledge*, Berkeley employs a style of short sections (generally less than a page) to begin or to advance arguments. This organizational style is similar to Marcus Aurelius and Ludwig Wittgenstein. It requires more work on the part of the interpreter because appearance and reality interact in the very act of reading. Thus, any reconstruction of these arguments is more interpretative than is the case among other philosophers whose arguments progress in a more linear fashion.

ARGUMENT 5.6
The Ground of Existence[19]

1. To exist is to be judged to exist by a mind – A
2. The only way a mind has objects (ideas or sensations) is through perception – A
3. The mind is a spirit – A
4. Ideas and sensations exist in as much as they are presented and judged by a mind or spirit – 1–3
5. If no mind is perceiving an object (ideas or sensation), the object is not in the state of being judged – F
6. There are two modes of judging an object: actual or potential – A
7. If no mind is actually or potentially judging an object, it does not exist – 5, 6
8. Objects have their being in a mind that contemplates them – 4, 7

This is perhaps Berkeley's most famous argument. It sets a standard for the distinction between appearance and reality that is based upon the empirical judgement of the observer. What is crucial here is that existence is relative to an observer. It is referred to as *pro se* existence since it asserts that to exist is to exist for someone on the basis of an empirical experience. For example, consider this page that you are reading right now. The page and the book that holds it in place are real to you as sensory impressions of white and black, and the outline of the book cover, the weight and solidity of the book in your hands, the olfactory experience of the page as it turns, and so forth. While you have that book in your hand and are looking at this page it exists to you *because* it is an object of your immediate sensory experience. Nothing more is known about that book. You don't know whether there really is matter that underlies the sense impressions and causes your sensations. No, this would be an unfounded assumption. What you do know is that your senses (assumed to be reliable) make a judgement about this page before you and the book that contains it. The judgement properly can go no further than the mere catalogue of those sensory reports. This is because it is only these impressions that are presented to you.

Berkeley's position can be called naïve or simple empiricism. Just like Sextus Empiricus in the last chapter, the call is to refrain from making inferences *from* the data but to let that data speak for themselves. We must resist the urge to create abstract ideas from the data and to speculate about non-empirical generalities. This is because the mode of the object's existence to us *is* as it is presented and no more.

One might be able to imagine such a worldview via the following Thought Experiment 5.4:

THOUGHT EXPERIMENT 5.4

You are a devotee of Berkeley (and Sextus Empiricus) and you want to adopt the worldview of naïve empiricism. You are looking for a job that won't cause you to create unfounded abstractions. What job possibilities are open to you?

This thought experiment is more open-ended than you might think. Almost any job could accommodate you so long as you are allowed to concentrate your attention upon the realm of the empirical and not go beyond it. For example, if you were a computer programmer you could work at the machine in front of you and manipulate the symbols of the computer language so long as you didn't speculate upon some deeper meaning. What you see is all there is. When you go home, your computer may be an object of potential perception (i.e. the next working day), but to you *at that moment* it no longer fully exists to you. It only exists contingently (based upon your assumption that no one will steal it or that the building will not burn down). If the 'gold standard' test of existence is that someone perceives something actually or potentially, then your computer's existence *to you* ceases to exist fully when you no longer directly sense it.

This can create a situation in which it appears that objects pop in and out of existence to perceivers. To *us* when we leave an empirical tableau the entirety ceases to exist – to us. Such a possibility is bothersome.

Further, Berkeley's criteria for ascertaining true existence (as opposed to illusion) creates a famous paradox: if a tree falls in the forest (and no one is around) does it make a sound? For Berkeley the answer must be answered from the *pro se* stance. To *me* the tree made no sound. To *you* the tree made no sound. This is because neither of us was there to hear it. For any individual on earth the tree made no sound because no actual person was there. Thus, relative to any actual person there was no sound.[20]

It is here that Berkeley brings in God to solve this non-realistic implausibility. If one were to posit God as perceiving everything on earth all at once, then *to God* objects don't pop in and out of existence. To God the tree falling in the forest makes a sound.

Therefore, something consistent with a realism worldview can be constructed in which empiricism is emphasized while maintaining a worldview that is plausible for a naïve empiricism standpoint.

A second argument of Berkeley examines another challenge to the appearance v. reality question.

ARGUMENT 5.7
Real Things and Objects of the Imagination[21]

1. [Metaphysical separateness can be determined by epistemological separateness] – A
2. Both real things and imaginary things are presented to us
   immaterially – F
3. [Those things that are epistemologically different consist of: (a).
   different for a reason, (b). can be distinguished as different] – A
4. Imagination begins and is formed in our minds in an irregular
   and inconsistent act – A
5. Real things are outside us and are presented to the mind – F
6. Ideas about real things are formed via regular, constant, vivid
   conjunction – A
7. Ideas about real things differ from ideas from the imagination
   – 1–6
8. [That which is strong, lively, and distinct is easily distinguished
   as more steady and orderly and coherent than the less lively,
   distinct, and weak] – F
9. Imagination is less strong, lively, and distinct than perceptions
   of real things – A
10. Ideas about real things are easily distinguished from imagina-
    tion – 3, 8, 9
11. Real things and imagination (though similar) are epistemologi-
    cally separate – 2, 3, 7, 10

12. Real things and objects of the imagination are metaphysically
    separate – 1, 11

Argument 5.7 is very interesting. At premise 2 Berkeley sets out
the posit that the medium of transmission of sense perceptions is
uniform. Everything (beginning with the object of perception to the
intervening space to the mind) is immaterial. All is immaterial.
Unlike Descartes (a dualist), Berkeley is a monist-spiritualist. There
is one sort of thing that exists (the ontological question) and it is
spirit. Only spirit is really known-to-be (the epistemological ques-

tion). The epistemological question decides the ontological question so that epistemology becomes the subject area of greatest importance. So long as we stay close to the empirical data and do not stray far, we're fine. That is, we are likely to be embracing truth and unlikely to be embracing falsehood (our goal, as per Chapter 4).

But then there is the pesky question of the source of illusion and error. Berkeley has already asserted that abstract reasoning leads to error (since it moves away from naïve empiricism). But what leads to abstract reasoning?

One possibility might be imagination. Now here Berkeley has a potential problem. If our minds are immaterial and the medium is immaterial and the object of our perception is immaterial, then how can we distinguish a direct encounter (sensation) from a moment of intellectual reverie (imagination)? Obviously, the intent of the argument is that if we were to consider our active sensation of an apple and our imaginary vision of the apple, the former is superior because we can eat it. The latter is less strong, lively, and distinct. This is because the imagination is a copy of something that is true (cf. Plato). Copies don't match the originals. On the principle of verisimilitude they are, at least marginally, fakes (see Chapter 4). Fakes are (to varying degrees) false. On the level of correspondence theory (understood as pattern resemblance), Berkeley's argument holds. Imagination is a springboard to abstract reasoning and imagination as a substitute for sensation leads us to error. On this account, imagination is a snare to embracing false propositions:

ARGUMENT 5.8
A Neo-Berkeley Argument

1. There are two ways to know: naïve empiricism and abstract reasoning – A
2. Naïve empiricism is the foundational source of truth – A
3. Abstract reasoning is the source of error – A
4. All of us want to embrace truth and eschew error – A
5. We should all embrace naïve empiricism and eschew abstract reasoning – 1–4

6. Imagination leads to abstract reasoning – A
7. We should all eschew imagination – 5, 6
8. Art is driven by imagination – A

9. We should all eschew art – 7, 8

Such an argument is reminiscent of one reading of Plato. If this is a plausible extension of Berkeley, then Berkeley's naïve empiricism is anti-art. When we consider the appearance versus reality problem from this perspective, only the brute force of sensations are properly presented to us. Very little interpretation will do. All else will incline us to error. Since art – especially narrative art such as poetry and fiction – relies upon abstract reasoning through fictive, composite characters and invented plot, it is the perfect model of abstract reasoning. Under this scenario, imagination is the bad guy.

The second way to confront one's sensory manifold is to search for regularities in the data and move towards abstract principles though the process of inductive logic. Here, Berkeley would demur and pull the circuit breakers. Abstract reasoning leads to error. Thus, though it would be impossible to exclude induction entirely, Berkeley (like Sextus Empiricus and the ancient medical empirics) believes that, as much as possible, we should stick to foundational sense impressions and interpret them as little as possible. When we do feel inclined to interpret, it must be done in a simple, conventional way that shows that we really don't think such conventional moves are really *true*. They may be useful for living, but like the pragmatist, one may employ various conventional designs without any commitment to truth.

In this context, imagination is fine so long as it makes no claims to being true. So long as it is mere image arranging in pleasing ways that cannot be further analysed, then so be it. The minute it makes a greater claim, then it moves towards falsity. Thus, those devoted to imaginatively-driven expressions of beauty are purveyors of falsehood. At best, the artists are like cooks that merely please the palate or not according to our conventional, transitory taste.

If this account is correct, then we should cut out the third section of this book and commit it to the flames of sophistry and illusion.

The Sources of Knowledge: Logic, Empiricism, and Emotions

The answer to our cliffhanger about the third section of this book lies in the sources of knowing. It is here that the appearance v. reality question will be answered. Like many important questions in philosophy, Plato and Aristotle originally surveyed the general topography.

Logic: Plato's Programme

Plato said in the *Timaeus* that there were two sorts of ontological entities: (a) those that always are and are apprehended by *noesis* (rational intellection) or *logos* (logical argument); and (b) those that are always coming-to-be but never actually get there and are apprehended by *doxa* (opinion) and *aesthesis* (sense perception).[22] Because Plato valued something being long lasting over something being short-lived, *noesis* and *logos* won the day. This was as true for the principles that governed the creation of the universe as it is for day-to-day cognition. For this latter process, Plato sets out what has been termed 'the divided line'.

ARGUMENT 5.9
The Divided Line[23]

THE LINE

Level One – The Intelligible:

A: Forms known through dialectical intellection (noesis)

B: Mathematical objects known through hypothetical reflection (dianoia)

Level Two – The Empirical:

A: Empirical objects known through grounded belief or trust (pistis)

B: Empirical facsimiles known through image arranging (e.g. advertising, rhetoric, et al., eikasia)

The Argument

1. The sources of knowing are empirical or mental – A
2. Empirical sources are easy to come by – A
3. [That which is easy to come by is trivial] – A
4. Empirical sources are trivial – 1–3
5. [Trivial and non-trivial are logical contradictories] – F
6. Mental sources are non-trivial – 4, 5
7. Direct propositional knowledge is relatively easy to come by – A
8. Direct propositional knowledge is relatively trivial – 7, 3
9. The highest form of knowledge comes from pure (dialectical and non-propositional) contemplation – 4, 6, 8

The source of knowledge that Plato endorses should begin in rational intellection. However, this is rarely the case. We must begin at the bottom of the vertical line. In the cave we are all presented with artificial depictions of empirical nature (instead of direct contact with nature itself) in our early years. Most people naively accept the package of conventional presentation given by the shared community worldview. The only modifications on this are through other conventional ad hoc agencies. In our modern world these agencies might be: advertising, media, and common opinion (largely conditioned by the whole of popular culture). By far the greatest numbers of people endorse the pop-culture view of empirical reality. If something appears differently, then that experience is often dismissed as being unrepresentative. Thus, falsification is impossible. The governing, shared community worldview (status quo) rests secure from any barbarians at the gate.

On the next level, a small minority wants to critically access the empirical images that have been arranged for them. The given paradigms of the community worldview are called into question on the basis of coherency and pragmatism. This is the realm of critical scientists. They challenge the given theories of the empirical realm with a view towards extending it. They devote themselves to jettisoning themselves from the popular paradigms in order to embrace a more esoteric understanding of nature. However, Plato asserts that as intelligent as these individuals might appear (especially to the *hoi polloi* at level II-B), they are constrained by backing the wrong horse in the race: empiricism. Empiricism can only take you so far – i.e. halfway.

The other source of knowledge begins with propositional intellection. This is the realm of mathematics and propositionally based philosophy. Here is the interplay between various hypotheses (thesis and antithesis). From this logical interaction, something akin to mathematical or logically based arguments result. These arguments owe their genesis to intellection and discursive propositional communication.

Most of Anglo-American philosophy of the last 150 years would be categorized at this level. Most of the exposition of *this essay* exists at this level.

The highest source of knowledge transcends propositional philosophy. It asserts that some sort of intellectual grasping is at stake that has no discursive account. One achieves it but cannot directly communicate *what* it is. Such discourse is internalist (by definition). Thus, all externalists will demur at this point.

Philosophers such as Kierkegaard, Camus, Sartre, Heidegger, and others who use a strategy of indirect discourse might fit at this level.[24] Also, theologians who purport narrative or other indirect strategies would fit here, too.[25] Indirect discourse can give expression in playfully contradictory philosophy,[26] or a philosophy presented in such a complex fashion that most readers are forced into an interpretative mode that creates a stratum above the text in which the rendering exhibits itself. Of course a third alternative is to sow one's seeds in literary gardens and use the narrative format (inherently indirect) to structure a domain for interpretation (more on this in Part 3).

So much for Plato's levels and what they mean. The argument for the same (very enthymemic) bases the levels of how we come to know on degrees of difficulty. This is given in a visual metaphor of relative clearness of obscurity. What is visually clear is the easiest to accept. What is obscure probably seems clear to most, but not so to the trained eye. Thus, we have the fictional Sherlock Holmes who 'sees' what others don't because he is a critical, empirical observer. For those who don't place all their chips on the empirical side, then the obscurity has another side. Some empirical presentation may be obscure because incorrectly it is thought to present a truth that is beyond its ken.

Thus, one might think about achieving true happiness and note that it takes money to eat, have clothing, and shelter. Under one inductive operation one might generalize that money confers happiness.[27] However, the grounds of happiness may have a different derivation than from the empirical realm. Plato thinks that this is the case. People were created to use their sense organs (primarily vision and hearing) to contemplate nature for the purpose of trying to apprehend the forms/ideas of what *is*.[28]

Because Plato's answer to the ontological question is that there are two sorts of things (invisible and visible) and that these also are connected to the ways that they are apprehended (intellection and logic v. sensation and belief), then it is the case that our purpose as humans is to connect to the higher (the invisible via intellection and logic) and to see the lower (the visible via sensation and belief) as – *at best* – a springboard to higher realities. Thus, all art and science is in the deepest sense instrumental to higher and deeper realities and never true ends in themselves. The Abrahamic religions of the world (Christianity, Judaism, and Islam) also see things in just this way. Thus, for Plato, if we relegate our sensory experience into the category of 'springboard' to more serious consideration, which will be the most effective way to embrace what is true and jettison what is false. The real mother lode is to be found in pure intellection. Though there are other advocates of a dominantly rational approach to the sources of knowledge, Plato offers an influential paradigm in the history of philosophy.[29]

Empiricism: Aristotle's Programme

A different approach from Plato's can be found from his student Aristotle. Aristotle was, in his heart of hearts, a biologist. Around a quarter of his extant writings are on biology. He was also keenly interested in other natural phenomena. Thus, from the beginning, Aristotle gives much more credence than Plato does to the role of sensation and status of empirical knowledge. In Aristotle's work *The*

Categories, Aristotle begins with actual individuals living in the world. These individual organisms are the most real for Aristotle. (Plato thought that the form/ideas of general classes was the most real – just the opposite.) Abstraction from the empirically existing individual is a part of what we do as humans as we try to understand exactly (scientifically).

Table 5.1 Aristotle's Categories[30]

	Substance	Quantity	Quality	Relation	Place	Time et al.
	Thing	Quantification	Form	Society	Locales	400 BC
	Living thing	*	*	*	Earth Locales	*
	Animal	*	*	*		Human measuring of motion
	Human	*	*	Husband duties	Cities	
	Male	Numbers	Colours	Social relation	Greek Cities	Solar-based Time
Start:	*Socrates*	One	White	Husband of Xantippes	Athens	399 BC

Now, Aristotle did not write down and fill out the above chart. This is my reconstruction after a common interpretation of it.[31] But Aristotle does give us the category titles and says that we start with Socrates and then, going upwards, we have a relation of predication such that male is predicable of Socrates. This sort of relation is one of abstraction from the most real (often called the primary substance) to the less real (the abstractions). By making the abstractions less real in this way, Aristotle echoes Berkeley and Hume.

Going horizontally there is a relation of being present in so that 'one', 'white', 'husband of Xantippes', et al. are all present in

Socrates. Notice that the properties present in Socrates do not exist by themselves. There is no existing 'white' aside from an existing white thing, such as Socrates.[32] These properties present in Socrates have traditionally been called 'accidents' because Socrates would still be Socrates if they were altered, e.g. if Socrates' wife died and he was no longer her husband, then Socrates would still be Socrates, albeit with one accidental change – from husband to widower.

Thus, the empirical existence of some individual is necessary for the predicables or accidents to be meaningful. When Socrates dies they all disappear. There is no eternal realm in which they all reside.

This general principle applies to animal kinds as well. For example, though it is useful to classify animals in hierarchical classes (and Aristotle offers functional principles of systematics that are largely consistent with modern systematics),[33] when all the members of said class cease to exist (like the dodo bird), then the class also disappears from our biological classification chart. For Aristotle, if you cease to be, then you are history. End of story.

The sorts of questions that Aristotle suggests for the source of empirical knowledge are given at the beginning of the second book of *Posterior Analytics*:[34] 1) *hoti* (the verification of the presented sense perception as an organized something), 2) *dioti* (the cause or reason why it is as it is), 3) *ti esti* (as a result of questions 1 and 2 an assessment of the essential definition of this sort of being), and 4) *ei esti* (an assessment of its mode of existence). Aristotle believes that when we ask these four questions of empirical phenomena, that we will gain a reliable method for embracing what is true and discarding what is false.

For example if we observed a rhinoceros, our detailed account of the animal would satisfy the first question. Say in that detailed explanation we were to set out its prominent horn that extends out from its forehead. We might wish to know the reason for this horn (question 2). The answer to this might require that we make reference to accepted scientific theories of causation. (For Aristotle this meant his theory of the four causes: efficient, material, formal, and final.)[35] Today, this would mean reference to accepted scientific theories – the projectibility of Goodman (see Chapter 4). The account of the reason why in contemporary terms might describe the evolutionary advantage of this appendage as a weapon within a given range of environments.

The third question follows from the second. Once we have found out the 'reasons why' of the prominent physical characteristics of the taxon in question, we may then formulate a definition for the animal based upon observed physical features and their functions.

Lastly, we need to speculate upon the modal force of these features/functions. Could the rhinoceros exist with a skin that was thicker/thinner? If a mutant had a longer horn, would it gain a reproductive advantage? Are any of the organs vestigial? The answers to these questions (in the modern context) may give us a better understanding of the species' phylogenic history and an opportunity to speculate on its relative fitness today.

The four scientific questions form the basis of a critical empiricism that Aristotle develops in the abstract in *The Posterior Analytics*, *The Physics*, and *The Metaphysics*. In *The Parts of Animals* and *The Generation of Animals*, Aristotle turns his attention to more concrete problems in the philosophy of biology such as the nature of reproduction (from humans to bees to insects). For the most part, Aristotle more or less follows his methodology, but the main point for our exploration is that Aristotle (unlike Berkeley) finds a way to merge rational concerns with empirical fieldwork. It is for this reason that he can be characterized as a critical empiricist. Though there are many other prominent empiricists, which have (save Berkeley) been characterized here as externalists, Aristotle's account of empiricism as the source of knowing truth stands as an important paradigm in the history of philosophy.[36]

Emotions: A pastiche

One result of contemporary feminist philosophy has been an emphasis upon the emotions as a possible source of knowing truth.[37] Of course, Aristotle famously dismissed emotions as a source of truth in the *Nicomachean Ethics*:

ARGUMENT 5.10
Aristotle's on Emotions and Virtue

1. To have virtue is to move within action [voluntarily, actively] –
   A (1106a)
2. In emotion we are moved [involuntary, passive] – A (1106a 1–5)
3. Virtue cannot be based upon emotion – 1, 2 (EN 1106a 6)

Though this argument is on virtue, for Aristotle virtue is dependent upon practical wisdom. Thus, his argument against emotion as a component for virtue would also hold for practical reason (and certainly, by extension, for theoretical reason). The knock upon emotion is that it is out of our control. (Though some defenders, in the Aristotelian tradition suggest that it is a logical consequence of our character that *is* within our control.) Recently, there has been a resurgent interest in emotion. It is not my intent here to enter into that discussion except to explore how emotion can be a source of knowledge.

In this respect, I will direct my comments on how emotion is crucial in one's understanding of beauty and that beauty (according to the general premise of this book) links directly to truth and goodness.

Though Aristotle was a detractor concerning the connection between emotion and the ground of practical reason, he does propose that it is one of the principal ways we understand tragic drama. The emotion here is *katharsis*. This is the emotional purging that the audience feels when one witnesses the decline of a fairly good man through that person's tragic flaw.[38]

A typical member of the audience creates a sympathetic attachment with the protagonist and then identifies with him. When the flaw brings him down, the reaction is similar to it happening to a friend or loved one. In cases of intense identification, the reaction might be directed to the possibility of it happening to her (the audience member).

After the performance, the audience member feels cleansed as the result of the emotional reaction. The emotional roller coaster and the recognition of what *could happen* creates a vicarious sense of experience that is real. Though the drama is artificial, the emotional experience by the viewer is real. As a result of this real experience, the audience member goes through an examination that is filtered by the personal worldview of that individual. For example, if the drama was about a brave abortionist (in the era before abortionists, such as *The Cider House Rules* or *Vera Drake*), and the audience member was against abortion, then the audience member would never engage in sympathy with the protagonist and thus never experience catharsis. However, if the audience member believed in a woman's right to choose an abortion for herself, then a sympathetic reaction would have occurred early on and the probability of catharsis would be very high.

The variable here would be goodness. One's understanding of the moral question of a woman's right to choose an abortion would be a precondition to the experience of the emotional catharsis. It is not sufficient for it, but certainly it is a necessary precondition. In this way, goodness (morality) acts as gatekeeper for possible emotional involvement.

Another obstacle might be the way the drama is presented. If it is not executed professionally with skill (causing the observer to willingly suspends her disbelief), then again, emotional involvement will be thwarted. This is to speak to the beautiful. We will not become emotionally involved in a dramatic presentation that is not beautiful. To be beautiful, the movie/play/short story/novel must (at a minimum) meet the professional standards that are set by the artistic tradition and/or current practitioners. This is because it is this tradition (aka the artistic canon) that conditions the audience in their expectations of just what such a work of art is supposed to do. For example, if one were writing English sonnets for an Elizabethan audience, then the expectation would be iambic pentameter lines with an interlocking rhyming pattern in the first ten lines that also sets out the problem with a rhyming couplet resolution. If the poet could skilfully execute these technical devices, then the audience will potentially engage. These technical skills (one aspect of the beautiful) are prerequisites for any emotional interaction.

When properly executed, the emotional interaction with the text, drama, movie, et al. can inform upon the personal worldview of the audience member and help them affirm, change, or modify their own worldview. For example, I have talked to many elderly people in the course of volunteer work who have told me that *King Lear* altered their view on estate planning. Why is this the case? Because in *Lear* the protagonist makes a grave error in listening to the petitions of two evil, flattering daughters (Goneril and Regan) against the unpleasant truth-telling of Cordelia. The consequences of such a mistake drives Lear to madness. The emotional reaction to this particular story interacted with the intellectual moral of the story in such a way as to validate it. Emotions here act as a concurrent validating condition to the proposition at hand. Because emotions spring from one's personal worldview holistically, they are often the tie-breaking element in our judgments on truth.

This is not to say that sometimes emotions can lead us astray. In the end, rationality must trump emotions. But this is not to say that emotions aren't very important. In the day-to-day operation of our lives, they are our surest and quickest way to guide action according to our personal worldview. The process of this interaction in the context of our personal quest will be the subject matter for the next chapter. Turn the page!

6   Integrating Truth
into the Quest

To strive, to seek, to find, and not to yield.

Tennyson, *Ulysses*

Truth and the Quest

This last chapter in Part II has as its aim ways to stimulate the reader to initiate his or her own quest for truth. The strategy of this chapter is to mix an integrative exercise with the personal and shared community worldview imperatives using the substance of the various distinctions already discussed in Chapters 4 and 5.

If it is true that all people, by nature, desire to be good, then there is an automatic consequent requirement that each of us also be engaged in a quest for truth. This is because the framework from which the good is understood requires a contextualization. For example, if one thought that to be good is to be a successful and wealthy businessperson, then the context for that normative structure needs to be established. What might such a structure look like? For starters, one would have to give specification to 'successful' and 'wealthy'. Some might contend that if one can keep his job over a decade or so and can pay all his bills with a little left over, then one is successful and wealthy. Others might contend that unless one were at the vanguard of management (director or above in a big company) and compensated such that she were able to obtain virtually all of the desirable material goods society has to offer, that one has not made the grade as successful or wealthy.

Obviously, these are two extremes. In the first case, the expectations are geared towards satisfying the functional criteria of job security and basic material comfort – say from the top three quintiles of societal income distribution. The goal is to be middle class and to be satisfied with it. In the second case, the aim is really at the top one-tenth of one per cent of job status and compensation. Obviously, 'success' and 'wealthy' take on quite different meanings depending on the understanding of the terms.

How does one decide between these two visions? A large part of the answer lies in what one holds to be *true* and the procedure for confirming or falsifying various candidates. Since the premise of this book is that the Good, the True, and the Beautiful are never entirely separable, there will (necessarily) be a bit of bouncing back and forth between the various concepts.[1] However, the avowed focus of this chapter is how coming to a personal understanding of Truth can assist us in our life journey – here called 'the quest'.

Personal Worldview and Truth

Our personal worldview is an amalgam at any given time of all that we hold to be true and normatively right in the world. Our personal worldview guides us each day as we set about the task of living in the world. It constitutes the ground of our personhood and power of autonomous choice. Without a personal worldview that we have individually fashioned – such that we may rightly claim ownership of it – we would necessarily be slaves to the slings and arrows of everyday fortune. With a personal worldview that we have consciously shaped (at least in part), then even *outrageous* fortune may be wholly or partially under our control. In this way, worldview is individual consciousness that is holistically understood as comprising all that we have chosen to identify who we are.

It is a fact that each of us lives in our own worldview and participates (to some degree) in various community worldviews. If we are engaged in a quest for truth, then it should be the case that both sorts of worldviews must have limiting criteria that are designed to discard false worldviews and embrace true ones.

The personal worldview imperative, though it was presented in the previous section on the Good, is filled with language that is all about truth. 'All people must develop a single comprehensive and internally coherent worldview that is good and that we strive to act out in our daily lives.' First, there are the components of 'comprehensiveness' and 'internal coherency'. These are formal criteria associated with the coherence theory of truth. And yet, as interpreted, 'comprehensive' refers to creating a good will that has an inductive interpretation that is connected with the notion of avoiding a 'sure loss contract'. To give meaning to such an admonition, one must bring in all sorts of externalist facts about the world in order to be sure that one's life strategies match those facts in such a way that probability theory and statistics support our various goals: working together synergistically and not counterproductively. This externalist link gives the coherentism criteria a decidedly correspondence theory spin.

This is reinforced by the requirement that our personal worldview be connected to a recognized ethical theory or religious account of being good. Because this requirement requires a matching, it is clearly oriented toward correspondence truth theory.[2]

Last, the personal worldview must be projectible into our lives. This means two things: (a) worldview aims must be possible; and (b) one must try to put his worldview into effect in his life.

The first interpretation means that aspiration models that are *tough but possible* are all right, but utopian models that are clearly impossible are disqualified. The second interpretation means that it is not enough to think and speculate about worldview. Those who hold the bar *that low* are hypocrites. The reason for this is that they intellectually endorse a position, x, and then go about doing ~x. This smacks of Sinclair Lewis' Elmer Gantry, who (in his public life) preached against fornication and challenges to conventional mores while in his private life he did exactly those things he railed against.[3] The reason that this is disturbing to most of us is that we implicitly accept Plato's dictum that if we know (believe) that x is true/good, then we will (descriptively) do that. This is a controversial principle of psychology that is consistent with my own foundational starting point of action, 'All people, by nature, desire to be good.'[4] To be a hypocrite (under such psychological interpretations) becomes unnatural (descriptively) as well as being wrong (normatively).

It should be clear from these brief remarks that we have entered the province of the pragmatic theory of truth. Here we are making the possibility and actuality of action the gauge of acceptability. We are not talking about formal characteristics or matching to establish verisimilitude. Rather we are engaged in dynamic application within the realm of action as an important component for truth judgement.

From this it should be clear that I am advocating a pluralistic utilization of the theories of truth according to the demands of one's personal worldview. Since (as we found in Part I) facts and values are rather intertwined, it should not be surprising that in our quest for truth we must often consult what we believe to be good. This interplay can be set out in a thought experiment.

THOUGHT EXPERIMENT 6.1

Take out four sheets of paper. On the first sheet, list the five most important events in human history. Next to each event give a short reason why it is on this list. On the second sheet of paper, list the five most important intellectual achievements in human history. Next to each event give a short reason why it is on this list. Then, on the third sheet of paper, list three to five of the most important events in your life; the two to three most important truths in your life; and the two to three most important people in your life. As with the other lists, support your choice with a brief reason why. When these are complete compare the lists composed on sheets one to two with page three. Then answer the following questions: (a) what patterns are there between all of your general choices?; (b) is there a connection between the personal list and the historical evaluation? If so, then what is it?; (c) What do you make of the synonymies between the two lists? What of the contradictions?

What is the point of Thought Experiment 6.1? It is an inventory list. Inventories are essential before one goes forward because they tell us *where* we are. What can we glean from such an inventory?

First, there is our personal connection to history. When we think in terms of the big picture, it is often an invitation to witness what we really think is true from our personal worldview perspective. These grand, sweeping perspectives allow us a simple way to reveal and express to ourselves what we believe to be the case. When the character Assef, in the novel *The Kite Runner*,[5] discloses that his favourite book is Hitler's *Mein Kampf*, it is clear to virtually every reader that this character's judgement illustrates that he is not to be trusted. One's personal worldview discloses what one takes to be true and often the way that this truth is supported.

Second, there is an element of judgement. How do we assess the events that we have experienced, studied, and thought about? It is this process of assessment one in which the theories of truth can come into play? Again, one's personal worldview often dictates just what sorts of propositions he is open to questioning or exploring.

Third, there is the evaluation of picking particular events over others. This can be most revealing (if we are honest). After you complete your own list, find a peer and discuss your responses to the three sample 'types' listed there. Are you similar to any of them in total? Are you similar to any in part? The comparison of yourself to others can be a springboard to self-reflection.

When engaged in retrospection one must be careful not to forget the careful scrutiny maxim that is a check upon internalist revisionism of the past. It seems to be the case that most of us colour our perspectives of the past via various internalist perspectives that form the architecture of our personal worldview. This can be so pronounced that some say that the popular genre of memoir writing should always be classified as fiction.[6]

The check on these excesses is the externalist approach that is the heart of the careful scrutiny maxim. This may require discussion with others close to you (who you trust and who know you) to go over the details of this list. Often the only times most people, in fact, go through such questioning is when they are faced with sweeping contextual changes in their lives. For example, adolescence is one such change that is triggered by significant biological alterations. Those who go away to college or those who enter the army or get a job just after high school also go through a significant change. Other such events include (but are not limited to) getting married, getting divorced, having children, losing your job, having a death in the family, retiring, and facing death. Even if we are not reflective, by nature, life has a way of forcing us to review things periodically.

Community Worldview and Truth

For three years, out of key with his time.
Ezra Pound, 'E.P. Ode pour L'Election de son Sepulchre'

Are *you* in key with the times? Sometimes I wonder about myself. The shared community worldview is often rather opaque to most of us. How do we really know what the commonly held values and understanding of facts really are? If we don't know, then how are we to react? What is the character of any given group of people? This is often the province of anthropology and sociology, but it is a question that all authentic agents living in the world must assess. It is a question about empirical truth. It is probably an easier question to answer when the focus is upon smaller communities (though the task of ferreting out the truth about our communities extends to even the largest communities in which we are members, the global community).

One way to find out what the shared community worldview is at any given time is to talk to people. Dialogue allows us to discover what others hold to be true. However, it is not definitive. This is because many people in social interactions do not put *the disinterested search for truth* as their priority. Self-interest and personal circumstances often colour our conversations. For example, if I asked Manuel whether he thought that local county government was working effectively to fulfil its espoused mission, it might make a difference to know whether Manuel works for county government or is benefiting in any way from the programmes I'm asking about. If Manuel *is* benefiting in one of these ways, then he is not going to give me a disinterested answer because Manuel possesses an *interest* in the question that goes beyond its truth. These interests that skew interpersonal dialogue can go beyond mere financial gain. For example, if I ask Fred what he thinks of stem-cell research and Fred is a Catholic who follows the Catholic Church's doctrinal position of describing stem-cell research as murder (since the embryos involved are, under certain conditions, potential living humans),[7] then Fred will demur. The source of his censure may not be the facts of the case, as such, but may be tangled up in other personal worldview positions – which explicitly include religious beliefs.

All this is to suggest that it is very difficult to understand what is the *spirit of the age*: the shared community worldview. In many ways the question becomes easier when the community becomes smaller. Thus, within one's own family, it might be easier to determine what the general feeling is on certain issues among the various family members. Also, within your division at work, various committees one serves on, volunteer groups, et al., it is easier to determine a sense of that group's understanding of facts and values concerning the world.

From the perspective of the shared community worldview imperative (each agent must contribute to a common body of knowledge that supports the creation of a shared community worldview – that is itself complete, coherent, and good – through which social institutions and their resulting policies might flourish within the constraints of the essential core commonly held values – ethics, aesthetics, and religion), the process of accepting truths and values as a community should be analogous to those undergone by the individual via the personal worldview imperative. They involve inductive and deductive logic that is coherent, complete, and good. The community's understanding of 'good' should be broad enough to include the top dozen religions and major theories of ethics – but is not expandable to every theory. Charles Mansion's and David Koresh's theories of religion (for example) would be excluded because they encourage rape and murder in their normal practice. As I have argued elsewhere, whenever ethics and religion contradict on the public stage, ethics must always trump because only ethics is grounded via externalist criteria upon which all can agree.[8] The boundaries of ethics set the terms by which intolerant groups should be allowed to practise their religion or political philosophy.

Besides conversation, the next best way to fathom the shared community worldview is through the media. In the media – internet, television, radio, books, newspapers – we are presented with investigators who attempt to present to us versions of what the collective consciousness *is* at any given time – generally with reference to some specific event (real or fictional). These various interpretations are presented to us to evaluate. Just as in conversation, there are often various vested interests that try to 'spin' events toward a particular direction for that commentator's (and the organization behind her) advantage. For example, an incumbent politician has a vested interest in his or her constituents believing that things are fine at present. Thus, by some application of association the voter might think:

ARGUMENT 6.1
Voting for the Incumbent

1. Things are fine just now – Fact
2. X is my representative in government – Fact
3. Representatives in government have a lot to do with the status of events as they are – Assertion
4. My representative has a lot to do with things as they are – 2, 3
5. I vote for people who create situations I like – Fact
6. I will vote for X – 1, 4, 5

Those who hold an argument similar to 6.1 will move quickly past premise 3 (that is highly controversial) and make their choice on election day. Of course, much of the understanding of premise 1 can be the result of media filtering. Everyone knows whether they can pay their bills each month and have a little left over for consumer consumption. No amount of media will change this understanding (though it is often the case that many family members may be ignorant concerning these dynamics, e.g. children and some spouses who do not pay the bills). There are also those who live in some level of denial that holds a rosy future – such as winning the lottery or some other means of escape from the grim externalist data that is confronting them.

However, these cases aside, it is difficult to get a take on the others who are in the various communities with whom we reside. This is largely due to the failure of adequate statistics to describe the factual nature of the community at any given time. For example, in the United States, there is an index that tracks unemployment. This would seem to be one good indicator of the state of the community. However, this index is skewed by the fact that it only records those who register with the state for unemployment insurance and list themselves as actively seeking work. There are obviously many who do not file for unemployment insurance and/or are out of the system and cannot be listed as actively seeking work. All of these people are not counted. Among the poor of America, there are many who are not caught by these statistics.[9] Other sorts of data (such as crime statistics and the cost of living) are also fraught with statistical anomalies.

Because of this difficulty of getting good externalist information by which we might make our judgements about the present state of our communities, it is hard to know where we are.

The situation only gets worse when we add values into the mix. For example, take the issue of abortion. In the United States at the writing of this book popular attitudes about abortion tend to vary according to the way the question is asked. If one asks 'would you favour or oppose a law that would ban all abortions except those necessary to save the life of the mother' only 36 per cent agree while 60 per cent disagree.[10] However, if you change the question to read, 'I am going to read a list of things that some people do. For each, thinking about your own values and morals, I'd like you to tell me whether you think it is acceptable or not acceptable . . . Abortion, is it acceptable or unacceptable? Do you feel that way strongly or some-what?' 15 per cent felt it was strongly acceptable, 26 per cent some-what acceptable (sub-total positive = 41 per cent); 14 per cent thought it was somewhat unacceptable, 39 per cent strongly unac-ceptable (subtotal negative = 53 per cent).[11] So does the American community worldview support abortion or not? Each poll seems to give opposite results. Obviously, each question asks something dif-ferent, but the point still remains that the data presented to us all requires interpretation to resolve an apparent contradiction. Without interpretation, the data are meaningless.

These are significant hurdles to face. It is certainly very important to understand the facts and values of one's community. The shared community worldview imperative demands this. In our quest for truth, it is always important to register internally the strength of the claim presented to us. In the case of garnering information on the various communities in which we live, it is probably the case that the closer we are to actual day-to-day empirical interaction, the closer we are to being correct in our conclusions. However, we cannot shy away from trying to access the larger macro communities in which we reside: city, state, country, hemisphere, and world. All of these associations hold weight. Even though our understandings become less reliable as we proceed to the larger groups, it is nonetheless very important to situate ourselves as best we can. We are members in all of these communities and we must establish an interactive structure that falls within the province of the shared community worldview imperative.

However, such truth searching can be difficult. For example, so often, in recent years the wealthy countries of the world (G8 nations) have sought to extend their own vision (via neo-colonialism) over the dispossessed nations of the world. This is wrong because it skews the search of truth (which must be disinterested) into a contentious rhetoric of vested interests. The shared community worldview imperative suggests an equality of group worldviews subject only to the criteria: consistent, coherent, good, and workable. The G-8 nations (who are the most powerful nations on earth) must recognize that 'might does not make right' from the point of view of truth seeking. It is a fact that in global politics that the powerful can (at least in the short term) exert their will upon others, but in fashioning our search for global truth, we must follow the methodologies advocated in Chapters 4 and 5 by being interactive, engaging and respectful.

The shared community worldview imperative also enjoins us to be active members of the various communities in which we live in order that we might help shape the community worldview. As we have seen above, assessing the nature of community worldview is rather more artificial and amorphous than understanding our own personal worldview. Various members of the community often view this l'éspirit du corps differently. Through use of the careful scrutiny maxim we must engage diligently to try and understand what the worldview is and then what we intend to do about it.

In order to illustrate what I have in mind, let me offer an example from my own life. I have always been very keen on sport. I played on many teams in grammar school, high school, college, and adult leagues. My interest in sport, however, did not cloud my vision about what I saw as the metamorphosis of team sports from what I took to be wholesome exercise, that was in a context of fair play and sportsmanship, to a hyper-competitive activity of 'win at all costs'. Many adults (especially those who weren't very good at sports themselves) wanted to revise their childhood through their children's successes. Only victory counted. Fairness and sportsmanship were ornaments that only came out of the drawer so long as victory was assured. When it came to ranking values, victory always came first. This was not the sporting community with which I had been associated with as a player. The community had changed, and I didn't like the change.

I spent some time thinking about this state of affairs when one of my children became old enough for team sports. I still believed in the positive influence of sports within a community dominated by fair play and sportsmanship. If the community had changed, then I needed to do more than gripe about it, I had to make my own contribution.

I decided to be a coach.

Now I had been a coach of youth teams before (when I was in high school and college to make money). This time I was entering the volunteer ranks of parents who make youth sports leagues possible. This particular league was a 'select' youth basketball team. There were team try-outs and all the boys who made the team were skilled at basketball. Our community mission was threefold: 1) everyone on the team would improve so that at the end of the year each player was better than he was at the beginning – in a significant way; 2) everyone on the team would engage in a season-long team charity project directed toward children of their own age with severe (often terminal) diseases on the principle that boys with highly talented bodies should be mindful of their peers who weren't so blessed; and 3) everyone on the team would compete to win every game we played within the parameters of fairness and compassion. I had everyone sign a pledge after the team try-outs that they and their parents believed in and would support these goals. If they didn't, then there were other teams to play on.

Playing with fairness, sportsmanship, and compassion also means not flaunting one's success on the floor in the face of your competitors. It means not 'trash talking' your opponents so that they become disturbed by your insults with the result that their level of play diminished. It means not cheating (even if you can get away with it). It means not running up the score to make your opponent feel totally vanquished by your superior skill. No one should leave his humanity on the sideline when he steps onto the basketball court. Everything that we do in sports should be within a context of restraint. We shouldn't aim at one hundred and ten per cent. Because when we over exert, we lose our power of moderation and control. And these are necessary in order to maintain an ethical community.

I can truly say that though none of those teams I coached (three in basketball and two in baseball) were league champions, they did exhibit a sporting community that had a defined worldview (with respect to that activity) and the boys identified with that worldview and were proud of it.

My role in all of this was that I responded to what I saw as a flaw in the community worldview of youth sports and I did my small part to try to alter it. I didn't single-handedly change the community for everyone, but I made modifications among my players and many other teams in the league who heard about our vision. Perhaps when some of my former players become volunteer adult coaches, they also will try to integrate fairness, sportsmanship, and compassion into the way their teams play the game.

This is one example of what a single person *can* and *should* do as a part of their community membership. Recognizing a truth does not occur in a vacuum. It is always clothed in a normative garment that requires a response. Thus, the search for truth within the community sphere is not a separate activity all to itself. What we see and discover has implications in our lives.

THOUGHT EXPERIMENT 6.2

On a sheet of paper, list three communities in which you are a member.

On a *second* sheet of paper, describe the worldview of that community as it is presently constituted and practised. Next to each practice, list whether you think the practice is fine the way it is or whether it could be improved.

On a *third* sheet of paper, list the improvements that you would recommend and what you personally could do to help initiate these changes – even if the suggestion is very modest.

At the end of the day, it seems to me that our ultimate criteria for judging ourselves and judging communities/nations in our quest for truth is whether the unit in question has undergone the sort of philosophical questioning advocated here.[12] The way we should normatively evaluate any society is via our assessment of their philosophical inquiry into truth – as opposed to viewing the True unreflectively qua our animal natures concerning merely power and pleasure.

In Part 2 we have explored the human quest from the vantage point of truth. In the process we have found ourselves talking about the good and the beautiful. This is inevitable. These three paradigms are inextricably intertwined. However, each also possesses some singular integrity of its own. What remains is to explore the final leg of our triangle: the Beautiful – from there the process of realizing who we are and what we should do truly begins.

Part 3
The Beautiful

7   Finding Out What is Beautiful – Classical Theories

> O how much more doth beauty beauteous seem
> By that sweet ornament which truth doth give.
> William Shakespeare, Sonnet 54

The Problem: Art and the Beautiful

When was the last time you purchased art? Did you rent a DVD, download some music for your iPod, buy some jewellery? The next question is: why did you do it? Ever asked yourself that question? It's a pretty important question when you consider how often we purchase art in some form: movies, music, books, jewellery, paintings, furniture accents, fashionable clothes, attractive cars – the list can extend to almost every facet of our lives. When students buy a backpack for school, many take a look at the way it is styled and purchase the better-looking backpack over the doughty rucksack that your dad might have had. Even if the stylish backpack is a few dollars more, most are willing to pop for it if they can. Being in fashion makes a difference to us. It's a difference that we are willing to pay for.

But what is fashion? Who determines what's hot and what's not? This is a perennial question that falls prey to the rationality incompleteness conjecture. It is impossible to know for sure. Two popular candidates are: 1) the fashion industry (whoever they are and however they meet to set these things), and (2) the buying decisions of the general public (if you like it, you'll buy it). Obviously, these two choices are in opposition. The first has a small clique making the decisions, while the second makes fashion a democratic result of the economic marketplace.

Regardless of how that particular question pans out, there is a deeper question underneath it. This question concerns the relationship between the artifact and what the artifact signifies. To get at this let's consider a thought experiment:

THOUGHT EXPERIMENT 7.1

You are a college student. Your parents live in the Midwest and you bought some new clothes that you felt were trendy for college on the East Coast. Now say that what you thought was trendy and would send a positive message to everyone who saw you, actually made everyone laugh and declare you to be a freak from some rural farm. You go to your closet and gather your new clothes and stuff them in your storage trunk – not to see the light of day until you go home for the summer. What's happened? On a sheet of paper, try to describe the relationship between the Midwest student and her new wardrobe. Are the clothes attractive or not? Upon what do you base your judgement?

This thought experiment moves us directly into the problem with art: how do we decide which art is good and which art is bad? Let's say (to make things a bit more difficult) that if the Midwest student had worn her clothes where she bought them that people would have been impressed. The people in the East weren't impressed. Who is right and why?

One quick way to respond to these queries is to return to the theories of truth presented in Part II. If we consider the correspondence theory of truth, then the clothes via their fabrication display principles of design that connect or do not connect to something like the Platonic form of the Beautiful. If there is verisimilitude between object and form, then it is truly beautiful – no matter what anyone says. If there isn't, then no amount of popular praise will make the artifact *truly* beautiful. Art under this approach is judged according to some universal standards.

A second approach would be to judge art through the coherence theory of truth. Under this approach, there are certain random posits that are set down about the nature of the beautiful for some particular society or segment of society living in a particular time and place. These comprise an agreed upon standard of taste among the ruling art clique. This standard of taste rules the day. Thus, when an artifact is brought forward, it is judged to be beautiful or not according to whether it is squares with (i.e. creates no contradiction with) the prevailing standard of taste. Of course, since the standard is dependent upon random posits and a ruling clique, the standard, itself, will change over time. Thus, all such judgements about coherence are relative to time and culture. Art under this approach can only be judged to be beautiful subject to the prevailing conditions.

The third approach would be through the pragmatic theory of truth. Under this approach the practical success of something makes it beautiful. For example, at the writing of this book, one of the most successful series of books is the Harry Potter series by J. K. Rowling. Under the first two approaches, few would have judged these novels to be exceptionally beautiful, but under the pragmatic theory of truth (since they are the best-selling novels of the decade in any genre), they automatically become beautiful. This is also true of other novelists like Stephen King, Agatha Christie, Dan Brown, and others who bucked the standard of taste and also did not connect directly with criteria generally associated with the correspondence or coherence theories.

The problem of art and the beautiful is just this: how do we judge something to be beautiful so that we can make sense of problems like those raised in Thought Experiment 7.1? This chapter will present some popular answers to this problem.

Why Should We Bother about the Beautiful?

We all live with a desire to connect to the beautiful. This is because the beautiful brings us pleasure and because they connect us indirectly to our vision of the good and the true. We seek the beautiful as something outside of ourselves. In this way the quest for beauty in our lives has its origins in an externalist perspective. The artifact or natural object exists outside of us. We use empirical means to assess their physical characteristics in such a way that there can be inter-subjective discussion about them. For example, the last line of *A Farewell to Arms* by Ernest Hemingway is: 'After a while I went out and left the hospital and walked back to the hotel in the rain.'[1] No one could contest this because we could simply go to a copy of the book and open it to page 314 (first edition) and read it out loud. Likewise, if one were to assess Marcel Duchamp's *Fountain* (which consists in the situating of a urinal, fabricated by some industrial toilet-supply company), we could all agree upon its physical dimensions: height, angles, drain diameter, colouration of the ceramic material, and other measurable characteristics.

However, the judgement about the beauty of the artifact is a separate question (as per the last section). This may be externalist or internalist according to the theory of truth that one cares to apply. The correspondence theory tends to be internalist while the coherence and pragmatic theories are decidedly externalist.

It is important to recognize how much about the assessment of art is actually externalist in nature. So often people discount the status of art as being so radically relative as to have no real status of its own. Art, under this account, is a mere trifle of fancy that we indulge in as a luxury if we are in a position in life to indulge in such things as luxuries. Understanding how much of the assessment of art is subject to intersubjective externalist criteria may remove some, but certainly not all, of this criticism. To get to the heart of the attack one must revert to theories of human nature.

One thesis of this book is that human nature begins with the good. All people by nature desire to be good.[2] In order to understand *how* to become good each of us needs to create a worldview that we can call our own. This process throws us into questions about truth. We cannot create a worldview without some standards concerning the nature of truth. For most these standards are thrust upon us by the media and are naively accepted. These unfortunate souls are slaves to the machinations of the advertisers. For those intrepid few who are willing to endure the quest, the acceptance of truth *means so much more.* One need merely refer to the European romance literature of the Middle Ages such as *Roman de la Rose* or *Le Morte d'Arthur* or 'The Knight's Tale' in *The Canterbury Tales* for a sensibility concerning the necessity to devote one's self in the quest for truth. The quality of our life depends upon it.

These aforementioned texts mix up the quest for truth with the quest for beauty. This is because of the rationality incompleteness conjecture. As humans we are often confronted with claims that seem very rational but yet don't seem quite right. A good example of this are the paradoxes of Zeno of Elea.[3] There is something very rationally compelling about Zeno's arguments. They were not refutable under the mathematics of the time.[4] However, this did not mean that everyone should just accept the argument. The reason is that most people recognize some form of the rationality incompleteness conjecture. Reason, though the most powerful influence in governing our lives, is still not sufficient to convince people to change their worldviews.[5] What is needed in addition is something else: enter beauty.

Theories of Art and Beauty

There are many ways to discuss beauty. The two most profitable from our perspective are: (a) theories on the way people confront the beautiful (often called 'aesthetics') and (b) theories on the way to judge something to be beautiful (often called 'criticism'). These two approaches are, of course, different. However, it is useful pedagogically to present them together in this context because these concerns overlap in many respects. Most writers in this area have some particular expertise in one of the areas of art and tend to slant their examples in that direction. The same is true with me. I am most conversant in literature. But I do not want to monopolize the perspective from that standpoint. Therefore, the presentation will be dominated by the presentation of literature (as examples of art) with some other examples from painting, music, et al. as they apply. I will structure my presentation historically (in order of presentation). These vignettes are meant to present a depiction of the diversity of perspectives that have been set forth in the Western tradition. Though many figures are brought forward, the presentation (even in its brevity) is by no means complete. (This is further compounded by the fact that I am only representing the Occidental tradition. When one adds writers from other strong literary traditions in Asia, Africa, South America, Oceania, et al., the number of figures increases mightily.) I would suggest that readers use these synopses like a menu. Find a reasonable number of texts that are attractive and read further. This is a critical requirement in order to fashion your own aesthetic/critical theory of the beautiful.

Ancient Theories

This section of the chapter will focus upon two ancient authors: Plato and Aristotle. These classical writers formed the point of departure for the modern and contemporary writers (beginning at the end of the eighteenth century).

Plato: Art as the Imitation of Truth (aka Ersatz Truth)

Plato is a rather slippery character. This is because he makes several contradictory comments upon what art *is* and what it can do. To begin this short presentation, it is crucial to understand that there are at least two senses of art. The first refers to a rather large category of human activity that is ruled by a set of functional criterion (*ergon*). When one masters these functionally defined outcomes, then one is excellent (*arête*) in the activity that may be called an art or *techne*. This understanding of art might include medicine, shoe making, and athletic training. For the most part, this understanding of art will be consigned to a general background condition. What is more to the point is created (*poein*), imitative art (*mimesis*). This is the sort of art that the sculptors, painters, poets, and dramatists use. The artist imitates life/reality and presents it to the city.

The problem is that Plato believes that most artists get it wrong. This goes back to his epistemological assumptions discussed in Chapter 5 (Argument 5.9, 'the Cave' (514a–517b) and 'the Divided Line'). If an artist is a regular fellow, then he exists at the lowest level on the divided line and would be a cave dweller who assesses the shadows of the puppets as being true. This means that the reality presented to the artist is false. It is ersatz truth. The artist does not see the real truth. If it is assumed that there is a slippage in all imitations such that even the best imitation doesn't ever completely match up to the original, then the artist is attempting to present what he sees as true (but which really is false) and in that transmission the end product will be even more false. In this way, the artist becomes a re-enforcer of the status quo (ersatz truth). For example, many people see television in this way. Popular television takes popular culture as the norm. It seeks to imitate it to make it pleasing and plausible to the many. In this way, the status quo is reinforced.

But what if (à la Ibsen)[6] we assume that the status quo (as supported by the many) is always wrong. This position (which I believe Plato supports) suggests that on epistemological grounds the popular culture is based upon falsity (judged by the correspondence theory of truth as interpreted via the Cave and the Divided Line). Thus, those artists that begin here will be corruptors of the state. This is because they will make falsity (the ersatz truth) seem to be attractive. In the *Republic* Plato suggests that these artists be discouraged in favour of the didactic artists (who use the pleasurable adornments of presentation to bring forth a truthful message).[7]

This possibility of a truthful message is the other side of Plato. From this standpoint, he thinks that art can move many toward the truth. It might be like the fugitive from the cave who returns and presents a work that might free his comrades from their chains. In the way, the artist might actually do some good.

However, Plato is rather distrustful of the ability of artists, unaided, to do this. In the *Ion*, Plato thinks that the artists can present a vision of the beautiful (and *a fortiori* of the true) *if* it is divinely inspired.

ARGUMENT 7.1
Divine Inspiration in Plato's *Ion*

1. [Art (*techne*) requires knowledge to operate] – F (from earlier argument)
2. To have a *techne* of poetry is to judge all poetry – A, 532c 7
3. [Ion can only judge Homer] – F

4. Ion's ability to speak about Homer comes not from art (*techne*) and knowledge (*episteme*) – 1–3

5. Poetry as a whole is a *techne* – F, 532 c8

6. All *technai* operate in the same way – A, 532d1

7. All *technai* must be understood as wholes – 5, 6, 532 d3

8. [Poetry as a *techne* must be understood as a critical whole] – 5–7

9. Other arts, like painting, are also critically understood as wholes – A, 532d

10. [There are two aspects of art: criticism (relying upon *techne*) and production (relying upon divine inspiration)] – A

11. Poets (and other artists) are divinely inspired; critics, by *techne*, understand what they do – 4, 8, 9–11, 533e–534e

12. [Poets are imitators of nature] – A

13. Rhapsodists interpret poets – A, 535a

14. Rhapsodists are interpreters of interpreters – 12, 13, 535a 9

15. Divinely inspired artists are not in their senses [adikountos – untrained= ~ *techne*] and as such can only mysteriously string couplets together (much as the loadstone is a mysterious coupler) – A, 535d 5, 533e

16. The loadstone is the Muse and the artist, the work and the audience, are all like the iron rings that are caught together – A, 536 a–d

17. [Rhapsodists, and other artists, create what they do not by *techne*, but by divine inspiration which is a mysterious force that comes from the Muse and not from the artist] – 11, 14–16

18. Each separate *techne* (art) has its own separate *ergon* (a functionally defined work) – A, 537a–c

19. We know x by its functional definition, each with its own nature – A, 537d 1–4

20. We know each art, *techne*, separately on its own terms – 18, 19

21. [Homer and the rhapsodists are not charioteers] – F

22. Between Ion, the rhapsodists, and Homer (the poet), the charioteer only has the *techne* of the charioteer – 18–21/ 538b (the same is true of other arts, such as fishing, 538d–539d, and medicine 539d)

23. [Only the one who has the *techne* has knowledge of the
     techne] – A

24. [The poet or the imitators of the imitators speak about what
     they personally do not know] – 20–24

25. Any truth an artist might exhibit is by Divine Inspiration (the
    Muses) and not from any actual knowledge he, himself,
    possesses – 17, 24

In Argument 7.1 Plato finesses the problem of whether the artist, as such, is capable of (a) seeing and assessing what is true, and (b) representing that truth to others indirectly in the artistic mode. The trick is that the artist may not be able (unaided) to see and assess the truth. It is given to him. Thus, the invocation of the opening line of Homer's *Odyssey*, 'Sing to me, oh Muse, of the many twisting ways of man' (my translation). When the beginning of the process is *not* the unaided observer looking at the world, assessing it, creating a world-view, and then transmitting that worldview to others, *but* is instead the divine inspiration of God (aka the Muse), then the whole process changes. If God is in charge, then the artist is merely the conduit of a message. That message is (by definition) true. The artist is merely the conduit of God's truth to the many (in Greek the *hoi polloi*). In a real sense the artist under this model ceases to be important. He is merely the messenger. Plato and the twentieth-century French philosopher Michel Foucault hold the sort of position of the artist being less important than the artifact.[8] The artist is submerged to the appreciation of the work. For example, consider the cathedral of Chartres in France. The architect is unknown. But is that important? Doesn't the message of the cathedral speak for itself? But what is the source of the message? If one adopts the correspondence theory of truth, then the source is truth itself (also known by theists as God). The artist is the conduit between reality and an audience. The most modern example of this is the newspaper. How many of us actually read the by-line of the newspaper? Most of us are more interested in the content. What does the article say? Or as Will Rogers used to say that all he knew was what he read in the newspapers. The content is key. Who wrote it is irrelevant. The author is only the messenger.

This is the intermediate position. It mediates between the artist as the propagator of ersatz truth and the artist as the visionary. It is unclear whether Plato ever held this latter position, but the closest thing to it is in his dialogue *Symposium*.

ARGUMENT 7.2
Beauty as seen through Love

1. Love must have an object; be a lover of something – F, 199d
2. Love is a desire for something – F, 200a
3. [One does not desire what one has] – F
4. Love desires an object which it lacks – 1,2,3, 200b–e
5. Love is the love of beauty – A, 201a
6. Love lacks beauty – 4,5, 201b [note self-referential paradox]
7. The good is beauty – F, 201c
8. Love lacks the good – 6,7, 201c
9. Love is neither beautiful nor good – 6–8
10. *DIOTOMA INTERLUDE 202a–212c Kalon/aischron* and *agathon/kakon* are polar opposites – A
11. Love is at neither extreme – A
12. Love is between the two – 10,11, 202b
13. All the gods are happy and beautiful – F
14. Love is not a god – 9,13, 202d
15. [Love is greater than man] – A
16. Love is between god and man – 12, 14, 15
17. Love is the offspring of resource and need – A, 203b–204b
18. [Wisdom is the means to the beautiful and good] – A
19. Love is a *philo-sophia* – 9, 16–18, 204b
20. A lover of good seeks *eudaimonia* – A, 204e
21. All men desire the *agathos* – F, 205a
22. Love includes all longing and desire for *agathos* and *eudaimonia* – 20–21
23. Only the *agathos* and *eudaimonia* are most highly prized – A
24. [Love seeks only that which is most highly prized] – A
25. Love only seeks *agathos* and *eudaimonia* – 22–24
26. Eternal goods are more highly prized than temporary ones – F

27. Love seeks eternal goods – 24, 26, 206b
28. Nature urges us to procreation – A, 206c
29. Conception occurs in a male/female union – F
30. Within human procreation is a divine element – A
31. [All things that nature urges happen to all] – F
32. All people procreate (or desire to do so) – 28–29, 31
33. All people procreate (or desire to do so) in the divine element – 30, 32
34. Divine conception is a harmony – A
35. Beauty confers harmony; ugliness confers discord – A
36. Divine conception is concerned with beauty – 34, 35
37. All people procreate (or desire to do so) via beauty – 33, 36, 206e
38. To procreate is to bring forth some effect – F
39. All people bring forth (or desire to do so) a beautiful effect – 37, 38
40. Propagation is a longing for immortality – A [cf. long discourse on animal reproduction 207b–208a]
41. [All people in love seek immortality in bringing forth beautiful effects] – 27, 39, 40
42. [Propagation of the spirit is higher than the body] – A, 209a
43. Wisdom is the governor of the spirit – A
44. [Begetting the effects of wisdom is the highest form of propagation] – 42, 43
45. The propagation of wisdom is a divine conception – A
46. The propagation of wisdom is the highest and is concerned with beauty – 19, 36, 41, 44, 45
47. Pure beauty is revealed on a scale of perfection that has immortal and beautiful objects – A, 210a–211d
    a. Beautiful body, a7
    b. Beauty of form, b2
    c. Beauty of soul, b8
    d. Beauty of natural law/activity, c4
    e. Beauty of nature, exact science (episteme), c6
    f. Philosophy, d6
    g. Beauty, d7

    h. Everlasting and eternal loveliness
48. The highest perfection confers arête, *eudaimonia*, and
     agathos – F
49. All men seek this scale – 21, 25, 46–48
___

50. Love reveals pure beauty on such a scale of perfection that all
     men seek it, i.e. 'Love's activity is to reveal pure beauty on such
     a scale of perfection that all men seek it' – 42, 47, 49,
     211d–212b

In Argument 7.2 Plato makes a case for the role of Beauty in revealing Truth. This is an important argument in the triad of the good, the true, and the beautiful. It asserts that humans see in beauty an emblem of perfection. If Greek moral thought saw perfection as the achieving of an end via the excellent (*arête*) satisfaction of an art (*techne*), and if this achievement confers goodness (*agathos* – the possession of which makes life worthwhile), then beauty's part in this process makes it a critical component in being human. Beauty is no mere recreation, but a real way to actualize our human nature.

Argument 7.2 begins by giving some closure to the main theme of the dialogue: an exploration of the nature and activity of love (premises 1–25). Love is connected with desire for the good (*agathos*) and with the contented, balanced soul (*eudaimonia*). In this way Plato is identifying love to the attainment of the good (in abstract and for the agent personally). The response to such a quest is to *propagate* (here understood as artistic production – after the Hippocratic aphorism, 'Life is short, art is long').[9] If Plato is correct here that the natural human inclination to love is really about the search for the good and the balanced soul, which, in turn prompts propagation (in the case of interpersonal relations – children, and in the case of people who are lovers of wisdom – artistic production), then the rest of the argument also follows. In premises 34 and 35, one characteristic of Beauty is identified: harmony (that is connected to the Divine, aka to Truth). This leads us back to artistic production again (propagation) in 37–40. Beauty (now connected intimately with Art) then connects to wisdom, 43–46 (Truth). In 47 this is situated in both the physical object (artifact) and the beautiful (form). Finally, in premise 48 there is a return to the Good.

This is a complicated argument that has spawned entire books. However, for our purposes here, the point is to emphasize that Plato does confer a rather higher place to art and beauty than was evidenced in the earlier arguments we have discussed. Here art and the artist are exalted and earlier they were denigrated as corruptors. One way to make sense of this is apparent contradiction is that (following in the direction of the *Ion*) what makes all the difference is the nature of what is being imitated. When the subject of imitation is the ersatz truth of the lower levels of the divided line or the shadows of puppets on the cave wall, then the artist leads the *hoi polloi* astray. But when the object is the form of the beautiful, then the result is enlightenment (the acquisition of truth) and the good (both formally and in one's own life through a contented and balanced soul). This sort of artist might include the work of Plato himself. He wrote dramatic dialogues that purported (one may assume on the basis of his *Seventh Letter*) to stimulate indirectly his readers to think about the Good and the True via a Beautiful presentation.

When art is understood as imitation in this way, then the answer to the question 'what is good art?' as opposed to 'what is bad art?' lies in ferreting out the object that the artist was imitating. When ersatz truth is in the artist's eyes, then he is a purveyor of corruption and is not a positive member of society. When *real* truth (as defined by correspondence theory) is in the artist's eyes, then the result is the betterment of society and the instrument of individual salvation.

Aristotle: Art as Philosophy for Everyone
Aristotle's principal work on art is *The Poetics*. In his systemic fashion Aristotle connects the activity of art with philosophy in Chapter 4.

ARGUMENT 7.3
Why we like art

1. All men by nature desire to know – F, Ch. 4 (cf. *Metaphysics* I.1)/1448b 12
2. [When we imitate nature we learn about nature] – F
3. Imitation of nature is inherently interesting to man – 1, 2 /b16

4. Learning by imitation excites the audience to actively engage in the process of learning – A /b13
5. [Dynamic learning is stimulated by poetic imitation] – A
6. Poetic imitation is inherently interesting to man – 3–5

Premise 1 sets out Aristotle's understanding of the most basic fact of human nature: the desire to know. It is the first sentence of his prominent collection: the *Metaphysics*. If we grant Aristotle his famous definition of what it means to be human,[10] then what follows from this? In the enthymeme, premise 2, there is a conjecture that *imitation* of nature prompts *learning* about nature. Why might this be? One account might be that the *imitation* stimulates further inquiry. This is different from Plato's general supposition that the *hoi polloi* would stop at the imitation and take that as reality, itself. When the poet was imitating ersatz reality, the result would be the corrupting of the individual. For Plato, the artifact would be the final stop. The audience would see it as a stand-in for truth. When that stand-in was based on falsity, then evil resulted.

Aristotle saw things differently. His idea of the *hoi polloi* was rather more active. When the artist presented an artifact to the populace, Aristotle did not believe the process stopped there. He thought that there was stimulation to inquiry. Instead of being the *end* of the process, the work of art was the *beginning* of an investigation.

Aristotle concentrates in his work on epic poetry and dramatic tragedy.[11] Some of the devices of the process include Chapter 11, 'Reversal and Recognition'.

Reversal (*peripeteia*) comes about when the action veers to the opposite direction. For example, in *Oedipus Rex* the servant intends to cheer Oedipus by telling him of his origins, but the servant's words have just the opposite effects (leading to his downfall).

Recognition (*anagnopisis*) implies a change from ignorance to knowledge. The best sort of recognition or discovery is one that is linked to a reversal. This is the case when Oedipus finds out his origins and how he ended up killing his father and marrying his mother.

A third element is an emotional calamity (*pathos*) that entails suffering and perhaps death. The last stage of Oedipus' journey that starts with his self-inflicted blinding and results in his own walkabout through two other plays, *Oedipus at Colonus* and *Antigone*. This self-imposed punishment creates a cleansing of the soul of Oedipus and an emotional cleansing on the part of the audience (*katharsis*). This is quite important because Aristotle (the man who put forth the definition of humanity as being rational animals) here includes affective criteria via the emotional cleansing of the audience in the drama. What should we understand about the status of such cleansing? On the one hand, it could be merely a pleasurable boon. One feels better after the play. On the other hand, it could be that we are *emotionally* improved through the process (see Chapter 1 on the status of emotions in the quest for the good; Chapter 5 on the status of emotions in the quest for truth).

Thus, art/beauty can connect to our emotions that, in turn, relate to the good and the beautiful. The mechanics of this process is set forth in Chapter 13.

ARGUMENT 7.4
Pity and fear in tragedy

1. A good plot is one that is complex and works by creating a whole that arouses pity and fear – F, Ch. 13 (earlier argument)/1452b 25

2. [Pity and fear are aroused only through actions based partially upon desert] – A

3. Option – A: Portraying a good man who moves from fortune to misfortune through no fault of his own arouses aversion in the audience not pity and fear – 2/b30

4. [Aversion is unlike pity and fear and works against good art] – A

5. Option – A is not a good plot structure – 1–4

6. Option – B: Portraying a bad man who moves from misfortune to fortune by happenstance does not evoke pity and fear, nor is it sympathetic for the audience – 2/1453a

7. [Sympathy from the audience is a secondary factor by which to judge a plot] – A

8. Option – B is not a good plot structure – 1, 6, 7
9. Option – C: Portraying a bad man who moves from fortune to misfortune is to show a person getting what he fully deserves, i.e. punishment – F/1453a 5
10. Though there is sympathy in 9, there is no pity nor fear – 9, 2
11. Option – C is not a good plot structure – 1, 9, 10
12. Option – D: Portraying a moderately good man who moves from fortune to misfortune partially due to his weaknesses or character flaw (deserts) evokes pity and fear – 2/a10
13. Option – D is the best plot structure – 1, 5, 8, 11, 12

In Argument 7.4 Aristotle sets his cards on the table in the enthymeme, number 2, that desert must play a part in the proper arousal of pity and fear.[12] 'Desert' is obviously a moral term referring to the good. For example, in the case of Oedipus in the first play, did he *deserve* his fate? Well, let's think about it. Here is a person who, through no fault of his own, was raised as an orphan in another city without knowledge of the Oracle's declarations about his fate. But he is responsible for the character he has created for himself according to the personal worldview imperative. Thus, Oedipus meets a man on the road who will not yield. Sounds a bit like a male testosterone ritual, eh?

Oedipus rises (or degrades himself). He fights and kills the other haughty male (unbeknownst to him, his father). So what? Has Oedipus killed his father? Clearly he has killed someone. Under the state-of-nature rules of the age, he has not been overly egregious. He is guilty of justifiable homicide. But is he guilty of the far greater crime of *patricide*? Therein lies the tale.

The various options are trotted out and rejected. This is because art needs something different from philosophy: it needs some essential emotional tension. This can only come with the introduction of nuance. When a basically good man with a flaw goes down there is nuance. On the one hand, the protagonist is basically good, on the other hand, he is flawed – just as most of us see ourselves. We are flawed, but for the most part, we feel we are good (or at least striving to become such). Thus, when the protagonist falls, we sympathetically connect with him or her. It could be *us*.

Our *pity* is evoked through our sympathetic interaction with the protagonist. Because the protagonist is like us (in being basically good), we feel a connection. This connection (that I call sympathy) creates pity for the fate of the protagonist. Part of this feeling is for the protagonist and part is our own projection of self-pity – should we identify strongly with the protagonist.

Our *fear* is a consequence of our pity. Once we have invested ourselves in the main character, then we become anxious as the mechanical downfall takes place. We know what will happen. We know why it will happen. But because we feel sympathetic connection with the protagonist, we indulge in quixotic hope that something will save him. This tension is the anxious fear that Aristotle is talking about.

At the end of the day, the process concludes in an emotional release on the part of the audience, *katharsis*. Thus, though the purpose of art is to satisfy our rational natures (Argument 7.3), its operation is to employ plot, music, and spectacle[13] to emotionally connect with the audience in order to heighten the experience in such a way that they will remember the drama and speculate upon its meaning. In this way, art stimulates rational reflection for the many more effectively than philosophy because of this broader appeal.

The successful artist under this scenario is not only a philosopher on the model of the 'stingray' Socrates (who shocked others into thinking), but is also an artisan who is skilled at delivering mimetic pleasure driven by a realistic plot. Under this assessment, the drama is only the beginning. The subsequent discussions and controversy constitute the philosophy that many audience members will undergo in a search for meaning. The audience wants to know what the author's vision (aka worldview) suggests and whether they agree. It is an alluring conscription. Are you drawn into the artist's worldview? How do you like it once you are there? The answers to these questions entail considerations of the True and the Good as one assesses the Beautiful.

THOUGHT EXPERIMENT 7.2

1. First decide your favourite art form: literature, music, painting, architecture, et al.
2. Within your favourite art form write down three examples of superb artifacts (list A) and three of failures (list Z).
3. Compare lists A and Z. What makes them different in your opinion?
4. Do any of your responses in number 3 have anything to do with the Good or the True? If so, set these out. If not, then what are these criteria? How can they be described/depicted?

Plato and Aristotle believed that art balances pleasure and instruction. Instruction is either about the good or the true. Thus, among two competing artifacts p and q, if they are both equally pleasurable, the one that delivered *more* of the good or more of the true would be the better work. Thought Experiment 7.2 allows you to see whether you agree with these ancient writers on aesthetics/criticism. From the ancient point of view, the way we judge (criticism) the beautiful is from the point of view of: (a) imitation from either a true or a false point of view; (b) imitation that is meant to stimulate philosophy for the masses; (c) a recognition that the work of art can rival any other as an account of the good and the beautiful. Are the ancient authors right? Partially right? Totally wrong? The way we think about the Beautiful rests upon the outcome.

8   Finding Out What is Beautiful – Modern Theories

Beauty is truth, truth beauty, – that is all
Ye know on earth, and all ye need to know.
John Keats, 'Ode on a Grecian Urn'

Modern and Contemporary Theories

In philosophy, the modern age begins in the seventeenth century and extends for two hundred years. The nineteenth century marks another change. The final historical category will be the twentieth century. This final era contains the 'modernist' movement before and after the First World War and the contemporary era that extends from the soundings of the Second World War until 2000+ (the endpoint of our inquiry). Some exposition of theories of aesthetics/criticism will be examined from each of these three categories using a mixture of key figures and movements. Again, the purpose is to be suggestive rather than definitive.

Modern Theorists
Kant: Art as Disinterested Judgements from Contemplating the Beautiful

Immanuel Kant is a very interesting figure to write on art. He is an individual whose personal taste in art is rather suspect since he thought Frederick the Great to be an inspired poet and his taste in music most appreciated Prussian marching bands.[1] However, in Kant's favour is his fine work on epistemology and metaphysics.[2] These are used to ground his ethics and his work on aesthetics. Because Kant is a systematic philosopher, one cannot divorce his work on aesthetics from his other philosophy. Beginning with *The*

Critique of Pure Reason and *The Critique of Practical Reason*, *The Critique of Judgment*[3] is intricately bound up in the other two works. Since these remarks are meant to be brief overviews brought forward to present the reader with an ensemble of the various historical positions on art (especially literature), I will only refer to Kant's other writings when I think it is necessary to comprehend the sense of his presentation.

There are two major components in Kant's *Third Critique*: I. The Critique of Judgment, and II. The Teleology of Nature. These two parts work together as follows: The general point of it all: first, nature would be incomprehensible were we not to impose upon it various rules (1st Critique). If we assume that, in fact, these rules were imposed by an exterior force, nature (= God?), then our discovery of the rules (that are actually *in* nature but do not announce themselves) gives us great pleasure. This means that when something is teleologically created, (like nature from a theist's point of view) or like art from everyone's point of view, the discovery of the principles of organization is pleasurable.

When these principles are harmoniously ordered we have a sedate kind of pleasure. When they are ordered so that the harmony produces a great effect of the purposiveness of the artifact, then the outcome is the *sublime*. In this way the sublime is a dynamic force.

There is a link between this manner of formal recognition of the beautiful (via sense and reason) and the moral (which, according to Kant is without self-interest). Thus, if the artifact gives nothing more to the agent besides a pleasure that the agent himself must provide, then the artifact is morally appreciated as well (the Good). The connection between the beautiful and the good is not causal, but the correlation is high (especially when the agent is already good and looking at the beautiful).

Kant's judgements about Beauty involve several elements: (a) a disinterested, non-rational recognition of an artifact or of nature; (b) a free-form imaginative interplay with the artifact or with nature; and (c) a recognition of purposiveness within the artifact or within nature that stimulates an awareness of the harmony between purpose and the object's existence. The recognition of this harmony occasions a necessary satisfaction through which the observer makes subjectively based universal judgements about the artifact or about nature.

For many readers, this may seem to be a very Byzantine process. This may be true. But it is no more Byzantine than Kant's account in the *First Critique* of the way that the understanding is presented with sense data via *quality, quantity, relation,* and *modality.*[4] In the First Critique, Kant simply wanted to break down the process of how we come to know and the metaphysical consequences of this. The more detailed his empirical account ('The Transcendental Analytic'), the more plausible his speculative conjectures about the limits of knowledge ('The Transcendental Dialectic'). Detailed analysis was Kant's method. Yes, the process is ponderous. Yes, the sentences are rather convoluted (even in the German). The outcome point is whether Kant extends your ability to make judgements about art.

In order to evaluate this, let us consider a key controversial argument that Kant puts forward.

ARGUMENT 8.1
The Beautiful is that which pleases universally without requiring a concept

1. The beautiful is the object of an entirely disinterested satisfaction – F (last argument)/ chapter 6
2. There are no private grounds in a disinterested standpoint – A
3. Whenever there are no private grounds, it is reasonable to assume that all react the same way – A
4. All judgements that are grounded in disinterest are (in a way) universal for all men (*das es einen Grund des Wohlgefallens für jedermann enthalten müsse,* Chapter 6, ll. 13–14) and this universality does not depend upon the objects but is subjectively universal – 1–4
5. Everyone has his own private feeling of pleasure from sense – A
6. When one judges the beautiful his judgment is for everyone – A
7. Sensations of pleasure may induce valid generalizations, but they are not objective nor subjective universals – A
8. Morality sets universal judgements via concepts – F

9. Only aesthetic taste represents the subjective universal – 5–8

10. There is a taste of sense (private judgments) and a taste of reflection (judgements generally held to be true) – A [*Sinnen Geschmack* v *Reflexions Geschmack*, Chapter 8, l.11]

11. Reflective taste rests not on concepts of objects (*Begriffen von Objecte*, l.10) because it involves no objective *quality of judgement* (*Quantität des Urtheils*, l.11) – A

12. Only reflections that are based upon concepts of objects that represent the quantity of judgement (from the table of judgement, 1st Critique) are objective – F

13. The representation (*Vorstellung*) of pleasure is at best generally valid (*Gemeingültigseit*); the ethical is an objective universal; and the beautiful is a subjective universal – 9–12

14. If the beautiful were according to the concept, the representation of beauty would be lost (because source would be gone) – F

15. [Without a source, a judgement would lose its authority] – A

16. The judgement of beauty cannot be due to concepts – 14, 15

17. If pleasure from an object preceded our judgement that the object were beautiful, then sensation would rule our judgement – F/Chapter 9

18. Sensation does not rule the judgment of the beautiful – F

19. The judgement of taste concerning the beautiful precedes the pleasure we feel – 17, 18

20. The communicative power in this sort of representation is given by the imagination – F

21. The imagination plays two cognitive roles: (a) in the schematism of concepts and (b) in free-play (cases in which there are no concepts) – A (cf. 1st Critique for (a))

22. The free-play of the imagination is the vehicle by which universal subjective judgements of artistic taste are communicated – 20, 21

23. The ability to communicate the free-play of the imagination (once determined) conveys pleasure – F

24. The judgement of taste once determined by the free-play of the imagination yields pleasure – 19, 22, 23

25. The judgement of taste determines the object in respect of satis-

faction and the predicate of beauty (without a concept) – F

26. The activity of 25 stimulates the understanding in a harmonious activity with the imagination – A

27. The understanding can think about this relation (but this activity is different) – A

28. The understanding can observe that a judgement of taste coincides with the conditions of universality – A

29. [The union with the understanding heightens the dynamic union] – A

30. The understanding works in harmonious concert with the imagination in judgements about the beautiful – 25–29

---

31. The Beautiful is that which pleases universally without requiring a concept – 9, 13, 16, 19, 24, 30

This is an important argument for Kant. It rests on some controversial assumptions. For example, in premise 3, it is assumed that without private interests we all react the same way. This assumes that we are all the same (respecting tastes and worldviews). Now this can be understood as: (a) being all the same factually, i.e. we are *actually* all the same. When Wendy sees x (an artifact or a natural object), then any other person, say Juanita, will automatically judge it the same way – so long that neither party has some vested interest in the artifact or the natural setting. Or it may mean (b) that there is some more general sense that we are all the same – such as being rational animals. But where does this land us? So we are the same on a generic level. So what? How does this ground an aesthetic judgement?

Thus, (a) is very implausible. As humans we see more difference than we do similarity. Kant cannot have meant this. But (b) – though it is very plausible – is not very helpful. This is because even if we are the same qua rationality, this does not mean that *sans private grounds for self-interest* we would all agree that Duchamps' 'Nude descending the Staircase' is beautiful. Or take John Cage's '1′1/2″ For a String Player'. If self-interest were stripped away, would we all appreciate its minimalist structure? Virtually none of us have self-interest in any artwork's success or failure, but that does not insure a uniform response. Premise 3 is problematic.

Then there is premise 6, when one judges the beautiful one's judgement is for everyone. It is hard to assess this premise. In Kant's time, the European colonial age was at its peak. European nations (with their weapons of conflict) had divided and claimed most of the uncharted world (uncharted from the European perspective). They sought to bring Christianity and European values to the unwashed heathen. There was a sensibility of naïve universalism that was rampant.[5] It is hard not to speculate whether this shared community worldview is behind premise 6. There is a similarity between the subjective universality in cultural Euro-centrism and the sort of subjective universal here asserted. However, it is clear that a subjective universal is important to Kant's argument. It is one thing to say that the commands of ethics are universally binding because those commands are formed from an exploration of concepts and the commands themselves are concepts. Concepts lend themselves to exacting scrutiny and are objective. But this is not the case for subjective judgements made without concepts. If they are universal, then it must be so in a very contingent way that might include acceptance of some shared art community worldview along with an understanding of artistic or natural purpose. That is a lot to load into the antecedent of a conditional.

In premise 8 there is an explicit contrast and an implicit similarity with ethical judgements. Kant frequently argues that ethical judgements are universal because of their subsumption under various determinate concepts – such as 'the good will', 'autonomy', 'logical coherence', and 'human dignity', et al. This process of subsuming objects under concepts is outlined in the Transcendental Analytic of the *First Critique*. Thus, explicitly judgements of normative value in morality differ in kind from those of aesthetics. However, that is not the end of the story. Implied here is a sense that (at the very least) there are various coincidences of ethical judgements and aesthetic judgements. For example in Chapter 59, Kant says that the beautiful is a symbol for the morally good (cf. Chapter 42). These similarities are not explained. Kant has set out a difference in kind between judgements made via concepts (the true and the good) and those made without concepts (the beautiful). Kant recognizes that there is (at least) an apparent conflict in the notion of the subjective universal. This gives rise to an antinomy (Chapters 55–60): the antinomy of taste is not strictly resolved but follows as a symbol or schema of the resolutions of the antinomies involved in pure reason and ethics. Kant has the good and the true explicitly bumping up against the beautiful, but the underlying manner of this is mysterious.

Nonetheless, it is necessary for Kant that judgements of the beautiful not be subsumed under concepts. This is because there is something special about one's interaction with the beautiful. Such a position harkens back to Plato and Aristotle. Each also thought that the mode of presentation in the beautiful was unique and different from discursive presentations. In premise 14 Kant declares that *if* judgements of taste were under concepts, that the representation of beauty would be lost. In other words, this is not the way art happens. It is not a dry lecture in the classroom but a vibrant event directly experienced by the subject. This experience has two facets (premise 21). The imagination plays two cognitive roles: (a) in the schematism of concepts and (b) in free-play (cases in which there are no concepts). The imagination works both in processes that contain concepts and those in which a free-play of reflection allows one to feel pleasure and satisfaction. It is the imagination that is the link between the good and the true (on the one hand) and the beautiful (on the other hand). In the first group, imagination works in the schematism in a pivotal role (cf. *First Critique*, A 137–147, B176–187). Because of this dual role, the understanding works in harmonious concert with the imagination in judgements about the beautiful (premise 30).

It should be remembered that Kant regularly returns to nature as his touchstone for the aesthetic experience. This gives rise to speculations about natural purpose and mechanical execution (Second Part). In human artifacts there also is a purpose. When one speculates upon this purpose from his subjective standpoint, there can emerge nuance and harmony between the true and the good (under concepts, thus objectively universal) and the beautiful (the result of disinterested reflection that produces pleasure and satisfaction). But a wall does not separate these two realms. This is because the beautiful stimulates the imagination. The imagination (*Eindbil-dungskraft*) can create another nature (worldview) of its own (Chapters. 49–50).

In the end it is the role of imagination that ultimately gets the job done: (a) it intermediates between the concept-driven realms of truth and morality and the non-concept domain of the beautiful; (b) it allows the presentation of art in such a way that we are drawn into a reflective mode by which a playful imagination displays a pastiche for *quality*, a feeling of the furtherance of life (= play of imagination) and *quantity*, that checks vital powers to create a strong emotion (= an earnest exercise of the imagination, Chapters 23–28). Beneath all the turgid prose, Kant suggests that art is different from truth and ethics. Art entices us to feel and be struck by the artifact in such a way that the rest of our personal worldview is shaken and stirred by process. Though Kant was not an aficionado, he did recognize the major role that art plays in forming our personal worldview. His writings suggest various links between the beautiful and the good along with the beautiful and the true. Not too much can be made of this because of the rather ephemeral nature of aesthetic judgements.

Hume: Art as Refined Sentiment of Taste

David Hume offers the reader an approach to aesthetics that mirrors his approach to ethics.[6] Ethical norms begin with the sentiments, he declares. The sentiments can give rise to pleasure. Hume suggests that this stimulated pleasure (among those who have acquired delicate taste) is what should stand as the standard of taste within a society even though there are many relativistic challenges to such a standard.

Unlike science, in which the particulars are agreed upon but the inductive laws are subject to controversy, art (and ethics) can set out general principles to which all agree. These principles of universal normative assent are linguistically grounded: elegance, propriety, simplicity, spirit in writing, etc., but beyond this nominal linguistic concord, there is great disagreement on how to subsume particular works of art into these categories.

The answer to the problem of subsumption comes from the critic who develops a delicate imaginative taste so that he perceives:

(a) what is being attempted in the artistic endeavour, (b) a list of all the ingredients involved, and (c) how the ingredients work together in an attempt to satisfy the artistic design. In earlier cases, the social/historical context of the work is also considered. Pluralism and not monism thus becomes the critical canon.

ARGUMENT 8.2
The most beautiful artifact is one that delicately stimulates the imagination.[7]

1. [Sentiments are right if someone experiences them] – A
2. [Judgements are right only in those limited instances that they correspond to material, empirically based reality] – A
3. All sentiments are correct; only some judgements are correct – 1, 2, p. 6
4. The ascription of Beauty to an artifact is a sentimental reaction on the part of the observer – A
5. There are some rules of composition that (by experience) have been found to please over the ages and in all countries – F, p. 7
6. [Any invariant rules that are proven by experience are only quasi-objective] – A
7. The rules in art are quasi-objective – 3–6, p. 8
8. Poetry is often based on gross falsehoods – F
9. Exact verisimilitude is not artful – A
10. [Poetry is not an expression of truth] – 7–9
11. The stimulation of the observer's imagination is artful – 4, p. 10
12. The most effective stimulation is by delicacy (as shown by the *Don Quixote* example) – p. 8
13. Delicacy is when the organs [of the audience] are so fine and so exact so as to allow every ingredient to be perceived – A, p. 11
14. Beauty is what pleases; ugliness is what displeases – A
15. [The most effective stimulation of the imagination yields the most pleasure] – A

16. The most beautiful artifact is one that delicately stimulates the imagination – 11–15

In Argument 8.2 Hume grounds the entire process of criticism in sentiment. Sentiment is notoriously subjective. If I say that I experience anger when I read a scene in a novel at some time, t_1, then it is always the case that I am correct that I experienced anger at t_1. It is not relevant for the question to be asked whether I was mistaken in thinking that I felt anger. Individual empirical experience is taken to be foundational and not subject to further meaningful inquiry. For Hume sentiments are like this. The emphasis here is clearly upon the individual observer (though the criteria for the observer's choice are open and available for intersubjective examination, externalism).

Premise 5 is a segue from the individual observer to more general observations about art. The mechanism for this is a quasi-inductive argument that says there is good reason to believe that if such and such literary conventions have worked well in the past (such as in Chaucer, Shakespeare, and Milton), they will work today. This is a strange sort of assertion from the man who brought contingency into inductive logic.[9] However, it may not be so strange if one takes this only to be a rule of thumb and not some sort of law or statistical generalization. In this case, Hume could refer to simple handbook-style rules such as Strunk and White's *The Elements of Style*.[10] There are certain tried and true rules of good writing and some of these (partly on the basis of longevity) can be set out in a sort of rulebook.[11]

However, fiction is rather messier than the expository or persuasive writing of most handbooks. First of all, fiction is merely contrived by the artist (according to Hume). If that which owes its origin to the fancy of an artist (and not to the empirical affairs of nature) is false, then artifacts are false. The events recounted did not happen. But the artifact cannot be so removed from our experience as to make it irrelevant. No. The artist devises a careful ensemble that delicately arranges the elements into an assembled whole. In Argument 8.2, the story of the hogshead of wine with the key and leather thong is brought forth to give some objective backing to what seems to be a hopelessly subjective process. So long as the evaluation is made using one's empirical faculties, auditory (for music), visual (for painting), touch (for textiles and crafts), then one has a foundational, empirical point of connection for those wishing to establish a workable standard of taste.

This is no easy task, but in the end Hume turns his attention to those few whose developed tastes are to be trusted. They will be the high priests of artistic merit. Most of Western art criticism has developed just along these lines. It makes sense to many that they entrust the canon of taste to the esoteric few. But what of those others who are standing at the gates? Are they to remain as they are, hat in hand waiting for the high priests to toss them change?

Hume addresses the problem of evaluating art head-on within the contexts of his empirically mitigated scepticism. This makes normative standards (be they art or ethics) as derivative from his overall philosophy. They have some connections with experience (via the sentimental reactions of pleasure et al.), but that connection is contingent upon the degree to which those sentiments were given context by the standard of taste. Such contexts create expectations. If the artifact satisfies the given expectations, then it may occasion sentiments of satisfaction and pleasure. But the question then becomes whether those sentiments of satisfaction and pleasure have been occasioned by the beautiful or by a functional-fulfilment model randomly chosen and successfully executed (the coherence model for truth – though Hume is clear that art is not about the presentation of truth). That task is left to scientists and philosophers. However, in the end of the day, it is unclear whether Hume's solution does not devolve into the sorts of prejudice that he abhors elsewhere.[12]

As we consider our triad of themes in this book, Hume weighs in by saying that the true stands apart from the good and the beautiful. Truth is known via externalist, inter-subjective critical empiricism. This is the basis of science (which stands as the primary example of matters of fact). In contrast to the true, the good and the beautiful are known in a second way (via sentiments). This mode of knowing yields general normative categories but is rather incomplete when it comes to offering definitive answers as to which particular actions are good or which particular artifacts are beautiful. Instead, we are meant to trust a standard of taste that has been created by the high priests of ethics and art criticism. These keepers of the canon based their considered opinions upon the tradition of what has been considered to be good or beautiful in the past. Obviously, this strategy is rather conservative in that it tends to enshrine what has been while shutting out current work in the field. Hume does not have this difficulty with the true because theories of science must always measure up the empirical explanandum. But in the case of ethics and art, there is no objective measure. Thus, it is very possible that attitudes and norms might become entrenched without adequate means of self-renewal and critical examination.

Contemporary Theories: the Nineteenth Century

This section of the chapter will give brief overviews of selected pivotal writers in aesthetics/criticism with the purpose of elucidating certain important ways of raising and answering central issues concerning beauty. Again, the reader must distinguish between those who are engaged in aesthetics/criticism from those who are propounding a *method* for creating art. For example, the Impressionist movement in nineteenth-century painting would count as a method for creating art. Thus it is not recognized here. Some *method* advocates seem also to advocate a groundwork for criticism – such as Wassily Kandinsky and Der Blaue Reiter movement. However, on the basis of the objective ground of criticism, these writers will be omitted in this presentation.

Coleridge and Shelley: the Artist's Soul Leading Us to Truth

Samuel Taylor Coleridge was associated with the Romantic Lake Poets at the beginning of the nineteenth century. The romantic poets of this school were interested (like Longinus) in emphasizing the genius of the poet as the cornerstone of understanding and evaluating a work of art. 'Fancy' and 'imagination' are terms most associated with Coleridge. Under this schema, 'fancy' is thought to be mere novelty. For many, this is enough for pleasure. But if one were to use novelty so that it resonated more deeply with thought, then fancy transcends to imagination. These terms were bandied about at the end of the eighteenth century such that Dr Samuel Johnson in his *Dictionary* sets out 'fancy' to be a sub-category of imagination.

Coleridge separates the terms – thus breaking with standard usage. For Coleridge to make this sort of radical separation is to make a break with one of England's key critics (Dr. Johnson).

Fancy operates via the association of *fixities* and *definites* in an association that is merely pleasing. This source of pleasure comes from the emancipation from time and space. Imagination is rather more ambitious. There are two sorts of Imagination:

- Primary Imagination. The living power of God in the eternal act of creation. It is also to be found within the soul of each person.
- Secondary Imagination. This echoes primary imagination and works with the will and understanding to create a well-wrought whole.

Coleridge thought that the artist was engaged in a quasi-divine act that could bring both the artist and his audience closer to God. This is because artistic activity mirrors that of Divine creation. Creative activity is necessary in order for people to make sense of their lives (an important exercise). This is brought forth in his argument from the *Biographia Literaria*.[13]

ARGUMENT 8.3
How poets help humankind

1. The poet (through secondary imagination) brings the soul of man into activity – F
2. The activity of secondary imagination reconciles the disparate puzzles of human existence – A
3. [The purpose of all humans is to reconcile the disparate puzzles of human existence] – A
4. The poet helps humanity to fulfil its purpose – 2, 3
5. [To help any agent fulfil his purpose is to make that agent good and to cause him to flourish] – A (cf. Aristotle's *Poetics* and *Ethics*)

---

6. Poets and their poetry improve humankind and are instrumental to their flourishing – 1, 4, 5

In Argument 8.3, Coleridge posits that through the activity of secondary imagination the artist stimulates people in a positive way. This stimulation allows them better to be authentic people in the world. But what might the mechanics of this be? I would suggest something like the personal worldview examination that is demanded by the personal worldview imperative. As was suggested earlier, it is requisite for people to live satisfactory lives that they periodically examine their own worldview: a compilation of their values and the facts they hold to be correct (the good, beautiful, and the true). What such displays of the secondary imagination do is to put before the audience various possibilities: narrative, visual, auditory in order to make the audience reconsider their present arrangement of personal worldview. The reconsideration is undergone on the basis of the artistic standpoint that stimulated this examination. Thus, the artist not only gets people to undergo personal worldview renewal, but also dictates the direction from which these questions will be asked. If periodic personal worldview examination is essential to leading a worthwhile life, and if the artist is instrumental in providing the context and energy for this, *then* the artist is providing an essential social service in the presentation of the beautiful: stimulating the general reconsideration of the true and the good in the lives of the audience. This means that art provides an essential social function and is no mere frivolous extravagance.

A contemporary of Coleridge, Percy Bysshe Shelley, further explores the social role of the artist. Shelley was primarily a poet though, like all the Romantic English poets, he did some non-fiction writing as well.[14] In his essay 'A Defense of Poetry' (1821), Shelley suggests a mechanism that allows people to undergo positive worldview revision. One of the lynchpins of Shelley's critical tools is the process that mirrors Keats' doctrine of *negative capability*.[15] In negative capability a person is enabled by the artist to locate himself in a different place (alternative worldview). Thus, if I read a poem about the English Civil War, I can (via the artistic power of the maker) put myself into the tumultuous times of seventeenth-century England between the royalists and the Roundheads. The intrigue and challenge that they faced become my own. I am *there*. I am living *in the skin* of the protagonist and facing his or her situation. It doesn't matter if I cross time, space, class, race, or gender. Everything is possible within the realm of negative capability. It is a definable outcome of the artistic experience that enables worldview analysis and growth.

Many people around 1800 were questioning whether poetry was still relevant to the modern person. Wasn't poetry a relic of the Greeks, Romans, and those of a bygone age? In the twenty-first century I have heard people asking the same question. But Shelley demurred. He believed that poetry combines wisdom and delight that kindles the imagination sympathetically to locate us in the place of another. This is because poetry is so much at the pulse of society that it not only diagnoses community worldview health, but it is there potentially to break down arbitrary differences. The mechanics of this are based in a principle of disinterest (like Kant). Poetry (unlike science and business) is only concerned with discovering truth. It is not about practical outcomes (science => technology) nor about advantage (business). More on how this happens in the outline of one of his key arguments.

ARGUMENT 8.4
Poetry as social salvation

1. Poetry turns all things to loveliness (exalts existing beauty and adds beauty to the deformed) – A
2. [Interacting with Beauty creates in the observer a clear mind] – A
3. [A clear mind sees Truth] – A
4. Poetry enables people to see Truth – 1-3
5. All things are as they are perceived to be – A (cf. Berkeley and Protagoras)
6. The poet alters perceptions favourably towards beauty – 1
7. The poet enables people to see Beauty – 5–6
8. [Those who interact with the True and the Beautiful will also see the Good] – A
9. The poet makes people see the Good – 4, 7
10. [To know the Good is to do the Good] – A (cf. Plato)
11. The poet makes people better – 9, 10
12. The poet is largely unacknowledged in his societal role – A
13. The poet is the unacknowledged benefactor of society – 4, 7, 11, 12

In Argument 8.4, Shelley contends that in order for ordinary people to see truth, they need a clear mind. In premise 3 he declares that art (poetry) enables the audience to see with clarity that they may have lost in their day-to-day existence. This clarity is an outcome of interacting with beauty. Thus, beauty is philosophically therapeutic (cf. Aristotle's *katharsis*). It helps the patient re-examine life and the personal worldview that gives it meaning. By seeing the beautiful and the true, the audience will also see the good. Thus, all three themes of this book are put on par and can be obtained as a result of interacting with the beautiful. From this portal, everything is possible. Since the facilitator of this whole process is the artist, it is she who we must thank for making specific individuals better, but also for reforming society as a whole. When Zola wrote *J'accuse*,[16] he had a specific social message in mind (as per the novels *The Jungle* or *Invisible Man*, *Night*, or *Oxherding Tale*).[17] One need not stop there. 'Guernica' (a painting), 'Blowin' in the Wind' (a popular song), ' Жар-птица ' or 'The Firebird' (a classical piece of music), and *The China Syndrome* (a movie about a fictional nuclear-plant disaster) all had the same intent: to comment upon the current world situation with an aim at changing things. There is something about art's power that it enables us to begin anew in our personal worldview explorations as we quest for the truth and the good in our lives.

Nietzsche: Art as the Battleground between Dionysus and Apollo

There is something comforting and frightening about Nietzsche's vision of the purpose of art in society. Art is seen from the perspective of the artist (what she intends to do) and from the perspective of the effects upon the audience (how the intentions play out in the audience's reaction). Within this two-fold perspective, Nietzsche upholds both ethic of the noble and controlled aspect of art as well as the ethic of uncontrolled, wild intoxicating effects of a really effective art work. These tensions are present in his work *The Birth of Tragedy*.[18]

ARGUMENT 8.5
Apollo v. Dionysus

1. Apollo is (the emblem of) a careful craftsman image maker; Dionysus is (the emblem of) an imageless intoxicated maker – A/Ch. 1
2. Apollo is the god of prophecy – F
3. [Prophecy is the highest of powers] – F
4. Apollo [as a universal emblem of careful craftsmen with a controlled, prophetic message] is connected with the highest of powers – 1–3
5. The bond between humans is strongly renewed by magic – A
6. Singing and dancing bring participants in communion with a vibrant human realm – A
7. Dionysus (as an emblem of the human element of magic, emotion, and physical action) is understood individually as a key component in human enjoyment of art – 5-6
8. [Both the influences of Apollo and Dionysus are pivotal in human enjoyment of art] – 4, 7
9. When one gazes and contemplates upon truth (via art from Apollo) this is one legitimate outcome – A/Ch. 3
10. In ancient Greek tragedy there was an excitement in the Greek Chorus such that the Dionysus element was stimulated – A/Ch. 8
11. In Greek myths, the theft of fire by Prometheus is on one account a sin, but on another account a virtue [it's a sin because it disobeys the commands of God; it is a virtue because it promotes a sense of progress] – A
12. [Human progress in knowledge and technology is a good] – A
13. Human action in the spirit of Prometheus is a good – 9–12/Ch. 9
14. [Some view the spirit of the individual, without checks, as a sin] – A/Ch. 10
15. [Individualism trumps all else] – A
16. Art is ultimately the expression of the artist via both Dionysus and Apollo with the former's individualistic vitality being the most important element – 4, 7, 8, 13, 15

Argument 8.5 is a very influential argument in the framing of the contemporary view of aesthetics – particularly in narrative art. When the classical writers such as Aristotle or Horace or Longinus talk about pleasure and instruction, it is never made clear the sort of pleasure that is involved. One could equally call 'pleasure' the experience one gets from listening to a singer recite the *Odyssey* for five plus hours or the 'pleasure' one gets at the bawdy jokes of Aristophanes' *Lysistrata* in a two-hour time frame with costumes, sets, music, et al. Certainly the former pleasure may be much better crafted and full of many great thoughts and driven by a revenge-tragedy theme (always popular with audiences), but the latter is charged with sexual energy juxtaposed with images of war and gore. The *Odyssey* narrative is more Apollo-oriented while *Lysistrata* is more Dionysus-oriented.

In more modern terms, we all might admire the care of Joyce's *Ulysses* or *Finnegan's Wake* for their craftsmanship and comment upon the English/Irish/Western literary traditions, but they are a bit dry. There are few sweat stains on the pages of these books as opposed to D.H. Lawrence's novels such as *Women in Love* or *Lady Chatterley's Lover*. William Faulkner was always considered to be leaning toward Apollo while Ernest Hemingway was in the Dionysus camp.

What is additionally curious is that Dionysus is associated with individualism. In the United States, individualism has always been held in high regard. The immigrants who came and took the land by conquest over the native peoples saw themselves as striking out for an individual vision of life (the personal worldview). This was connected with a spiritedness that often overflowed to violence, sexual licentiousness, and the general force of über-personality to solve life's problems (as opposed to reasoned philosophical discussion). If Nietzsche is correct here, then we are drawn to the Dionysus's vision, but not to the exclusion of Apollo. We do not commend overly violent, overly sexual, overly phrenetic depictions – void of careful craftsmanship that is grounded in a rational sensibility. Thus, Dionysus alone is not enough. Though it positively tips the balance between two Apollo-based treatments, it is not singly sufficient as a presentation on its own.

The reader may remember that in the first part of this book, the personal worldview imperative was interpreted with respect to the requirements of completeness. This entailed that the agent acquires a good will. There were two interpretations of the good will: (a) the Kantian interpretation (that depended upon rationality considering its own criteria and the criteria of deductive and inductive coherence as an essential and ultimately trumping criterion), and (b) the Augustine interpretation (that called upon emotional input that was necessary but not sufficient for the good will). In this way, this author recognizes the same two categories as Nietzsche. The difference is that we reverse the order. Now, to be fair, my earlier discussion was in the context of the *good* and not in the context of the *beautiful*. But to be consistent with my understanding of the public practice of religion (that I hold to be parallel to one's disposition toward art), I still hold that *Apollo* and not Dionysus should hold sway. The reason for this, is that in the end, within the realm of action, is always the good. That is our salvation. This must be understood within the context of the true and the beautiful, but if one were to construct a triangle, the good would be at the apex with the true and the beautiful at its bases (see Figure 8.1).

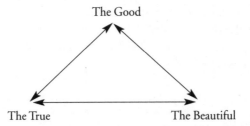

Figure 8.1 The relationship between the Good, the True, and the Beautiful

Nietzsche would schematize this rather differently. He might put the beautiful as a starting point in which the true and the good might find their character. From the standpoint of an individual, as such, this is understandable. The noble, *to kalon*, is a term of commendation that is very individually oriented. It can be tied to individual excellence and accomplishment or it can be tied to individual excess and narcissism.

In the end, Nietzsche offers an interesting model for the personal and shared community worldview perspectives. It has much support in sales figures for novels, movies, plays, and the explosion of interest in hip-hop and rap music. Though I disagree with Nietzsche's priorities, it is an issue that we all must confront in our quest to create a personal worldview that we believe in.

Contemporary Theories: the Twentieth Century

In the twentieth century, the critical game changed. The First World War shocked the Occidental world in a fundamental way. These shock waves resonated. One could easily write a two-volume work on simply the theories of the twentieth century. Since this exposition is a very highly edited overview, it is impossible to recognize many very fine and influential figures.

Clive Bell: Emotion and Significant Form

Clive Bell believes that art is concerned with emotion, but not *any* sort of emotion. It is a controlled sort of emotional response that he calls aesthetic emotion. This is similar to the sort of disinterested rapture that Kant describes. Good art is that which occasions in the audience this sort of aesthetic emotion. Bad art does not. The trigger of aesthetic emotion is what Bell calls significant form.

The argument for this is:

ARGUMENT 8.6
Significant form is that which charges aesthetic emotion[19]

1. When people view Cézanne, Poussin, Piero della Francesco, et al., their aesthetic emotions are stirred – A
2. The relations of lines and colours in their presentation is called significant form – A
3. In our experience of art we begin with our personal experience and from this various artifacts provoke aesthetic emotion according to individual taste – F

4. [When individuals view artifacts they are moved by their individual taste to aesthetic emotion] – 1–3

5. When people say something is 'beautiful' they mean that it is 'a combination of lines and colours that provoke aesthetic emotion' – A

6. When people say something is 'beautiful' they mean that it possesses significant form (though many use the word more broadly than this) – 2, 5

7. There are many different sorts of formal presentations, e.g. realistic form, mathematical form, compositional form, created (non-realistic forms) – F

8. All formal categories can become significant – F

9. What raises a depiction within a form category to significant is its ability to provoke aesthetic emotion within its audience – A

10. Significant form is that which charges aesthetic emotion – 4, 6, 7–9

Bell grounds his argument in painting. But the principles are generally applicable because the notion of significant form could be applied to other art areas as well. What is important here for our purposes is that art is judged as being effective or not based upon the reaction of the audience. Here this is stated as the ability to evince aesthetic emotion – presumably first among the critics and then among the *hoi polloi*. One can judge art by the way the audience receives it. But let us be perfectly clear about this approach: it is relativistic and possibly circular. Different societies and historical periods will judge art differently. The seventeenth century rated John Donne to be a minor metaphysical poet.[20] And yet when Sir Herbert Grierson decided to edit a modern edition of the *Songs and Sonnets*, all of a sudden, Donne became a major poet and the precursor to T.S. Eliot.[21] What mattered was the modernist tastes of the post-First World War period. The interests of various periods will occasion various aesthetic pleasures: realistic painting depicting religious scenes, or realistic painting depicting Greek and Roman myths, or realistic painting depicting domestic life, or realistic landscapes, or realistic still life, or impressionistic modifications of all of the above, or other schools presentations to the public. Thus, under this standard of criticism, a work of art is judged according to the shared art community worldview.

It's possibly circular because significant form is that which evinces aesthetic emotion and aesthetic emotion is the criterion for some artifact having significant form. One way out of this potential circularity is to pivot to the pragmatic theory of truth. Since outcomes of popularity can be measured (by critics or by the general audience), one might make the secondary assumption that people buy artifacts (paintings, novels, movie tickets, et al.) because they find them aesthetically moving. In some cases the critics will love a book or movie and the general public demurs. In other cases it is just the opposite. If we make this minor emendation to Bell, then what we are left with is a theory of audience criticism. A work of art is measured by the way the audience is affected.[22] Under this interpretation Clive Bell is really an advocate of audience criticism not too dissimilar to Monroe Beardsley.[23]

Martin Heidegger: Art and Truth

Martin Heidegger is a systematic philosopher (like Kant and Aristotle) meaning that his whole philosophical project is behind each initiative. Heidegger is an advocate of the correspondence theory of truth. Like Plato and the pre-Socratics, Heidegger posits being universally understood (*sein*) and its designation and individual connection (*da-sein*) as hovering in the vicinity of truth as a principle (or form) of unification (*Dasein*). The contrast with Plato is that there is less concern for the moral instruction of the State. For Heidegger (like Kierkegaard) it is the individual and her own personal quest that is the centre of attention. Political states come and go. They are transitory. Beyond these, each of us must find a way to find an authentic relationship to unification (*Dasein*).

ARGUMENT 8.7
The artist, artifact, and truth[24]

1. What something *is* constitutes its essence or nature; the origin of x is the source of x's nature – A/p. 17

2. [Whenever the origin of x also is the outcome of x, either circularity or a dialectical relationship is at play] – F

3. The artist is the origin of the artifact, and the artifact is the origin of the artist [in a non-circular manner] – A/p. 17

4. [The artist and artifact have a dialectical interaction that reveals the nature of each] – 1–3

5. Artifacts possess natural and artificial 'thing-ness' – A/pp. 21–22

6. In the process of making the artificial, thing-ness comes-to-be via *hule* (matter) + *morphe* (shape) bringing forth *eidos* (form) – F/pp. 26–27

7. The artifact bears the characteristics of its shape via a unity of the manifold of sensation as it discloses the formed matter – 4–6/pp. 28–29

8. Using the form of the subject matter (in this case peasant shoes), Van Gogh reveals what the shoes are *in truth* – A/p. 36

9. To reveal *truth* one is not merely reproducing images but is reproducing a thing's general essence, aka truth – 5–8/ p. 37

10. Art gets us closer to what *is* (an ontological revelation) – A/p. 43

11. The revelation of ontological reality occurs by presenting a world-view to the audience – A/pp. 44–45

12. The presentation of a worldview to the audience opens up a new worldview perspective that sets forth its own conditions of truth – A/pp. 45–50

13. Truth [known via worldview] reveals being – 10–12/p. 50

14. Art (from the maker's standpoint) requires craftsmanship (*techne*) that is a way of making public [the becoming of] that which is concealed – A/pp. 58–59

15. Effective art is the occasion of the 'happening of truth' for an audience – A/p. 71

16. Art is the becoming and happening of truth for an audience [from the perspective of the artifact and the mind of the artist] – 4, 9, 13–15/p. 71

Heidegger's argument must first be seen in the context of his other work. For Heidegger, the principal cause for authentic people living in the world is to return to the unity of their own selves *da-sein* with the being of other entities: *sein* (being universally understood) via a relationship with that other ground of being: *Dasein*.[25] Finding this relationship is necessary post-Aristotle who (on this account) created a schism between *sein* and *da-sein* that must be reconciled (according to the prescriptions of the pre-Socratics).[26] Thus, the human quest is defined in a searching for a connection with *Dasein*. One avenue to accomplish this is via art. Since artifacts and the artist interact such that each can be said to be the origin of each other (premise 4), then the audience can approach a dynamic unity that displays the artifact's thing-ness through a form that is the result of the shape and material constitution of the artifact (premise 6). For example, in a poem the material aspect might be the paper on which the poem is presented, the type fonts, type style, and ink colour. The shape might be the relation to various prosody forms (heroic couplets, Spenserian stanzas, sonnets, etc.). From the interaction of these emerges the form of the experience that conveys the reader to another worldview (premise 11). This new worldview presents its own conditions of truth (premise 12). Ultimately, Heidegger sees this as revealing *Dasein* (premise 13). In this way, Heidegger sees the artistic enterprise as assuming a correspondence theory of truth in order to instruct (get the audience into a relationship with *that being* (outside the agent): *Dasein*). If this reading of Heidegger is correct, then art plays a crucial role in beings living on the earth. Like Plato's *Symposium*, beauty is uniquely situated to lead people to truth. Like Aristotle, there is a connection to ratiocination. Art is a means of philosophy for the masses. Such a conclusion works for Aristotle. On the other hand, since Aristotle is the first analytic philosopher, and since analytic philosophy separates the subject and object and compartmentalizes it (the source of our human alienation), then in the larger sense Heidegger would reject Aristotle. This same sort of criticism might be levelled against Kant.

Coleridge and Shelley separate the author from others by attributing genius of vision to the artist so that he or she is the *other*: separate and apart from the rest of humanity. This is probably true of Nietzsche as well (though one must patch together passages on the *überman* with those on the artist who portrays the Apollonian or

Dionysian vision for the audience). Heidegger does not do this. For him the author and text are origins of each other via a dialectical interaction (premise 4). This means that the understanding of the author becomes more complicated than was imagined by Coleridge, Shelley, and Nietzsche.

Heidegger, via a dialectical process, both elevates the work and lowers the artist. Because these are in dialectical interaction, neither can claim ascendancy or 'origin' status. This standpoint resonates with Michel Foucault, who creates a similar worldview appreciation of the author–work amalgam.

In the end, the audience will judge a work of art according to the truth of presented worldview. When one enters the projected worldview, one must evaluate it. Heidegger is a little vague on the mechanics of this process – leaving it to an internalist sensibility to connect with *Dasein*. I would propose a more transparent approach. Deciding on whether to accept a new worldview is analogous to the way we accept novel normative theories (see p. 115, n. 24).

If this ascription is correct, then Heidegger's account of the nature of art as truth fits in well with my account of normative worldview in Part I. This would then be one way that the Beautiful bumps into the True and then subsequently to the Good in interesting and productive ways.

Jacques Derrida: Rhetorical Flourishes in Interpreting the Work
Like Arthur Danto, Derrida elevates the role of the critic. But at the same time he lowers the intent of the artist as critic. This is because the work, and not the author, takes centre stage. It is not the work as intended by the author, but the work taken for its exhibited characteristics. There are two main interpretative devices that Derrida uses in this quest. The larger umbrella can be termed the deconstruction method – a brief, simplified summary of this method is as follows:

1. Find the limits of the text by identifying and overturning conceptual metaphysical oppositions within the work through uncovering polar oppositions.

2. The critic inserts his own ideas in the void created in number 1.
3. The critic re-assesses the work after having emended it as per number 2.

Often, Derrida fulfils number 1 by his use of neologisms. Derrida is famous for his neologisms. These are deep inquiries into words. For example, *supplement* in French means 'substitute' or 'addition'. Rousseau used the word consistently in the first sense (presumably on purpose) but Derrida says that the second sense waits in the wings and must be employed as well – even in this case when the writer explicitly did not intend it. In this case Derrida sets out Rousseau as being between the Enlightenment and Romanticism – this on the basis of an alternative reading of a meaning not intended by the author! Obviously, in this circumstance the critic re-creates the text in his own image.

A commonly used term to signify examining a work, as such, is 'textuality'. Textuality assumes the stance in which the written work is the starting point from which the interpretative process begins. For Derrida this interpretative process is a *play of differences*. This is a key phrase. Let's explore some meanings of the phrase. One meaning of 'play of differences' mirrors Derrida's own playful self.[27] For Derrida the difference means to: (a) differentiate and (b) to postpone.[28] In deconstructionism the connections are made outside the work of art. The critic supplements the art work himself. This can be called the principle of supplementarity. After the process of supplementing the work of art, the new amalgam contains both the work of art and the critic's emendations.

For Derrida the critic works between the *signified* (what is meant) and the *signifier* (the vehicle for conveying the meaning). The signifier functions as a trace that leads the critic to what was signified prior. This distinction goes back to the Swiss linguist Ferdinand de Saussure. Saussure says in *Course in General Linguistics* (1916)[29] that language is a system of differences without positive terms. Derrida borrows this idea of differences and adds a temporal dimension. Whereas Saussure keeps language fixed in time, Derrida doesn't.

Derrida juxtaposes two senses of the word *différer* (which translates both as 'to differ' and 'to defer'). When we create the noun forms the split is apparent by sight but not by sound (since they are pronounced the same): *différence* and *différance*. The first form is synchronic (static in the sense of Saussure) while the second implies a diachronic process that unites both senses. This is because, in speech, both come together. But only in writing is the variation seen. This means that writing is more primary than speech. Derrida abhors the fact that in the Western tradition speech is more privileged than writing by the hoi polloi, but in the logical order just the opposite is the case.

ARGUMENT 8.8
'Plato's Pharmacy'[30]

1. Theuth, the inventor of writing presents his invention to King Thamus of Egypt – F
2. Writing lasts quite a long time – F
3. Memory, the outcome of speech, often lasts a short time – F
4. [There are often points that we wish to use, but we forget them and so miss the chance] – F
5. The writing invention of Theuth is a 'drug' (*pharmacon*) that will extend memory – 1– 4
6. [If one knows she has a crutch to protect against lost memories, then one will not try so hard to remember] – A
7. '*Pharmacon*' is also a poison – F
8. [A crutch poisons its possessor instead of helping him] – A
9. Writing is a poison to be avoided – 6–8

10. Writing is both a helpful drug as well as a poison – 5, 9

This battle between writing and speech is illustrated in the essay 'Plato's Pharmacy' through the story in Plato's *Phaedrus* in which Theuth, the so-called inventor of writing, presents his invention to King Thamus of Egypt as a cure for forgetfulness. The king believes just the opposite will be the result, i.e. forgetfulness. This is because 'pharmacon' means both 'drug' and 'poison'. Was there ever a logic prior to the split of meanings that united the two? This sort of question is the suggestive diachronic of Derrida.

To know the limitations of a text is very useful. There are *many* limitations of a text that may prove to be relevant. It is impossible to know what they are in an a priori fashion. Deconstruction, however (as per Derrida), opens itself up to trivial word play. This is just like Socrates' dismissal of Prodicus in Plato's *Protagoras*.[31] A possible problem is that there are no externalist signposts to all for intersubjective evaluation. The critical theory rests upon internalist apprehensions and the attribution of meanings and their consequences that may not be a part of the original design of the art work. This is reminiscent of the London artist and her posters for her lost cat. The famous artist put up posters in Bloomsbury for her lost cat. However, people collected the posters as art – even though the artist's intention was to retrieve her lost cat.[32] If her posters (contrary to her intention) can be called art, then why not the critic's reconstruction based upon criteria totally foreign to the intention of the author?

Derrida is thus representative of the elevation of the critic as he or she playfully finds angles of cleavage within the work in order to take it apart for the purpose of rearrangement according to the critic's own worldview within a coherence truth theory re-constructed.

Conclusion

These last two chapters have covered a lot of territory. Its purpose is to present a brief glimpse of some theories of aesthetics and criticism from some of the great thinkers in history (giving some concern to variety of expression and points of view). It will be the province of the next chapter to present criteria by which we might be able to fashion a critical theory in the context of the true and the good.

9 The Quest for the Beautiful

> How beautiful is all this visible world!
> How glorious in its action and itself!
> Byron, *Manfred*

All of us are drawn toward the beautiful. This inclination is both natural and acquired. The natural side aligns itself with its origins: nature. We are overcome with the beauty of the human body and the shapes of other living creatures, flora, and the land. With this given we begin the acquired appreciation with imitations of the natural – both in form and in spirit. These reactions can be simple statements or convoluted presentations that mix comment with presentation. As the element of interpretation increases, the truth represented is less the given truths of nature, as such, but more the artist's reflections upon nature. Each of us, as humans, is drawn to the works of nature and to the works of artisans, first because they are pleasing to us, and second because we feel that they are connected to the true and to the good. But the ways these all are connected are complicated – as the number of prescriptions set out in Chapters 7 and 8 attest. In this chapter, it will be the goal to circumscribe the mode of discourse and to offer several meta-principles that will help guide us in our quest.

Setting out

The first step in our quest is confronting all the theories set out in the previous chapter, synthesizing this massive amount of information into some useable forms. I challenge the reader to make some sense of these through the following exercise.

THOUGHT EXPERIMENT 9.1

Think about the authors presented in Chapters 7 and 8 and evaluate these authors according to the following criteria:

- The source of the artistic vision
- The role of the artist in the artistic process
- The role of the critic in evaluating the artistic process
- The perspective of the audience
- The relevant truth theories implied
- The path to the good presented by the theory

Set out your thoughts in a way that will allow you to make comparisons.

Thought Experiment 9.1 is meant to be a synthetic exercise that
forces each of us to try to combine what is valuable in each of these
important writers. It is my opinion that such an exercise will also call
upon our personal worldviews as we make choices and set out combinations that we think are useful in moving forward to describe the
beautiful.

In the spirit of Thought Experiment 9.1, I have taken it upon
myself to do this. What I come up with is shown in Table 9.1. What
this table shows is a combination that is highly idiosyncratic. It seeks
to follow the rules of the Thought Experiment 9.1 with a view of
integrating the central themes of this book. Obviously, Table 9.1 is
not exhaustive. It represents what I take to be the most suggestive
amalgams from Chapters 7 and 8. Let's run over the candidates.
There are four central types that are set forth: art from genius artist,
art from nature imitated, art from clever craftsman, and art from
artisan with a common touch. Each organizes the central questions
differently. It is a divided line – in the tradition of Plato. On the top
level of the line are the realist perspectives (those favoured by
myself). On the second-level are the anti-realist perspectives. Let's
explore all four possibilities in order, beginning with the top.

In the art from *genius artist approach*, it is assumed that the artist's

Table 9.1 A synthesis of Chapters 7 and 8 into four critical perspectives: a divided line

Art from the Genius Artist	Art from Nature Imitated
Source: From artist's intended purpose to prescriptively declaim. **Role of Artist:** Artist is genius seer and purveyor of truth. **Role of Critic:** Handmaid to the artist. **Audience Perspective:** Makes own decision with input from critics. **Truth Theory:** Internalist Correspondence Theory. **Path to the Good:** Finding the truth makes one good.	**Source:** From Nature imitated/interpreted. **Role of Artist:** Medium to imitate Nature. **Role of Critic:** Alongside artist as interpreter of Nature. **Audience Perspective:** Alongside artist and critic as interpreter of Nature. **Truth Theory:** Externalist Correspondence Theory. **Path to the Good:** Nature is good (given), distance from Nature is bad (given). Follow Nature.
Art from the Clever Craftsman	**Art from the Artisan with a Common Touch**
Source: From empirical patterns of harmony and nuance that deliver pleasure in the work. **Role of Artist:** Artisan who can construct pleasing patterns that are pleasurable. **Role of Critic:** One representative consumer. **Audience Perspective:** Reacting from personal preferences for pleasure given their worldview perspective. **Truth Theory:** Internalist/Externalist Coherence/ Pragmatic Theory. **Path to the Good:** The good is identical to or separate from the true and the beautiful (according to one's own view of pleasure).	**Source:** From shared art community worldview. **Role of Artist:** A member of a community creating work valued by the rules of the community. **Role of Critic:** A high priest of the community in charge of the artistic canon. **Audience Perspective:** The community in a love–hate relationship with the critics. Sees the author as one of their own. **Truth Theory:** Externalist Pragmatic Theory. **Path to the Good:** Utilitarian. Assimilating oneself into the shared community worldview according to general pleasure.

central purpose is to prescriptively declaim. This means that the artist wants to communicate truths to his audience that she believes to be true. Since this is also the province of philosophy, an artist from this approach could be called a popular philosopher. Art is generally more accessible to large audiences than is philosophy. Thus, it would not be unfair under this account to declare the artist to be a popular philosopher. Artists in the tradition are instructing through the pleasure they present. Those who entice and instruct the best are greatly revered. Writers such as Homer, Virgil, Chaucer, Shakespeare, and Milton are often seen as falling within this group. This group of authors is given high marks for their ability to communicate important truths to a wide audience. Not every practitioner in this ilk has been as successful. Dryden, Pope, Johnson, and Tennyson are certainly competent poets, but at times the instruction overtakes the pleasure.

The critic and the audience role in this first model are to assess how successfully the artist fulfils her own purpose. The point of attention is upon the artist and her work. This may include biographical information about the artist. However, such information is useful only as it allows the critic and audience to assess how the author's vision has been transferred to the book, movie, painting, or symphony. Words of assessment such as: 'vision', 'voice', and 'authorial worldview' are key. It is not enough merely to hear a distinctive voice, but the voice must convey a worldview that is inviting to the critic/audience. How do you like living in such a worldview? If the presented worldview is significantly different from that of the contemporary audience/critic, then a choice must be made. Should the readers press to make that worldview reality? When Charles Dickens writes from the standpoint of changing child-labour laws in nineteenth-century Britain, enough of his readers concurred and created the political will to change. When Richard Wright and Ralph Ellison set forth a vision that depicted a racially unjust US society, many concurred and set the stage for the civil rights movement of the 1950s.

The truth theory presented is the correspondence theory of truth. The artist (from the internalist perspective) has a vision of *what is* and *what should be* and exhorts us to follow him. If the critic/audience agrees, then personal transformation and social change can be the result. If the author's perspective (as judged by the correspondence theory) is correct, then we are all improved as a result.

The second amalgam is art from *nature imitated*.[1] This has been a very powerful approach – especially in the visual arts. The leading player here is nature that provides a model for the artist. The artist, in turn, tries to reconstruct and imitate nature. When this is a painting, then the result is some sort of representational art (from photographic exactness to impressionistic and expressionistic comments on the same).[2] In poetry the expression of representational art is generally in the form of highly lyrical, imagistic displays. An example of this is Wordsworth's poem 'Daffodils':

> I wander'd lonely as a cloud
> That floats on high o'er vales and hills,
> When all at once I saw a crowd,
> A host, of golden daffodils;
> Beside the lake, beneath the trees,
> Fluttering and dancing in the breeze.
>
> Continuous as the stars that shine
> And twinkle on the Milky Way,
> They stretch'd in never-ending line
> Along the margin of a bay:
> Ten thousand saw I at a glance,
> Tossing their heads in sprightly dance.
>
> The waves, beside them danced, but they
> Out-did the sparkling waves in glee:
> A poet could not be gay,
> In such a jocund company:
> I gazed – and gazed – but little thought
> What wealth the show to me had brought:

> For oft, when on my couch I lie
> In vacant or in pensive mood,
> They flash upon that inward eye
> Which is the bliss of solitude;
> And then my heart with pleasure fills,
> And dances with the daffodils.

This is a wonderful poem. What it seeks to do is to imitate to the critic/audience a field of daffodils. The poet aspires to make us see such a field in early spring and say in response, 'Wordsworth got it just right!' That is the ultimate compliment for an artist working in this quadrant. The truth theory is correspondence and the standpoint is externalist. We can therefore meet as audience and decide whether the poet got it correctly.

The nature of verisimilitude need not be exact imitation. Just as painting can look 'just like' the object (one extreme of representational painting) *and* be an interpretative rendition (the other extreme of representational painting), so also can poetry. Consider Ezra Pound's famous poem 'In a Station of the Metro'.

> The apparition of these faces in the crowd;
> Petals on a wet, black, bough.

This poem is also imagistic. It seeks to imitate rush hour on the Paris Métro. The first twelve syllables[3] concern one realm and the last seven another. Each interacts imagistically – though not in the same way as Wordsworth's 'Daffodils'. However, in each poem there is a vision of truth that is presented via representation/imitation. The underlying assumption of each is that there is something good here. In a field of daffodils there is something natural and good about its appearance. The disclosure to the poet and his resultant artifact signifies something real: nature. Nature is good (unexamined assumption). If we project ourselves into this worldview, then we also are saying that nature is good. If we are to follow this prescription, then we (also) will have to attest that nature is good and is to be followed in our lives. Thus, the beautiful, the true, and the good unite again in an interesting way.

The third approach is that of *art from the clever craftsman*. Like the second model, the focus is upon the artifact, as it publicly exists. The critic and the audience can look upon the work and ascertain its character. The artistic role is one of pattern maker. In music, this might mean exact-counterpoint as per Bach. In painting, it might mean a very clever scheme of presentation such as Hans Holbein's 'The Ambassadors' (with the conceit of the skull) or Georges Seurat and his complementary dot-matrix system of painting as in 'Un Dimanche après-midi à l'Ile de la Grande Jatte'. Each of these paintings employ patterned conceits that principally depend upon a particular pattern and nuance for their effect.

There are two modes of pattern making: the exoteric and the esoteric. The distinction can be shown through literature. The first (the exoteric) is best described via the genre novel: mystery, romance, and science fiction, et al. These novels depend upon the audience's expectations of the genre for the judgement of pattern. For example, in the mystery novel one expects there to be a foul person with a flaw who might be an excellent candidate to be murdered. Then there is a killer (who also has a flaw) but is both doing the world 'a favour' by killing Mr X, but is also exposing herself to her own flaw. In the investigation there are many red herrings (false leads). Finally, an astute detective (police or private citizen – Miss Marple or Hercule Poirot or Philip Marlowe) sorts things out and the order of the universe is maintained with a red ribbon.

The internal consistency of this form is addicting. It is not unusual for devotees of the internal consistency form to consume novels by the bagful. Mystery, romance, and science fiction together constitute a large share of books published.[4] The reason for this, I think, is that people flock to these artifacts because they present a stable, coherent vision that is true to each genre type. When one buys a mystery novel one can feel some assurance that even though the bad guy is very clever, the detective is even cleverer. Order is maintained. All is right with the world.

The great popularity of television also owes its success to these principles. Creativity and originality (though important) are subsumed by the *formula*. Thus, the genre types of sitcom, reality TV, bizarre game shows, et al. are sold on the basis of an internally consistent pattern. If the pattern is still popular, then so will be this iteration (or so the story goes). True, in this sense, is being consistent within the guidelines of the established pattern. Beautiful means that one has worked within the pattern in a supremely innovative way so that the many loose ends are elegantly accounted for within the general scheme. The status of the good is rather dicier. This is because 'good' under this account would be merely attending to a pattern. Because this standpoint makes no assertions about the way things are (from a correspondence perspective), it is anti-realist. Those philosophers who feel that there is no real good, but only perceived adherence to patterns that are in a deep way arbitrarily intuitionistic would feel a comfort level here.[5] Unlike the first two critical perspectives of beauty that were connected to the *other* (that is real and exists, viz., truth and nature), this third group is situated differently. The good is rather embraced as a genre element. The genre is: social construction. In a particular culture, the good is identified without reference to anything other than these attitudes/dispositions/maxims that are accepted givens. The words that describe the good are linked to the construct.[6]

The second sort of pattern maker is really a puzzle maker. This is the highbrow version of the clever craftsman approach. The artist creates an intricate pattern and the audience's job is to sort through the pattern via painstaking close reading. James Joyce's *Ulysses* and *Finnegan's Wake* fall into this mode. The intricate etymologies and external referral to the canon of literature make the study one of detective work. The same may be said of Thomas Pynchon's *Gravity's Rainbow*. Many would also insert composers like John Cage and abstract expressionist painters with their own private theory of composition. This second variety within the third approach of artist as clever craftsman is often popular only among a clique of those who enjoy the esoteric pleasures of puzzle construction.

Thus, the third approach can be very precise in its audience (in its esoteric mode) just as it is extremely popular in the exoteric mode. The exoteric is in demand because it is very much in touch with the culture and its mercurial changes. The good, true, and beautiful are set in reference to human preferences in the context of coherence. By itself, coherence asserts no realistic claims (thus is 'anti-real'). For proponents, this is an advantage because there is less to defend.[7] Detractors claim that this is purchased at the price of nothing being there. Without a tether beyond itself, the real possibility exists of arbitrary conventionalism (which is only a criticism if you are inclined toward the first two critical positions).

The esoteric is popular to the small cadre of the initiate. The good and true often turn inward reflecting not only on the puzzles and their eventual solutions, but also upon the esoteric group themselves as supporters and admirers of the complex pattern making (that only they and a small group of fellow travellers can comprehend).[8]

The final critical stance is *art from the artisan with the common touch*. The standpoint of this critical perspective begins with the shared community worldview. Like Hegel in *The Philosophy of Right* one can set out the community perspective as paramount.[9] This standpoint normatively endorses the community perspective. Since the worldview is anti-realist there is no real concern to link to a correspondence theory but rather to a pragmatic theory of results. Because we've moved away from skilled pattern maker to merely a creator of a product that people buy, a business model takes over. Art becomes just one more item of fashion and personal expression like mood rings and lava lamps that can go in and out of popular favour. When these artifacts are hot, they are immensely popular and revered (because they are popular).

The *New York Times* list of best-selling books is one such index. What is a good book? The answer is what is currently on the best-selling list. When some book, such as *Love Story* or *The Da Vinci Code*, is at the top for some extended time, it is adored. When it falls out of favour, the book is remaindered and public libraries sell their copies for pennies. Permanence is not a feature of this last critical standpoint. This is because what is popular to the community is based upon nothing else than resonating with the common touch. The common touch is like Heracleitus' river: it is always changing. To seek for permanence is a vain endeavour. The pragmatic truth theory that underlies this approach belies it. Instead, there is the latest hit song, the latest in-painting group, or the latest fashion style in clothes. The only thing permanent is change itself.

Of course there is the canon. But to enthusiasts of this critical stance, old works are dusty. Housecleaning requires dusting them off with modernization or redoing that section of the room (terribly tacky, darling).

And who is the critic in all of this? He is a sales consultant. The public critic predicts which book, movie, painting show, or musical opus will make it with the public. Because 'making it with the public' *is* the standard of success. Under these guidelines, a novelist like Iris Murdoch would be given the boot.[10] She rarely sold more than 20,000 copies of her novels (not the benchmark for a best-selling author).

The critic, as sales consultant, guesses what will be popular with the book-buying public. Such critics view themselves as the high priests of the artistic canon because they have their finger on popular taste. If *Frankenstein* seems a little non-politically correct, then it drops from the canon. If Ezra Pound has offended too many people for his idiotic political views, then he goes, too.

The audience often has a love–hate relationship with these critics. For example, if Mary Lou Sue asks her steady boyfriend what movie they want to go to, he might reply by flipping open his cell phone and pulling up the latest critical opinions on the current top-grossing flicks. Fred wants to see what's popular because what's popular must be good (because it's popular). Mary Lou is not so sure. She thinks that the particular critic from the *Washington Post*, mentioned in the survey, is often at odds with her ideas. She might say, 'No. Let's not go just because X says so. I often hate the movies she likes. I mean she liked that movie – what is it called? – last week, remember? The one in which the dog died. You know I really hate movies in which the dog died. My dog, Fido, was a companion to me when I was growing up. I really hate movies that show a dog dying. Any critic who likes it is trash, as far as I'm concerned. Unless you can get me another critic's idea, I just want to show up and buy a random ticket.'

Mary Lou Sue expresses the opinions of many consumers. They have some very private reasons for liking a movie that cannot necessarily be generalized. For this reason, they often find themselves battling the high priest of artistic taste, the critics (aka sales consultants). These critics often describe their gut feeling or other intuitive reactions as if they were the gold standard of artistic taste. In the end, it is a shouting match of sorts among competing marketers.

The ethical theory that associates itself most closely to this critical perspective is utilitarianism. In utilitarianism, the authority becomes the shared community worldview perspective. What the shared community worldview advocates is correct. 'Correct' in this sense is taken in both the descriptive and the prescriptive sense. One must first ascertain what the community advocates (this can be determined by various externalist devices such as sales figures). In the end, some measurement of the popular pulse is necessary in order to give assent or dissent.

THOUGHT EXPERIMENT 9.2

You are the city manager of ANY-town. The town council has several proposals for a public sculpture in front of the town hall. You are not sure how to proceed.

On the one hand, you think that you should consider applicant-A because most people say that she has exhibited a real vision of the true. Unfortunately, in your town, this view is rather uncomfortable. Then there is exhibit-B. Though it depicts an aspect of the town, as it is, some are unhappy because the town wants to move forward. The third candidate is very interesting. Its patterns intrigue and captivate. Yet, many ask, what does it mean? Finally, there is an entry that has a naked baby being raised to the sky by its father. Everyone says, 'That's life today; the father interacting with his son! We are a community that supports the intervention of men in the child-rearing process.'

You are the city manager. You must make the decision. Which project will you choose and why?

Evaluation of the Critical Perspectives

It is difficult to discern what is good art. It is the contention of this book that the answer to the question is intertwined with the issues of the Good and the True. Without these other perspectives, there is no way to judge between these in an authentic way.

The critical perspectives segregate themselves as follows:

Realist perspective: Art from Genius Artist and Art from Nature
    Imitated
Anti-realist perspective: Art from Clever Craftsman and Art from
Artisan with the Common Touch

So put on your thinking caps. Do you think that we can *know* reality? Or is the whole process just a tale told by an idiot, full of sound and fury, signifying nothing? Perhaps, I should have been a pair of ragged claws scuttling across the floors of silent seas? What do you think? This is the first step in this divided line. Is realism possible? If so, you are in the Art from Genius Artist camp or the Art from Nature Imitated camp. If not then you reside in the Art from Clever Craftsman camp or the Art from Artisan with the Common touch camp.

I am a realist. I see benefit from both perspectives depending upon the context. Since I hold a theory of the true that is correspondence-theory oriented, the top two levels (the realist perspective) are most amenable. Since I also hold a theory of the good that is both dependent upon the personal worldview imperative (internalist) and the shared community worldview imperative (externalist), it is impossible for me to choose between art from genius artist and art from nature imitated. Each may have distinctive advantages, but there is no decisive way to choose between these on the grounds of truth. However, when one mixes in the good, then the more direct road to truth is more attractive to me. This is because when nature intervenes between the artist and truth or between the audience/ critic and truth, then there are multiple possibilities for miscommunication to occur between one of the levels to the other. Thus, in the end of the day, the art from genius approach is my preferred critical perspective.[11]

I would advise my readers to think for themselves. Go back to the first and second parts of this book in order to ascertain your standpoint concerning the realist and anti-realist positions. Then review your positions on the various theories of truth. These may push you toward one box or the other.

Finally, look at the theory of the good that you espouse. How does that theory connect to truth? If there is a disconnect, then one or the other should be modified (as per the personal worldview imperative). After this process, I would suggest that most readers will be able to choose a preferred critical perspective. This is important, because the role of beauty in our lives is important and the way we judge beauty constitutes our critical perspective.

Art as Essential to Life

Earlier in the book there was a speculation on how important art is in our lives. If our starting point in answering this question is the table of embeddedness (from the good – Chapter 2), then the reader might be surprised that art is not mentioned in that listing.

Some would assert that art is a level-three secondary good. For those individuals art is a pleasurable extra – much like an ice-cream cone. We all enjoy ice-cream cones, but we can all live without them, too. This author has certainly met a large number of people who profess this attitude. If we consider Table 9.1, then this attitude could definitely be supported by the anti-realists (art from the clever craftsman and art from the artisan with the common touch). Since under the anti-realistic perspective, neither the beautiful nor the good are, at base, about something that really *is*, then it is an easy move to the inference that art is a pleasurable extra in life, much like the ice-cream cone. Even the true is deflated by the anti-realist position. Thus, from Table 9.1 the art from clever craftsman and the art from the artisan with a common touch would both support the contention that the status of art in the table of embeddedness is as a level-three secondary good.

On the other hand, are the realist positions. These hold that art is about something that really *is*. If art is about something real, then the artist's expression through the artifact also *is* (either via internalist or externalist correspondence theory). This ontological status is important. For if art is really about nothing, then it can have no status on the table of embeddedness – except as a light source of pleasure. The realist perspective is more robust. It holds that the good, the true, and the beautiful are about *something that is.* From Figure 9.1 this would mean either that an artist has direct contact to truth or that an artist's has indirect contact to truth via nature. In either case, the good has a higher status on the table of embeddedness. This is because it is more than a transitory luxury. The connection to correspondence theory truth supports this claim.

But what sort of good is it? What sort of rights claim flows from this? These are the critical questions. Obviously, one cannot say that any artifact is like: food, clothing, shelter, and protection from unwarranted bodily harm. In the strict biological sense of staying alive to be a functioning agent in the world, art seems not to be there. But *wait*. I am being too cavalier. Think of the case of African American slaves. From 1619 until 1863 (by strict law – and some say 1965 by practice)[12] these unfortunate souls were treated as property. They were set into severe toil and pain to work so that others might live in luxury. However, one of the daily context tenets that kept them going was singing. Much of this was double edged: on the one hand they overtly sounded like Christian hymns but on the other hand they were really against their tyrant slave-holding 'masters'.[13] After work, Alex Haley (author of *Roots*) said that evening history lessons were played out through story telling connecting the family in a lineage back to Africa.[14] These are all examples of how art makes life bearable. In this case, I would contend that art (used in this way) is integral to survival. It can be categorized as 'protection from unwarranted bodily harm'. As such it would be a level-one basic good. No rights claim is higher.

From my experience as a college teacher, I can attest that many students also use popular music to survive. These students are certainly not in actual servitude. Au contraire, they are often very privileged. But they still confront the world in which they live. Even among the privileged there is pain involved in being a human on the earth. One way to protect one's self is through art.[15] This is a remedy for all people. Thus, it is my contention that even a person of privilege seeks out art as a refuge that makes existence possible. Life is hard for all people at all stations of life. It may be harder for some than for others at particular times, but in the end, hard times face us all. Art is there to help us continue.

This view of the nature of art as a good is rather palliative. Art helps us live with the pain. There are other more positive functions of art.

First, art is very useful in providing the familiarity with the history and culture of the society in which we live. This would put art at a level-two basic good. Art under this interpretation would transform from being intrinsically good to being instrumentally important for adapting to the society in which one lives. (This is rather what Plato thought.)

Second, art is that which fulfils humans in such a way that it is essential to forming and supporting their plans of life. In this case, art would be a level-one secondary good. I believe that for the vast majority of people, this is where art makes its impact upon us. We use art to entertain and instruct us. Art acts to lead us forward on our life quest. It is an imaginative beacon to what we believe is possible. It inspires us toward the good and the true.

Since I believe that in a just society the government ought to intervene to provide its citizens all of the basic goods (levels one and two) and secondary goods (level one only), any of the preceding depictions of the way that art impacts our lives are extremely serious.[16] These are claims about which there is a strong correlative social duty. I believe that it is possible that different aspects of art affect people differently and connect at different levels.

It is probably true that art can (in some form) plug in at any level. This makes the assessment of the beautiful in terms of the good rather tricky. For example, at the writing of this book several companies are selling decorated mobile phones. These designs take the form of personal statements about life. They in no way enhance the performance of the phone as an instrument of telecommunications. On the inside of the phone are the customized ringtones. Again, there is no functional value to these. Both the exterior decoration and the customized ring tones have to represent an art that is a level-three secondary good. Like the ice-cream cone we could all live without it. Life is marginally more pleasurable with these glittering accessories, but they cannot be compared to the value given by the spirituals sung by the slaves in the fields or the tales of wonder told by Jews in the Nazi death camps so that they might keep hope alive.[17]

Thus, the answer to what sort of good art is within the table of embeddedness cannot be made categorically. Art can fit into any category. The real deciding criteria surround the function that art is playing in the lives of individuals and social groups. This is variable and can be misconstrued by those outside of that particular group. For example, the slaveholders might hear the singing in the fields and think that the value of the singing to the people in the fields is not great (say level-two or three secondary goods). Likewise, in the case of the Nazi concentration camp guards who hear mumbling Yiddish stories from within the squalid quarters. The guards might think that the stories are just nonsense.

Since the operation of art is individual and socially variable, the question should be addressed from another level of generality: the society as a whole. Because of art's potential to be an essential element in someone's life: that palliative key that makes it all bearable (a level-one basic good), the rulers of society must take this into account. On the positive side it may be a beacon to inspire us toward a particular direction in our personal quest (level-one secondary good related to realizing a life plan).

But, of course, it can also take the form of fake diamond arrangements on a mobile telephone (a level-three secondary good). How should society assess the sort of good that art represents? The best practical principle (in cases in which there is a variable normative value that cannot be adequately assessed from an externalist perspective) is *the precautionary principle*. Under the precautionary principle one is very conservative in one's proposed actions because one considers being *wrong* in the implementation of some policies is so great as to warrant considerable attention. Thus, under this precautionary principle the system of jurisprudence in the United States and Great Britain says that they would rather let a guilty man walk free from a trial than to convict an innocent man. Or in medical ethics, we advocate keeping a person on life support systems for a time (even though he may be brain dead) until we are very sure that there are no possibilities of recovery. As we can see, the precautionary principle is rather inefficient. It accepts certain inefficiencies for the sake of the good.

If we apply the precautionary principle to social policy towards art, then we must accept that: (a) any artifact/performance/exhibition may relate to individuals or groups within the society as a level-one basic good. It may be integral in their ability to survive in society. Now we have to be careful about this. If the art itself (in its creation or its presentation) violates the personal worldview imperative or the shared community worldview imperative, then it need not deserve consideration. For example, in the 1980s there was a reputed phenomenon of 'snuff movies' in which one of the characters in the movie was actually murdered (or so the story goes). Even if some group said that they needed 'snuff movies' to support their existence, the very fact that the premise of the movie involves *murder* (which by all accounts is immoral), then the claim of that group – even at the highest level (level-one basic goods) – cannot trump the victim's own level-one basic good and so the movie should be banned. The same holds true for child pornography et cetera.

Because of the possibilities of abuse, censorship is a difficult topic of discussion. Many might stretch the boundaries of 'art' to include detailed instructions on how to construct an atomic bomb. Since the entomological origins of art via the Greek word *techne* includes all functionally defined enterprises, one might claim that putting the detailed instructions on how to construct an atomic bomb and the ways to contact suppliers of the materials necessary is an *art*. Thus, its suppression would involve the censorship of *art*. Whether these instructions constitute art or not is *not* the primary question. When *creation of* or the *presentation of* any body of information (art, science, et al.) involves an immoral act or the explicit[18] invitation to do the same, it is not permissible.[19] For sake of clarity, let us describe these cases as human-rights censorship (following the protocol of embedded human-rights claims). This sort of censorship means that censorship is allowable just in case the externalist case for harm within the table of embeddedness exceeds or equals the level of the original rights claim. For example, one might say that the person who wished to put the formula for an atomic bomb onto the internet (along with ways to procure all necessary materials and perhaps some assemblers) is a level-two basic good (a liberty right of expression). The balancing rights claim attaches to all the people that will probably be killed by a consumer of such a proposal (200,000–800,000 dead and 5,000,0000 or more physically affected relative to where it is detonated). This involves a level-one basic good loss on a large scale. A level-one basic good trumps a level-two basic good. Therefore, censorship of this via filtering or suppression of websites devoted to such a theme is obligatory.

The utility of the artifact/performance/exhibition cannot involve a similar violation of the basic goods of the subject group upon which the project was created. This standard is the basis of public censorship of art. Art is not entirely free. It cannot involve the *actual* deprivation of rights of the subjects of art or *encourage* others to do so on the level of imminent harm. This latter half is controversial. It is obviously open to all sorts of interpretation. But let me give some examples of what I have in mind.

Context: An African American in the United States from 1890 to 1940 (in which there was slavery, then there was ubiquitous oppression via *de jure* and *de facto* human-rights violations including lynching, apartheid rules governing opportunity, and general distain). Now consider any moviemaker, novelist, painter, or other narrative-content artist (and the subsequent performance artists) and that artist creates (or performs in) an artifact that encourages others in the society to lynch African Americans, then that artist should be suppressed. But what is the manner of this suppression? The most lenient is to leave it to the marketplace to decide who will buy the tickets. But this can only encourage the evil already present. Another tactic would be to suppress the artifact/performance/exhibition. But this is also very problematic because it enables the state to control art. However, the principle of precautionary reason demands it. Since art is a level-one basic good to many, the society should not deny its availability *except* in the most extreme cases – such as the 'snuff movies' and child pornography, et al.

The result is a policy that seeks to allow as much information as possible – subject only to the standard of clear and present danger that may result in irreparable harm as the result of the display of such art. I think that every community would accept such a doctrine. We must be very careful in executing such censorship. This is because of the possible nature of art as a level-one basic good (and even the level-two basic good as well as the level-one secondary good – those goods within the state's province), it is necessary that the state exercise precautionary reason to its most reasonable extent (limited only to the standard of real and imminent danger). The principle of precautionary reason protects society against politicians using the principle of human-rights censorship to their own nefarious purposes because it is centred upon externalist correspondence theory. Under these standards there is a burden of proof that must be met *demonstrating* an empirically justified clear and present danger exists that will cause irreparable harm just in case one were to permit the adoption of such and such artistic expression (aka prior restraint).[20]

Thus the conclusion of the discussion on whether art is essential to life is that art and artifacts (from the standpoints of artist, critics, and general audience) affect people at all the levels on the table of embeddedness. It is also possible that art can involve a possible harm that can be classified as a clear and present danger that will cause irreparable harm (according to externalist, correspondence theory criteria). This possibility of censorship should be tempered by the principle of precautionary reason. In effect, this amounts to giving all 'ties' to the artist.

The dynamics between artists and their artifacts in society is robust. They act in a palliative way to help us endure the pains of existence and in an imaginative way to inspire us to the best that all of us can be. In this way it is clear that art is essential to life.

Art and the Imperatives of Worldview: the Quest for the Beautiful

There is not a specific directive in the personal worldview imperative governing the beautiful (except as it might connect to becoming complete and coherent and as it might connect to becoming good). This is because we are all different. The quest for the good often is best approached via the true. This is especially the case for those who find the empirical realm their personal calling. These sorts of people include almost everybody: scientists, doctors, businesspeople, government workers, soldiers, and social workers, et al. In everyday life, most of us (on one level) are first interested in earning enough money to pay our bills and then to get materially ahead a little bit. This means entering the great externalist contest of economic striving. There is, of course, a very stark definition of this: food, clothing, shelter, and protection from unwarranted bodily harm. In much of the world, the economic struggle begins and ends there. This is a terrible reality.

For most of my readers (within the richest countries of the world) the economic quest is at level-two and level-three secondary goods: keeping up with the Joneses and getting beyond the Joneses.[21] But is that all there is to the quest? I hope not.

As our mercurial Socrates says in the *Symposium*, beauty can reorient our worldview standpoint so that we look for more. We need not be content with the images that Madison Avenue flashes to us on the television and the internet. Life is about something greater than the largest house/car/television among one's peer group. Absolutely! But what?

Art is uniquely positioned to suggest answers. In my position as a college teacher I often observe students who are 'turned on' by novels, poems, music, and visual art. It shakes them out of their complacency. Because art first comes to us affectively, it is the most effective method for stimulating personal worldview reflection.

Indeed, when groups of people simultaneously read/view/listen to an artistic presentation it is also possible that the individual worldview reflections are shared with others in the community. There is something about the artistic experience that is social and not exclusively private.

It is unnatural to attempt to horde the artistic experience of pleasure/thinking/connecting to the good. When we read a good novel, we lend it to someone else to read. When we see a good movie, we get on the email or mobile phone and tell as many of our friends as possible that they 'have to see it'. When we see a great art exhibition or attend a dynamic concert, our first instinct is to share the experience with others. This is because art is a building block in social discourse. It is a shared experience that promotes cohesion within the shared community worldview (the good). It is an experience that often shakes us to our core so that we feel compelled to discuss and reflect about its meaning with others (the true).

In many very essential ways, art promotes healthy communities in which individuals re-visit their personal worldview standpoint and the social context in which we all exist in micro and macro communities. Since I believe that is what our life quest is all about, then art is the healthy stimulus for positive personal renewal and community growth. Nothing could be more practical or essential for living. Art *is* practical. Art *is* essential. This is because art stimulates reflection of one's personal worldview and of the shared community worldview. Part of this reflection will also entail pondering about truth and the good.

Since art's pleasure grabs us immediately and gives us a shake, it has an advantage over other devices of the good and the true that are often more prosaic and require a greater personal investment to conquer the initial learning curve that stands in the way of individual involvement. The beautiful has no such entry fee. It is constructed to be readily accessible to all with eyes that see and ears that hear. Art provides the entryway to the human quest. As such, art is indispensable.

Conclusion: Integrating the Beautiful into our Lives

Though I claim in the last section that art and the beautiful come and grab us come what may, there is a difference between being a passive consumer of whatever art is placed before one and being a discriminating aficionado who develops her own personal taste according to a plan of her own devices. One example of this can be seen in the previews for movies. Most American movies have five to seven previews before the main feature. These are advertisements of what is to come. (Videos and some DVDs do the same thing.) Most people in the audience react to the ninety-second clips such that they determine to watch the movie or to avoid it. This is an example of what I am talking about. Others make choices on subscriptions to acting companies, symphony series, ballet seasons, or opera calendars based upon the same principle: they want to plan their quest towards the beautiful. It must be an ensemble. Now the shape of such a plan is often budget driven. In the lowest budget mode, it might be creating a reading list for the next year based upon going to the public free lending library (in those few countries that have such a valuable resource).

The quest for the beautiful can even express itself through the time-honoured tradition of families passing down stories, songs, and dances to the next generation. All of this counts: it is a way to construct the portal to the good and the true that we all naturally seek.

This book is meant to be a guidebook for all who strive to undertake the quest. Like any guidebook, it has tried to suggest various attractions along the way that will assist the traveller in life to experience and find that which will make existence worthwhile. It is a valuable quest. Each of us will be better off for the effort. Our communities will be improved when its members become knights of the quest. All of us: male, female, Asian, European, African, South and North American, Australasian (or descendants from these) are enjoined to begin – right now! The time is growing late.

Glossary

Aesthetics Theories on the way people confront the beautiful.

Careful scrutiny maxim One maxim advises that we do not act unless we have sound, empirically based reasons to do so.

Criticism Theories on the way to judge something to be beautiful.

Daily context thinking Pursuing choices that will lead us to truth in the midst of day-to-day decision-making.

Dogma of empirical rectitude The dogma that asserts that that our sense experience is correct unless we are given very strong reasons (rational and empirical) to the contrary.

Imagination Presents novel possibilities to one's worldview for consideration. Imagination recognizes broad patterns and assesses their possible significance. Of course the pattern and their significance can later turn out wrong. On the other hand, they can turn out right! The imagination offers a powerful connection between the Good, the True, and the Beautiful.

Liberty, the strong approach We are all responsible for everything we do regardless of the circumstances. (NOT BOYLAN) v. **the strong determinism approach**. We are never responsible for anything we do because the source of our action lies outside our will (NOT BOYLAN). Boylan is in between leaning towards liberty and determinism (both environmentally and genetically).

Most plausible hypothesis maxim In those situations in which the rationality incompleteness conjecture holds, one may employ the selective faith maxim to accept the most plausible hypothesis based upon all relevant information given to the agent (relevance here is defined via the personal worldview imperative).

Precautionary principle Under the precautionary principle one is enjoined to be very conservative in one's possible actions because one considers being *wrong* in the implementation of some policies is so great as to warrant considerable attention.

Quest for knowledge Each of us as people living in the world quests for knowledge; this means that we all (a) want to embrace all that is true and (b) reject all that is false. To deviate from this quest is to degrade our human nature.

Rationality incompleteness conjecture Rationality seeks demonstrably to prove all propositions. However, in cases in which there is no empirical, non-question begging, test for verifying a principle, all the best reason can do is to offer various plausible alternatives. The resolution can only come about through appeal to the personal worldview imperative and its application in the way we confront novel normative theories. (See the **Most plausible hypothesis maxim**.)

Selective faith maxim In those situations because of epistemological constraints upon empirical knowledge (in principle or in fact), we should set down the most plausible truth (grounded by our personal worldview) and act upon that.

Strategic context thinking Pursuing rules that will frame our daily context thinking through a longer-term perspective. Strategic context thinking underlies the standpoint with which we face the world (our personal worldview).

Theories of Truth

Coherence theory of truth Coherence theory stipulates that a given body of knowledge is true if and only if there are no internal deductive contradictions. (Sometimes people also add the stipulation that the body of knowledge is also complete – meaning that one cannot pose a problem from the covered universe and not generate an answer.) *Truth* here means that everything works smoothly together such that an artificial whole is produced that has boundaries and symmetry. Proponents of the coherence theory of truth often point to symmetry and elegance as properties attaching to true bodies of knowledge.

Save the phenomena approach This is to create a coherent account that squares with observation or utility (such as travelling to Naples with Ptolemaic star tables). Whatever had to be done to the base theory is OK so long as (artificial) coherence is maintained.

Elegant coherence approach A theory must work purely – without addition (for the most part). This is a doctrine of simplicity. But simplicity is essentially an aesthetic, normative judgement. It is *not* enough to save the phenomena. Instead, one must consider coherence in a broader sense: conceptual coherence. This would suggest that a system is coherent only if its broad conceptual commitments fit together without artificial gerrymandering.

Correspondence theory of truth Correspondence theory states that a proposition is true when it accords with the actual state of affairs.

Synonymy When two or more propositions (one or more of which may be logical interpretations of an empirical entity that claims to be accurate of that entity) mutually commit themselves to logical tautologies, then the two propositions are synonymous.

Pragmatic theory of truth This asserts that a theory is true relative to the work it can perform. There are two distinct ways to understand this: 1) Relating to mere personal expediency (the internalist perspective), and 2) Relating to intersubjective scientific confirmation in the experimental method (the externalist perspective).

Thought experiment fallacy This occurs when the artificial nature of the thought experiments distorts our understanding of a practical outcome. Most thought experiments try to focus upon some extremely narrow point in order to evaluate it. However, when the thought experiment makes some unrealistic assumption about human nature, etc., then the result may be false.

Value/duty doctrine Whenever agent X studies P and discovers various properties about it (seen in light of his personal worldview), then if X decides that P is elegant, then X values P (where P is an artifact, a natural object, an agent, or a human institution). As a result of this process of observing and classifying that leads to the judgement of elegance and its resultant valuing, X takes on a corresponding duty to protect and defend P subject to the constraints of the principle of human survival and the 'ought implies can' doctrine.

Worldview Imperatives

Personal worldview imperative 'All people must develop a single comprehensive and internally coherent worldview that is good and that we strive to act out in our daily lives.'

Shared community worldview imperative 'Each agent must contribute to a common body of knowledge that supports the creation of a shared community worldview (that is itself complete, coherent, and good) through which social institutions and their resulting policies might flourish within the constraints of the essential core commonly held values (ethics, aesthetics, and religion).'

Notes

1 Being Good

1 Fragment from Simonides of Ceos (circa 556–468 BC), a lyric poet best known for his poems celebrating the Greek victories at Marathon and Thermopylae. See Plato, *Protagoras* 339b 1–3, my translation.

2 Eugène Ionesco, *Four Plays*, tr. Donald M. Allen (NY: Grove Weidenfeld, 1982). The quote cited is from the end of *The Bald Soprano*.

3 Attribution: Andy Warhol photo exhibition, Stockholm, 1968: Justin Kaplan (ed.), *Bartlett's Familiar Quotations*, 16th edn (New York: Little, Brown & Co., 1992): 758: 17.

4 See especially *Return of the Jedi* and *Revenge of the Sith*, George Lucas Films.

5 This is a much-debated issue. For a contemporary discussion see: Thomas I. White, *In Defense of Dolphins* (Malden, MA and Oxford: Blackwell, 2007).

6 Plato, *Republic* II, 359d–360-b, cf. Herodotus, *History* I, 8–13.

7 Cf. the Table of Embeddedness in my *A Just Society* (Lanham, MD and Oxford: Rowman and Littlefield, 2004), Chapter 3.

8 I should note that this analysis does not imply an identification of pleasure and good or pain and bad.

9 I do want to give a cautionary note on thought experiments. Though this book will present quite a number of them, they must never be so artificial that they create a false metaphorical depiction of the dynamics that would face real people in the real world. Most often thought experiments try to focus upon some extremely narrow point in order to evaluate it. However, when the thought experiment makes some unrealistic assumption about human nature, etc., then the result may be false if they seek clarify a claim about the world. Though I do not attempt to mislead readers in this way, I want to put you all 'on guard' to make sure that I haven't committed what I call the thought experiment fallacy (that is to modify the boundary conditions artificially in order to assure the outcome one wants).

10 Plato, *Republic* II, 359d.

11 Bobby Fischer's tortured and erratic behaviour has been discussed recently in Hans Bohm and Kees Jongkind, *Bobby Fischer: The Wandering King* (London: Batsford, 2005).

12   Some of Fischer's opinions can be found at: http://home.att.ne.jp/moon/fischer.

13   My apologies to the pop singer Billy Joel for this loose paraphrase of one of his song lyrics.

14   In a *USA Today* pool published on 27 March 2007– A1, it showed that the aspirations of people 18–25/26–40 in the USA on what they wanted: Get Rich 81%/62%; Famous 51%/219%; Help Others 30%/36%; Become Community Leaders 22%/33%; and Become Spiritual 10%/31%.

15   Petrarch, *The Sonnets, Triumphs, and Other Poems of Petrarch*, translated by several hands (London: G. Bohn, 1859).

16   At the writing of this book this is an ongoing issue. But one report that supports this supposition comes from R. Jeffrey Smith, 'Hussein's Prewar Ties to Al-Qaeda Discounted', *Washington Post* 122.5 (Friday 6 April 2007), A-1.

17   I go into further depth in this analysis of the substance of these theories – their strengths and weaknesses – in my book, *Basic Ethics* (Upper Saddle River, NJ: Prentice Hall, 2000).

18   The literature on non-cognitivism in ethics is quite large. For an introduction see: A. J. Ayer, *Language, Truth and Logic*, (London: Gollancz, 1936); Simon Blackburn, *Spreading the Word* (Oxford: Clarendon, 1984); Peter Geach, 'Imperative and Deontic Logic' in *Analysis*, 18.3 (1958): 49–56; Peter Geach, 'Assertion', *Philosophical Review*, 74 (1964): 449–465; Alan Gibbard, *Wise Choices, Apt Feelings. A Theory of Normative Judgement* (Oxford, Clarendon Press, 1990); R. M. Hare, *The Language of Morals*, (Oxford: Clarendon, 1952); and C. L. Stevenson, *Ethics and Language*, (New Haven, Yale University.Press, 1944).

19   Ludwig Wittgenstein, *The Blue and Brown Books* (New York: Harper-Collins, 1986): section 1.

20   The group of experimental psychologists in the twentieth century were largely influenced by behaviourism – see B.F. Skinner, *About Behaviorism* (New York: Vintage, 1976) – but they had other key influences as well – cf. James C. Goodwin, 'Reorganizing the Experimentalists: The Origins of the Society of Experimental Psychology', *History of Psychology*, 8.4 (2005): 347–361.

21   Boylan, *A Just Society*, pp. 22–25.

22   For a discussion of some of the most prominent deontologists see: Boylan (2000): Chapter 4.

23   The particularist objection comes from Jonathan Dancy, *Ethics without Principles* (Oxford: Clarendon, 2006); cf. Joseph Raz, 'The Trouble with Particularism', *Mind*, 115.457 (2006): 99–120, and Mark N. Lane and Olivia M. Little, 'Defending Moral Particularism' in *Contemporary Debates in Moral Theory*, ed. James Dreier (Malden, MA: Blackwell, 2006). The second objection comes from G.W.F. Hegel, *Werke. vol. 8 Grundlinien der*

Philosophie des Rechts, ed. E. Gans; translated by T.M. Knox, *Hegel's Philosophy of Right* (Oxford: Clarendon Press, 1942), Section 153, p. 90ff. See also: Allen Wood's explanation of this critique in 'The Emptiness of the Moral Will', *The Monist*, 72 (1989): 454–483. For a defence of Kant on this point see Marcus Singer, *Generalization in Ethics* (New York: Athenaeum, 1961), pp. 279–295 and David Cummiskey, *Kantian Consequentialism* (Oxford: Oxford University Press, 1996), pp. 47–50. For a compromise opinion see Christine M. Korsgaard, 'Ethical, Political, Religious Thought' in *Creating the Kingdom of Ends* (Cambridge: Cambridge University Press), pp. 14–16.

24 See Boylan, *Basic Ethics*: Ch. 8; cf. Boylan, *A Just Society*, pp. 10–16.

25 A more systematic expression of this would be as shown in the chart 'The Way We Confront Novel, Normative Theories', in Boylan, *A Just Society*, Ch. 1.

26 An insincere agent is not fully autonomous because he is not seeking to act according to the best information he can assemble. He is content merely to slide along with anything above some perceived minimal level of execution. The inauthentic agent is not fully autonomous because he has not chosen a background condition for his choice that gives full weight to his most deeply held values as he tries to assemble a worldview. Instead of choosing a worldview according to the boundaries of completeness, coherence and goodness, he chooses according to some other overriding principle, such as power, sex, or money.

27 Of course, any true betting house would also figure in something for the business to cover overheads, salaries, profit, etc.

28 For a classic discussion of this see: G. W. F. Hegel, *Phenomenology of Spirit*, tr. A. V. Miller (Oxford: Oxford University Press, 1977), pp. 104–118.

29 In a critical situation in which the two are in opposition and the sides are equal, I suggest that the rational part plays the decisive role.

2 The Self and Others

1 For an excellent discussion of the biological basis of the altruism debate see Elliott Sober and David Sloan Wilson, *Unto Others: The Evolution and Psychology of Unselfish Behavior* (Cambridge, MA: Harvard University Press, 1998).

2 There are obviously various statements of the psychological-egoistic worldview. The one presented is meant to capture important common features of each.

3 Subject, of course, to the rules governing the thought-experiment fallacy.

4 For an exploration of the reductionistic inclination in psychology see, first: Sigmund Freud, *The Basic Writings of Sigmund Freud*, ed and trans. by A. A. Brill (New York: Random House, 1938); Duane P. Schultz and Sydney

Ellen Schultz, *A History of Modern Psychology*, 7th ed. (Fort Worth, TX: Harcourt College Publishers, 2003); and David G. Myers, *Psychology*, 7th ed. (New York: Worth Publishers, 2003).

5 Of course, this is another unproven primitive posit that could be wrong. All theories of human nature are of this sort.

6 If *kalon* is the intersection between the ethical and the beautiful in a positive way, then the *eischron* is the same intersection in a negative way. Some synonyms might be 'sleazy', 'ugly', and 'despicable'.

7 'Embedded' in this context means the relative fundamental nature of the good for action. A more deeply embedded good is one that is more primary to action.

8 Others may emend this hierarchy. If these corrections are in the spirit of the table itself (meaning that they are meant to describe the goods necessary for human action), then such additions are a welcome improvement to basic purpose of describing the relative embeddedness of goods regarding action. Others have made similar attempts at distinguishing the goods of agency. Some have said that the Table of Embeddedness reminds them of Abraham Maslow's hierarchy (see *Toward a Psychology of Being*, 2nd ed. (New York: D Van Nostrand Company, 1968)). Others have seen similarities with Alan Gewirth, *Reason and Morality* (Chicago: University of Chicago Press, 1978), pp. 53–58, in which Gewirth sets out three classes of goods that might be claimed by agents. I will argue that there are two general classes: basic and secondary goods. Each general class has, in turn, sub-classes that begin with those goods necessary for any action at all and ending up with luxury goods. For a discussion of this see my article, 'Justice, Community, and the Limits of Autonomy' in *Social and Political Philosophy: Contemporary Perspectives*, ed. James Sterba (London: Routledge, 2001). I am also indebted to Henry Shue, *Basic Rights: Subsistence, Affluence and U.S. Foreign Policy*, 2nd ed. (Princeton, NJ: Princeton University Press, 1986), pp. 15ff. Similar appeals have also been made by John Rawls with his doctrine of primary goods, in *A Theory of Justice* (Cambridge, MA: Harvard, 1971), section 15, and by Amartya Sen with his capability sets, in *Inequality Reexamined* (Cambridge, MA: Harvard, 1992), Chapter 3.

9 This is generally called the libertarian approach, but since this has several different meanings, I think this is a less ambiguous way of labelling.

10 It should be noted here that group selection theory is not, at present, the dominant theory of evolutionary biology. However, some of these points may be amenable to individual selection models, punctuated selection models, and others as well.

11 See Barbara McClintock, *The Discovery of Characterization of Transposable Elements: The Collected Papers of Barbara McClintock* (New York: Garland Press, 1987); see especially pp. 117–154, 335–344, 444–465, 478–515.

12   Of course this is still a rather controversial hypothesis. Two recent studies
     that support the hypothesis are: David Goldman, Gabor Oroszi, Stephanie
     O'Malley, et al., 'The COMBINE Study: Conceptual, Methodological,
     and Practical', *Journal of Studies on Alcoholism*, 15 (2005): 56–58; Stephen
     M. Malone, Jeanette Taylor, Naomi R. Marmorstein, et al., 'Genetic and
     Environmental Influences on Anti-Social Behavior and Alcohol Depen-
     dence from Adolescence to Early Adulthood', *Development and Psy-
     chopathology*, 16.4 (2004): 943–947.
13   A more systematic defence of this argument can be found in Michael
     Boylan, *A Just Society* (Lanham, MD and Oxford: Rowman and Littlefield,
     2004), Ch. 3.

3 Self-fulfilment

1   Thomas Hobbes, *Leviathan*, ed. Richard E. Flathman and David Johnson
    (New York: W. W. Norton, 1997), Chapter 13, p. 69.
2   Friedrich Nietzsche, 'Beyond Good and Evil' in *Basic Writings of Nietzsche*,
    tr. Walter Kaufmann (New York: Modern Library, 1968), II. 36, p. 238.
3   Those who would like to see some questions here from the point of view of
    the author should see Michael Boylan, *A Just Society* (Lanham, MD and
    Oxford: Rowman and Littlefield, 2004), pp. 148–149.
4   For an introduction to authors advocating for the endpoints in the liberal-
    ism (individualism)/communitarianism (general will) continuum see: John
    Rawls, *A Theory of Justice* (Cambridge, MA: Harvard University Press,
    1971) and Alan Gewirth, *Reason and* Morality (Chicago: University of
    Chicago Press, 1978) v. Michael J. Sandel, *Liberalism and the Limits of
    Justice*, 2nd edition (Cambridge: Cambridge University Press, 1998) and
    Amitai Etzioni, *Rights and the Common Good: The Communitarian Perspec-
    tive* (Belmont, CA: Wadsworth, 1994). In *A Just* Society, I argue for a view
    midway between these poles, pp. 123–133.
5   It is a difficult number to set out, but somewhere between 200 to 500
    would be the maximum size of a micro community.
6   The full argument for this is found in my *A Just Society*, Ch. 6.
7   For a full discussion of this see: Sarah Karush, 'Old and New Hamtramck
    Clash in Debate over Muslim Call to Prayer', Associated Press Release, 19
    April 2004, Monday BC Cycle; Sarah Karush, 'Hamtramck Vote A Victory
    for Those in Favor of Allowing Mosques to Broadcast Islamic Call to
    Prayer', Associated Press Release, 21 July 2004, Wednesday BC Cycle;
    Philip Zaleski and Carol Zaleski, 'Muslims and Christians Sharing Public
    Space', *The Christian Century* 122.23 (15 November 2005): 8.
8   The modern understanding of game theory has been greatly influenced by
    John Von Neumann and O. Morgenstern, *Theory of Games and Economic
    Behavior* (New York: John Wiley, 1964). For a more contemporary view of

the developments in game theory see Robert B. Myerson, *Game Theory: Analysis of Conflict* (Cambridge, MA: Harvard University Press, 1997).

9 Aristotle sets out in the *Nicomachean Ethics* that happiness is functionally defined through fulfilling what it means to be a human, a rational animal; cf. *Nicomachean Ethics*, Book Seven, Chapters 11–14 and Book Ten, Chapters 1–5 and *Metaphysics*, Book One, Chapter 1. Rawls famously jumps on board in *A Theory of Justice*, section 65. Gewirth famously demurs in *Self-Fulfillment* (Princeton, NJ: Princeton University Press, 1998).

10 This would be contra philosophers like John Rawls who made it the cornerstone of constructing a rational life plan; see *A Theory of Justice* (Cambridge, MA: Harvard, 1971), Chapter vii. 65.

11 The origins of kin selection theory rest in W.D. Hamilton's article 'The Evolution of Altruistic Behavior', *American Naturalist*, 97 (1963): 354–356 and 'The Genetical Evolution of Social Behavior', *Journal of Theoretical Biology*, 7 (1964): 1–16 and J. Maynard Smith, 'Group Selection and Kin Selection', *Nature*, 201 (1964): 1145–1146 and 'Group Selection', *Quarterly Review of Biology*, 31 (1976): 277–283. For a contemporary discussion see Elliott Sober and David Sloan Wilson, *Unto Others: The Evolution and Psychology of Unselfish Behavior* (Cambridge, MA: Harvard University Press, 1998), pp. 58–79

12 For Immanuel Kant, principles that form the boundaries or limits of reason's capacities are different from those that describe internally how reason is constituted (*Critique of Pure Reason*, translated by Norman Kemp Smith (New York: St. Martins, 1929), 210–211, 258, 450ff., 455ff. *et passim*). A mere formal boundary principle is not sufficient as a philosophical grounding or foundation. These are often confused.

13 Bayes Theorem is used in statistics to estimate the probability that various hypotheses are true. It is commonly used as part of inductive logic. It sets forth the following ratio: the probability of observing X *if* H (the hypothesis) is true/the probability of observing X. Readers with an interest in mathematics might like to read further in Peter M. Lee, *Bayesian Statistics: An Introduction*, 3rd edition (London: Hodder Arnold Publishers, 2004).

The point to be made here is whether inductive logic is in any way question-begging. Obviously, the mechanism for assessing the truth of the hypothesis in the numerator of the ratio dictates the result. But what is the basis for this claim? The grounds for answering this will be the subject matter of Part II.

4 Finding Out What is True

1 This is adapted from William Kingdom Clifford, 'The Ethics of Belief' in *Lectures and Essays*, Vol. 2 (London: Macmillan & Co., 1901), pp. 163–205.

2   Adapted from William James, "The Sentiment of Rationality" in *The Will to Believe and other Essays* (New York: Longmans, Green & Co., 1897), pp. 63–110.

3   The reader is reminded that with all thought experiments, one must be wary of the thought-experiment fallacy (see Chapter 2). If the artificial nature of the set-up distorts (rather than simplifies) the dynamics of actual instances in the world, then the thought experiment should be rejected as being misleading.

4   This example is a rather free adaptation from Nicholas Wolterstorff, 'Can Belief in God be Rational if it Has No Foundations?' in A. Plantinga and N. Wolterstorff, eds, *Faith and Rationality* (Notre Dame, IN: Notre Dame University Press, 1984), pp. 135–186.

5   Roderick Chisholm, *The Foundations of Knowing* (Minneapolis: University of Minnesota Press, 1982).

6   Leibnitz's theory of the identity of indiscernibles can be found in *Primae Verites* C 518–20 in *Philosophical Writings*, translated by M. Morris and G. H. R. Parkinson (London: Dent, 1995), pp. 87–88.

7   This discussion owes itself partly to Ludwig Wittgenstein, *Tractus Logico-Philosophicus* (Franfurt: Suhrkamp Verlag, 1982): 5.5423ff., and to Gestalt psychology: Christian von Ehrenfels, 'Ueber Gestalt qualitaeten', *Vierteljaresschrift fuer wissenschaftliche Philosophie*, 14 (1890) and Max Wertheimer, *Source Book of Gestalt Psychology*, tr. Willis D. Ellis (New York: Harcourt Brace and Co., 1938).

8   A tautology is a term in logic that asserts the logically obvious, such as a = a. This means that the truth values of one of the compared terms is identical to the other. For those who construct truth tables to analyse propositions in symbolic logic, all and every truth functional stand-in of one proposition is identical to the other.

9   Immanuel Kant, *Critique of Pure Reason,* tr. Norman Kemp Smith (New York: St. Martins, 1929 [1787]), B106.

10 The all-together part is to avoid the voters' paradox in which voters prefer A to B and B to C and yet prefer C to A – this going against the law of logical transitivity.

11 There are some exceptions here when the issue is the truth of some novel scientific paradigm. Though the data are externally observable, their relation to the organizing principle may not be. Thus, in these cases, though in time intersubjective confirmation and falsification are possible, at the outset even empirical theories may be in practice overwhelmingly internal.

12 There are obviously many versions of correspondence theory. The version presented is meant to give a flavour of some of the common principal features.

13 *The Principle of Human Survival* says that humans may be obliged in their

struggle for survival to kill animals, plants, and to alter the natural land-scape. In this way, humans are acting just as other animals do in their own quest for survival. It is further assumed that humans are justified to con-tinue in these practices past the point of basic, primitive survival to some level of moderate, comfortable living; see Boylan, 'Worldview and the Value-Duty Link' in *Environmental Ethics,* ed. Michael Boylan (Upper Saddle River, NJ: Prentice Hall, 2001).

14 'Ought implies can' refers to a limitation on moral duty that begins when one is unable to perform the task commanded by the statement of duty.

15 Sometimes, for example in the case of logic or mathematics, there are many isolated individuals accepting the same doneés but all their mechanizations are private. It's like a truck load of egg cartons packaged together and going to market.

16 A classic treatment of this problem somewhat along these lines is Thomas S. Kuhn, *The Copernican Revolution* (Cambridge, MA: Harvard University Press, 1957).

17 This is an immense area but a little flavour of several ancient and modern instantiations of this issue can be found in M.A. Finocchiaro, 'To Save the Phenomena: Duhem on Galileo', *Revue Internale de Philosophie* 46.1 (1992): 291–310; Michael Boylan, *Method and Practice in Aristotle's Biology* (Lanham, MD and London: UPA/Rowman and Littlefield, 1984), Ch. 1; Marc Lange, 'Scientific Realism and Components: The Case of Classical Astronomy', *Monist,* 77.1 (1994): 111–127; Frederic Adams, 'Of Epicy-cles and Elegance', *Canadian Journal of Philosophy*, 24.4 (1994): 637–641; Robert G. Hudson, 'Classical Physics and Early Quantum Theory: A Legitimate Case of Theoretical Undeterminism', *Synthese*, 110.2 (1997): pp. 217–256.

18 There are, of course, at least two understandings of simplicity in the litera-ture. One concerns the *explanans* (theoretical account) and the other refers to the *explanandum* (that which is explained: nature). In the case of saving the phenomena the emphasis is upon the former. If one held a correspon-dence theory of truth, then the latter would also be roped in. For an intro-duction to some of these issues see: Mario Bunge, *The Myth of Simplicity* (Englewood Cliffs, NJ: Prentice Hall, 1963); Elliott Sober, *Simplicity* (Oxford: Clarendon Press, 1975); and Arnold Zellner, Hugo A. Keuzenkamp and Michael McAleer (eds), *Simplicity, Inference and Model-ing* (New York: Cambridge University Press, 2001).

19 William James, *Essays in Pragmatism* (New York: Hafner Publishing Co., 1948), p. 170.

20 One influential argument along these lines was offered by Edmund L. Get-tier, 'Is Justified True Belief Knowledge?', *Analysis*, 23 (1963): 121–123. Other key articles on this question are: Keith Lehrer, 'Knowledge, Truth,

and Evidence', *Analysis*, 25.5 (1965): 149ff.; Marshall Swain, *Reasons and Knowledge* (Ithaca, NY: Cornell University Press, 1981): 149ff.; Fred Dretske, 'The Pragmatic Dimension of Knowledge', *Philosophical Studies*, 40 (1981): 363–378; Glibert Harman, *Thought* (Princeton, NJ: Princeton University Press, 1973); Paul Moser, *Knowledge and Evidence* (New York: Cambridge University Press, 1989); Robert Fogelin, *Pyrrhonian Reflections on Knowledge and Justification* (New York: Oxford University Press, 1994); Richard Greene and N. A. Balmert, 'Two Notions of Warrant and Plantnga's Solution to the Gettier Problem', *Analysis*, 57.2 (1997): 132–139; Michael Levin, 'Virtue Epistemology: No New Cures', *Philosophy and Phenomenological Research*, 69.2 (2004): 397–410; L. Floridi, 'On the Logical Unsolvability of the Gettier Problem', *Synthese*, 142.1 (2004): 61–78.

21 Richard Rorty, *Philosophy and the Mirror of Nature* (Princeton, NJ: Princeton University Press, 1979), p. 176.

22 Donald Davidson, 'On the Very Idea of a Conceptual Scheme', in *Inquiries into Truth and Interpretation,* 2nd edn (Oxford: Oxford University Press, 2001), p. 183.

23 This example comes from Carl Hempel, 'A Purely Syntactical Definition of Confirmation', *Journal of Symbolic Logic*, 8 (1943): 122–143, and 'Studies in the Logic of Confirmation' reprinted with a postscript in *Aspects of Scientific Explanation* (New York: The Free Press, 1965). A rich literature developed around this thought experiment that is noted in Clark Glymour, 'Relevant Evidence', *Journal of Philosophy*, 72 (1975): 403–426.

24 In logic the contraposition flips the order of subject and predicate and adds complements to both the subject and predicate. It is only a valid transformation in universal affirmative and particular negative proposition.

25 I owe this thought experiment to Karl Popper, *The Logic of Scientific Discovery* (New York: Harper, 1965 [a translation of *Logik der Forschung*, 1934]), especially Chapter IV.

26 Popper's critique of psychoanalysis isn't shared by all: see Adolf Grunbaum, *The Foundations of Psychoanalysis* (Berkeley, CA: University of California Press, 1984).

27 This example comes from Hilary Putnam, 'The "Corroboration" of Theories' in The Library of Living Philosophers, vol. XIV *The Philosophy of Karl Popper,* ed. Paul A. Schilpp (LaSalle, IL: Open Court, 1974), pp. 221–240.

28 I have adapted this example from Nelson Goodman, 'A Query on Confirmation', *The Journal of Philosophy*, 43 (1946): 383–385 and *Fact Fiction and Forecast* (Cambridge, MA: Harvard University Press, 1955), Chapters 3–4.

29 By 'projectible' I mean that we can apply the proposition in question to some accepted scientific theory such that the accepted theory can subsume

(= cover or explain) the proposition through the conceptual space marked out by the accepted scientific theory. Since the accepted scientific theory provides intersubjective confidence (= justified belief) on the part of community, being able to project some proposition into the theory allows us to predicate that same confidence to the proposition (on the basis of axiomatic heritability). For a discussion of these relations see: Michael Boylan, *A Just Society* (Lanham, MD and Oxford: Rowman and Littlefield, 2004), Ch. 1.

30 Davidson, 'On the Very Idea of a Conceptual Scheme', p. 194.

5 Scepticism, Illusion, and the Sources of Knowledge

1 For a quick overview of these positions see my article on the Internet Encyclopedia of Philosophy on Galen: http://www.utm.edu (last accessed on 1 June 2006). For a classic print version see Ludwig Edelstein. *Ancient Medicine.* (Baltimore, MD: Johns Hopkins University Press, 1967). For a thorough discussion of several eclectic issues see Philip J. Van der Eijk, *Medicine and Philosophy in Classical Antiquity* (Cambridge: Cambridge University Press, 2005).

2 Moral particularism has been a much debated topic over the past twenty years. The most notable proponent is Jonathan Dancy, *Ethics without Principles* (Oxford: Oxford University Press, 2004); cf. B. W. Hooker and M. Little (eds), *Moral Particularism* (Oxford: Oxford University Press, 2000).

3 Augustine, *Against the Academicians*, ed. tr. Mary Garvey (Milwaukee, WI: Marquette University Pres, 1941), especially Book II, vols. 11–12, and Book III, vols. 23–26.

4 For our purposes, 'Facts' will be taken to be relative to the communication flow: speaker (about a point of contention) => audience. When these two sides are in accord, then it will be tagged as a 'fact'. Cf. Michael Boylan, *The Process of Argument* (Englewood Cliffs, NJ: Prentice Hall, 1988), Chapters 1–2.

5 The most plausible hypothesis maxim: In those situations in which the rationality incompleteness conjecture holds, one may employ the selective faith maxim to accept the most plausible hypothesis based upon all relevant information given to the agent (relevance here is defined via the personal worldview imperative).

6 The role of intuitive grasping here has a rich history. For an introduction to the primary sense to which I am referring see Michael Boylan, *Basic Ethics* (Upper Saddle River, NJ: Prentice Hall, 2000), Chapter 1.

7 René Descartes, *Meditations on First Philosophy*, tr. Elizabeth Haldane and G. R. T. Ross in *The Philosophical Writings of Descartes,* vol. 1 (Cambridge: Cambridge University Press, 1911). I also make reference to the standard edition of Descartes edited by Adams and Tannery (A&T) (Paris: L. Cerf, 1897–1910).

8   David Hume, *An Enquiry Concerning Human Understanding* (London: A. Millar, 1748).

9   Plutarch, *Plutarch's Lives*, 11 vols, translated by Bernadotte Perrin (London: Heineman, 1917), V. 472.

10 Though a famous argument, (I think; therefore, I am), Descartes never enunciates it as such. Rather it works this way: Meditation II (A&T VII, 25–28):

    1. An evil deceiver tries to trick me or not – F
    2. [I] think or 'thinking' is – F
    3. [All verbs require subjects and objects] – F
    4. *I* exist without a deceiver – 2, 3
    5. If there is a deceiver he tries to trick *me* – A
    6. I exist with a deceiver – 3, 5
    ——————————————
    7. Deceiver or not I exist – 1, 4, 6

11 Descartes even wrote a book on creating these rules from the ground up, *Rules for the Direction of the Mind.*

12 Plato, *The Republic,* translated by G. M. A. Grube, rev. C. D. C. Reeve from *Plato: Complete Works,* ed. John M. Cooper and D. S. Hutchinson (Indianapolis, IN: *Hackett*, 1997), VII, 514a ff.

13 Plato is very systemic in this claim. He holds the same principle on the inferiority of imitation in the context of the creation of the universe, *Timaeus* 28b.

14 The sun can be understood as the form of the Good that acts to unite all other forms into a whole that is the object of all learning (Truth).

15 This has led some, such as Karl Popper to suggest that Plato is a champion of non-democratic forms of government, *aristocracy* (rule of the best – non-inherited). The mass of people (*hoi polloi*) are just not to be trusted because of the assumptions of the Divided Line: Karl R. Popper, *The Open Society and its Enemies*, 2 vols (New York: Harper & Row, 1962).

16 The Bell Curve is a controversial worldview construction. For a popular discussion of these issues see: Steve Fraser, ed., *The Bell Curve Wars: Race, Intelligences, and the Future of America* (New York: Basic Books, 1995) and Joe L. Kincheloe, Shirley R. Steinburg, and Aaron David Gresson (eds), *Measured Lies: The Bell Curve Examined* (New York: St. Martins, 1996).

17 This is a controversial point whether Nietzsche was noble or despotic (via his eliticism). For a discussion of some of these issues see: Christopher Hamilton, 'Nietzsche on Nobility and the Affirmation of Life', *Ethical Theory and Moral Practice: An International Forum*, 3.2 (2000): 169–193; Edith Erlich, 'Frederich Nietzsche: Der Mensch und die Maske', *Synthsis Philosophica*, 13.1 (1998): 253–268; Rod Coltman (ed. tr.), *A Century of Philosophy: Hans-Georg Gadamer in Conversation with Riccardo Dottori* (NY: Continuum, 2004); and Alan Gewirth, *Reason and Morality*

(Chicago: University of Chicago Press, 1978), pp. 30, 89.

18 Cf. Raskalnikov in Fyodor Dostoyevsky, *Crime and Punishment*, ed. tr. Jessie Coulson and George Gibian (New York: Norton, 1975).

19 *Of the Principles of Human Knowledge* (Dublin: A. Rhames for J. Pepyat, 1710), sections 3, 6, 22, 24, 33.

20 Of course, the tree may make a sound to some animal nearby. But the status of the animal's experience is subject to speculations aligned to the problem of other minds. Best here to only consider humans and God.

21 *Ibid.*, sections 30–33.

22 *Platonis Opera*, ed. John Burnet, vol. IV (Oxford: Oxford University Press, 1902): 27d 6 and 28a1, cf. 28a. My translation.

23 From *Republic* 509d–511e.

24 I also throw my hat into the ring at this level – see *The Extinction of Desire* (Oxford: Blackwell, 2007).

25 For example, one might point to religious teachers such as Jesus and Siddartha in this regard. They often taught in teasing stories that defied simple, direct interpretations. If Plato is right about the sources of knowledge, then any discourse at this level must, of necessity, be indirect.

26 Such as Jacques Derrida, *Writing and Difference,* translated by Alan Bass (Chicago: University of Chicago Press, 1980) and *Of Grammatology*, translated by Gayatri Chakravorty Spivak (Baltimore, MD: Johns Hopkins University Press, 1998).

27 For a different view of the relation between money and happiness see Michael Boylan, *The Extinction of Desire* (Oxford: Blackwell, 2007).

28 *Timaeus* 47b–d.

29 Some other prominent figures include the Stoics, many of the medieval philosophers, Descartes, Liebniz, Spinoza (among modern philosophers) and then largely the idealistic tradition (in the UK) and much of Continental philosophy post-Hegel.

30 *Categories*, 1b 20.

31 I am thankful to Richard McKeon for this rendition of the categories in conversation.

32 I note that though this is a traditional reconstruction of Aristotle's categories, it is unlikely that Socrates as a 70-year-old man (as per the date) would be white. Athens is near to the equator and would have been considerably darkened. There is even a tradition that says that Socrates came from Egypt and was Arab or Black. This thesis is discussed (in the negative) by Mary Lefkowitz, *Not out of Africa: How Afrocentricism became an Excuse to Teach Myth as History* (New York: Basic Books, 1997).

33 The big caveat here is that Aristotle explicitly did not embrace evolution (as set out by Empedocles). For a discussion of this see Michael Boylan,

Method and Practice in Aristotle's Biology (Washington, DC and London: UPA/Rowman Littlefield, 1983).

34   *Posterior Analytics*, 39b 23ff.

35   These causes often group together with the first two providing a mechanical/material account and the last two providing a teleological account, see Boylan, *Method and Practice in Aristotle's Biology*; R. J. Hankinson, *Cause and Explanation in Ancient Greek Thought* (Oxford: Clarendon, 2002); and Philip J. Van der Eijk, *Medicine and Philosophy in Classical Antiquity* (Cambridge: Cambridge University Press, 2005).

36   As already mentioned in Part II, the ancient empirics, the modern empiricists – Locke, Berkeley and Hume – and the nineteenth- and twentieth-century philosophers beginning with Reid through the philosophers of science are all contributing members of this tradition.

37   From the side of feminism as such see: Virginia Held, *Feminist Morality: Transforming Culture, Society, and Politics* (Chicago: University of Chicago Press, 1993); Alison Jaggar, *Feminist Politics and Human Nature* (Totowa, NJ: Roman and Allanheld, 1983); Nel Noddings, *Caring: A Feminine Approach to Ethics and Moral Education* (Berkeley, CA: University of California Press, 1984); Susan M. Wolf, *Feminism and Bioethics: Beyond Reproduction* (New York: Oxford, 1996); Rosemarie Tong, *New Perspectives in Healthcare Ethics* (Upper Saddle River, NJ: Prentice Hall, 2007).

From the side of exploring emotions, as such: Annette Baier, *Moral Prejudices: Essays on Ethics* (Cambridge: Harvard University Press, 1995); Simone de Beauvoir, *The Second Sex*, translated and edited by H.M. Parshley (New York: Bantam, 1952); Jon Elster, *Alchemies of the Mind: Rationality and the Emotions* (Cambridge: Cambridge University Press, 1999); Allan Gibbard, *Wise Choices, Apt Feelings: A Theory of Normative Judgment* (Oxford: Oxford University Press, 1990); Patricia Greenspan, *Practical Guilt: Moral Dilemmas, Emotions and Social Norms* (New York: Oxford University Press, 1995); William James, 'What is an Emotion?', *Mind* 19 (1884): 188–204; Robert Solomon, *The Passions: The Myth and Nature of Human Emotions* (New York: Doubleday, 1984); Richard Wollheim, *On the Emotions* (New Haven: Yale University Press, 1999).

38   The scholarly version of Aristotle is: Aristotle, *Arisotelis Opera*, ed. Immanuel Bekker, rpt. Berlin: de Gruyter (1960 [1831– 6]), Chapter 6 on *katharsis* and Chapter 13 on the definition of a tragic character.

6 Integrating Truth into the Quest

1   Obviously, this was only the most preliminary of questions. If one were evaluating being a successful businessperson as a way of becoming good, then other pivotal questions must also be asked in order to gather an adequate amount of data upon which the input of truth might inform upon

the good. The above is merely a beginning nod in that direction.

2   Not all religious epistemologists are advocates of the internalist perspective. Alvin Plantinga makes a case for an externalist understanding of religious epistemology in his *Warrant: The Current Debate* (Oxford: Oxford University Press, 1993) and *Warrant and Proper Function* (Oxford: Oxford University Press, 1993).

3   Sinclair Lewis, *Elmer Gantry* (New York: Harcourt Brace & Company, 1927).

4   Michael Boylan, *A Just Society* (Lanham, MD and Oxford: Rowman and Littlefield, 2004), p. 1.

5   Khaled Hosseini, *The Kite Runner* (NY: Riverhead, 2003).

6   This point has been a popular topic for years. For a couple of contemporary public media takes see Christine Halse, 'Writing/Reading a Life: The Rhetorical Practice of Autobiography', *Auto/Biography*, 14.2 (2006): 95 and Matthew Flamm, 'Truth, Fiction and Frey', *The Nation*, 282.6 (13 February 2006): 5.

7   I should note to readers that I do not hold this position. For an overview of this and other bioengineering issues see my co-authored book, *Genetic Engineering: Science and Ethics on the New Frontier* (Upper Saddle River, NJ: Prentice Hall, 2002).

8   Boylan, *A Just Society*, Chapter 4.

9   Among those in this situation are sociological groups that over-represent themselves in the poverty classification such as African Americans, Latino Americans, Native Americans, and those individuals who are undocumented yet trying to work in the United States.

10 This poll was taken by the Gallop organization for CNN/USA today within the United States between 10 and 12 March 2006.

11 This poll was taken by ICR, International Communications Research for the Henry J. Kaiser Family Foundation at Harvard and the *Washington Post*. The poll was taken between 20 March and 29 April 2006.

12 Plato makes a similar point in the *Statesman* 272c when he says that one may evaluate a society according to its commitment to philosophy as part of the public discourse.

7 Finding Out What is Beautiful – Classical Theories

1   Ernest Hemingway, *A Farewell to Arms* (New York: Scribners, 1929), p. 314.

2   Michael Boylan, *A Just Society* (Lanham, MD and Oxford: Rowman and Littlefield, 2004), p. 1.

3   An example of this are Zeno's paradoxes. For a discussion see Boylan, *A Just Society*, pp. 12–13.

4   See especially G. E. L. Owen, 'Zeno and the Mathematicians', *Proceedings*

of the Aristotelian Society, 58 (1957–58): 199–222; J. F. Thomson, 'Tasks and Super-Tasks', *Analysis,* 15 (1954): 1–13; Gregory Vlastos, 'A Note on Zeno's Arrow', *Phronesis,* 11 (1966): 3–18; Gregory Vlastos, 'Zero's Race Course', *Journal of the History of Philosophy,* 4 (1966): 95–108; James Watling, 'The Sum of an Infinite Series', *Analysis,* 13 (1953): 39ff.; Ian Mueller, *Philosophy of Mathematics and Deductive Structure in Euclid's 'Elements'* (Cambridge, MA: M.I.T. Press, 1981), p. 234; cf. T. L. Heath, 'Greek Geometry with special reference to Infinitesimals', *The Mathematical Gazette,* 11 (1922–1923): 248–259; Simplicius, *Commentary on Aristotle's Physics,* ed. H. Diets, 2 vols (Berlin, 1882, 1895). Simplicius gives an account of Antiphon's reasoning on page 54.2: 55–58.

5 I discuss these paradoxes in reference to worldview change in Boylan, *A Just Society,* pp. 12–13 and in *Basic Ethics* (Upper Saddle River, NJ: Prentice Hall), Chapter 8.

6 Henrik Ibsen, *An Enemy of the People,* tr. James McFarlane (Oxford: Oxford University Press, 1983), Act V.

7 *Republic* X, 603b–605c.

8 Michel Foucault, 'The Archaeology of Knowledge' in *The Archaeology of Knowledge and The Discourse on Language,* tr. A. M. Sheridan Smith (New York: Pantheon, 1972). Note, that I am not trying to make Foucault to be a theist but merely to say that the artist is subsumed by the message.

9 Hippocrates, 'Aphorisms' in *Hippocrates,* selections in four volumes, Vol. 4, edited and translated by W. H. S. Jones (London: Heineman, 1931).

10 Some, including myself, would assert that Aristotle's definition of human nature is too thin. Certainly, we may be the only animal on the planet with rational powers so highly developed. However, there may be more to being human than merely the actualization of these rational powers. For example, say we were to switch the starting point to 'desire to be good'. What would follow from this? Well, for one, anything else that would bring about being good – including various affective aspects of who we are – such as philosophical love. For more on this sort of argument see: Boylan, *A Just Society,* Ch. 2.

11 There are internal references to a work on comedy that (unfortunately) has not survived. For those readers who love to pine about such things, I strongly advise reading philosopher Umberto Eco's erudite novel *The Name of the Rose* (New York: Everyman, 2006 [1994]) in which the lost treatise plays a crucial role in this medieval murder mystery.

12 This, of course, puts emotion somewhere in the realm of reasoned parameters. For more on this see note 37 in Chapter 5.

13 Chapter 14, 'Pity and Fear Through Spectacle and Plot'.

   1 Pity (*eleeivov*) and Fear (*phobon*) may be stimulated by: (a) the spectacle of the production or (b) by the arrangement of incidents – A

2 [The amount of sensory stimulation necessary to produce pity and fear is rather gory and monstrous] – A

3 When pity and fear are stimulated by spectacle the play risks being monstrous (sensational) – 2

4 Stimulating pity and fear through the arrangement of incidents will appeal to reason – F

5 [Reason is hidden and therefore less likely to be monstrous (sensational)] – A

6 It would be better to stimulate pity and fear by the arrangement of incidents than by spectacle – 1, 3, 4, 5

7 The arrangement of incidents may involve: (a) friends, (b) enemies, (c) those neither friend nor enemy – F

8 The discord between enemies is well deserved – F

9 [Pity and fear are aroused only through actions based partially upon desert] – F (earlier argument)

10 The discord between enemies will not stimulate pity and fear – 8, 9

11 The discord between those who are neither friend nor enemy is without desert – A

12 The discord between those who are neither friend nor enemy will not stimulate pity and fear – 8, 11

13 The discord between friends is based partially upon desert – A

14 The discord between friends (or family, e.g. Clytemestra being killed by Orestes) is the only arrangement of incidents that stimulates pity and fear – 7, 10, 12, 8, 13

15 The act itself can be performed in knowledge (as when Medea kills her children) or in ignorance (as when Oedipus kills his father and marries his mother) – F

16. The best sort of plot is when the incidents arouse pity and fear through an action that is knowingly or unknowingly performed between friends or loved ones – 6, 14, 15

8 Finding Out What is Beautiful – Modern Theories

1 Chapter 49, AK 315–316, B. 159; Rudolf H. Weingertner, 'A Note on Kant's Artistic Interests', *Journal of Aesthetics and Art Criticism*, 16 (1957): 261–262.

2 *Kritik der reinen Vernunft* in *Kants Werke* Akademie Textausgabe vol. 4 (Berlin: Walter de Gruyter & Co, 1968 [1781).

3 The traditional translation for *Kritik der Urteilskraft* could usefully be amended as the Critique of the Power of Judging. What is important here is to ascertain the grounds for making any judgements about beauty. The text referred to here is Principal text: Kant, *Critique of Judgment*, tr. J. H. Bernard (New York: Macmillan/Hafner Press, 1951), *Kritik der Urtheil-*

skraft in *Kants Werke* Akademie Textausgabe vol. 5 (Berlin: Walter de Gruyter & Co, 1968 [1790]).

4   Immanuel Kant, *Kritik der reinen Vernunft* (Berlin: Walter de Gruyter & Co., 1968 [1781/1904], A70, B95.

5   The dynamics of colonialism are enormous. A few recent books on various aspects of unjustified universalization include: Muhammad Sani Umar, *Islam and Colonialism* (Leiden: Brill, 2006); William Roger Louis, *Ends of British Imperialism: The Scramble for Empire, Suez, and Decolonialization* (New York: Palgrave, 2006), Hamid Irbouh, *Art in the Service of Colonialism* (London: L. B. Tauris, 2005); and Ann Renée Cramer, *Cash, Color, and Colonialism* (Norman, OK: University of Oklahoma Press, 2005).

6   David Hume, *An Enquiry Concerning Human* Understanding, ed. Eric Steinberg (Indianapolis, IN: Hackett, 1977 [1748]), especially XII.2 and 3, pp. 107–114.

7   David Hume, 'Of the Standard of Taste' in *Of the Standard of Taste and Other* Essays, ed. John W. Lenz (Indianapolis, IN: Bobbs-Merrill, 1965 [1742]).

8   From *Don Quixote*, Part II, Ch. 13. The example is that there are two experts asked to evaluate a hogshead of wine. The first said it was fine except for a faint leathery taste. The second said it was fine except for a faint taste of iron. It was found that at the bottom of the cask was a key with a leather thong.

9   *Enquiry*, IV.2, p. 22ff.

10 William Strunk and E. B. White, *The Elements of Style*, 4th edn (New York: Longmans, 1999 [1918]).

11 Some might contend that, in the realm of fiction, handbooks are rather more difficult. Of course, there are several classics such as John Gardner's *The Art of Fiction* (New York: Vintage, 1991), but there seems to be less unanimity on these as guidebooks to successful style.

12 For example, Hume's argument against miracles in *Enquiry* II.x.

13 Samuel Taylor Coleridge, *Biographia Literaria and Aesthetical Essays*, ed. J. Shawcross 2 vols (Oxford: Oxford University Press, 1949 [1817]), Chs 13–14.

14 Shelley's most prominent poems include 'Prometheus Unbound', 'Hymn to Intellectual Beauty', 'Mont Blan'c, and 'Ozymandius'. His fiction and non-fiction writing can be found in his collected works, ten volumes edited by Roger Ingpen and Walter E. Peck (New York: Scribners, 1926–1930). On a personal note, readers should be aware that Shelley was a free thinker who wrote a tract advocating atheism and alternative family arrangements. His wife, Mary Godwin (daughter of Mary Wollstonecroft and William Godwin – both free thinkers in their own right), was later to write the gothic novel *Frankenstein*, the introduction to which was written by Percy.

15   John Keats's doctrine of negative capability is very similar to what Shelley is advocating. In both, the viewer is transported into the worldview of the artist or narrator so that he/she might be transported into another way of approaching and solving the problems of the world. For a current understanding of this concept in the context of Keats see Christoph Bode, 'Hyperion, The Fall of Hyperion, and Keats's Poetics', *Wordsworth Circle*, 31.1 (2000): 31–37.

16   Emile Zola, 'J'Acuse: Lettre au Président de la République', *L'Aurore* (13 January 1898).

17   Upton Sinclair, *The Jungle* (New York: Doubleday, Page, and Co., 1906); Ralph Ellison, *Invisible Man* (New York: Random House, 1952); Elie Wiesel, *Night*, tr. Stella Rodway (New York: Pyramid Books, 1961); Charles Johnson, *Oxherding Tale* (Bloomington, IN: Indiana University Press, 1982).

18   Friedrich Nietzsche, *The Birth of Tragedy*, tr. Raymond Geuss and Ronald Speirs (Cambridge: Cambridge University Press, 1999).

19   Clive Bell, *Art* (London: Trafalgar Square, 1927 [1914]).

20   Samuel Johnson, *Lives of the English Poets*, 2 vols (London: Henry Froede, 1906 [1779, 1781]), p.13ff.

21   Sir Herbert Grierson, *The Poems of John Donne* (London: Oxford University Press, 1912).

22   My inference is that the other way around, viz., that the significant form by itself stimulates the aesthetic emotion, is prone to the suggested problems. I am offering a way to read Bell that will solve these objections.

23   Monroe Beardsley, *Aesthetics: Problems in the Philosophy of Criticism*, 2nd edn (Indianapolis, IN: Hackett, 1981).

24   Martin Heidegger, 'The Origin of the Work of Art" in *Poetry, Language, and Thought*', tr. Albert Hofstadter (New York: HarperCollins, 1971).

25   These concepts are first set out by Heidegger in *Being and Time*, tr. Joan Stanbauch (Albany, New York: SUNY Press, 1996 [1927]).

26   *Ibid.*; cf. Martin Heidegger, *Hegel's Concept of Experience*, tr. Kenley Royce Dove (New York: Harper and Row, 1970) and *Introduction to Metaphysics*, tr. Gregory Fried (New Haven, CT: Yale University Press, 2000).

27   A personal anecdote illustrates this. In a discussion period at a conference at Villanova University, I pointed out a contradiction in his presented argument and Derrida replied, 'So what? Isn't life a little more fun that way?' He both meant and did not mean this. Part of his strategy was (like Socrates) pedagogical.

28   It is instructive to compare this function of the 'Play of differences' to others in his tradition. For Gadamer is the activity of interpreting. For Saussure it is the linking of objective seminological functions.

29   Ferdinard de Saussure, *Course in General Linguistics* (New York: McGraw Hill, 1966 [1916]).

30 'Plato's Pharmacy' is a key essay from *La Disséminations* (Paris: Éditions du Seuil, 1972).

31 Prodicus of Ceos made careful verbal distinctions that amounted to nothing (nominalism – according to Plato). He also worked on morality (see Xenophon, *Memorabilia* II.1 21–34). He is a supporting actor in Plato's *Protagoras*.

32 This example was given to me in conversation by Simon Blackburn.

9 The Quest for the Beautiful

1 Let me make it clear that I believe that individual artists can participate in more than one of these amalgams in the course of their career.

2 Of course there are always those playful souls such as Gerhard Richter who pretends to offer a photographic presentation on one level until the audience observes that part of it is out of focus. For more on Richter, see Kai-Uwe Hemken, *Gerhard Richter: 18 Oktober 1977: Eine Kunst-Monographie* (Berlin: Insel Verlag, 1998).

3 Since this is thought to be one of the early English language Haiku poems, we must consider the first line to be an enjambment of a seven-syllable first line with a five-syllable second line: the apparition of these/faces in the crowd/petals on a wet, black bough. Under this reading, the entire interest is upon the two sorts of apparition: faces in the crowd and petals (presumably cherry blossoms) on a wet black bough. The contrast between bustling and unnatural (the Métro) and the natural (short-lived cherry blossoms) makes for a robust Apollo-style interaction.

4 This is a difficult question. Much of it is trade proprietary. However, what I have been able to determine via a biased source (the Romance Writers of America) is that the fiction-reading public in the USA during 2005 breaks out as: romance = 39.3 per cent, mystery = 29.6 per cent, science fiction = 6.4 per cent. Thus 75.3 per cent of fiction sold in the USA according to this survey was genre. Less than 25 per cent was not. Source: www.storyforu.com. Accessed on 20 December 2006.

5 In contemporary moral philosophy there is a deep divide between the anti-realists who adhere to a programme of analysis of language and others (realists – like myself). Since the anti-realists do not believe that there is a real basis for moral or truth or beauty claims, as such, they deflate these options and embrace intuitionism as their garb. For a contemporary exponent of this position see Simon Blackburn, *Truth: A Guide* (Oxford: Oxford University Press, 2005).

6 From the social construct side see Helen Longino, *The Fate of Knowledge* (Princeton, NJ: Princeton University Press, 2002). From the nature side and his 'memes' see Richard Dawkins, *The Ancestor's Tale: A pilgrimage to the Dawn of Evolution* (Boston: Houghton Mifflin, 2004).

7   Those who deflate the correspondence theory of truth – such as Donald
     Davidson, *Inquiries into Truth and Interpretation* (Oxford: Clarendon
     Press, 2001) and Blackburn, *Truth*, do so because they believe that all that
     we can really know is found in coherence or pragmatic theories of truth.

8   At times, Western philosophy has fallen prey to such esoteric rights. At the
     end of the medieval period, complex nominalism held sway such that only
     a very small number might count themselves as appreciating the presenta-
     tion. Whenever philosophy becomes too esoteric, it isolates itself to only
     the sophisticated pattern makers – whether it is medieval philosophy or
     contemporary analytic or Continental philosophy.

9   Georg Wilhelm Friedrich Hegel, *The Philosophy of Right*, tr. T. M. Knox
     (Oxford: Clarendon Press, 1942); Michael Oakeshott, 'The Tower of
     Babel' in *Rationalism in Politics* (London: Methuen & Co., 1962); and
     Alan Donagan, *The Theory of Morality* (Chicago: University of Chicago
     Press, 1977).

10   I hope it is clear to readers the high regard in which I hold Iris Murdoch.

11   Notice that I say, 'preferred perspective'. I think that in certain contexts,
     each of these four can be very useful in our quest for beauty. When one
     adopts a preferred standpoint this does not exclude other standpoints
     under different descriptive conditions.

12   This is an anecdotal point of shared community worldview. My African
     American friends (to a person) believe that the Emancipation Proclamation
     was only the first step towards freedom and equal rights in America.

13   A standard repository of American slave songs can be found in William
     Francis Allen, *Slave Songs of the United States* (New York: P. Smith, 1951).
     The case for double meanings is discussed by: Gavin Jones, 'Signifying
     Songs: The Double Meaning of Black Dialect in the Work of George
     Washington Cable', *American Literary History*, 9.2 (1997): 244–267; and
     in reference to 'Steal Away' and other Underground Railroad songs at the
     Kentucky Underground Railroad site: http://www.ket.org/underground/
     resources/music.htm (last accessed 20 December 2006).

14   Alex Haley, *Roots* (New York: Doubleday, 1976).

15   Some might contend that I am not talking about defence, but about
     escape. Under this approach, art is an escape that may help one cope, but
     does not assist in coming to terms with essential issues that might change
     the underlying conditions. This is an interesting argument. If one were to
     accept it, Art would descend from basic goods level-one to at least level-two
     (if not below that).

16   Boylan, *Just* (2004), Chapter 7.

17   Stories, poetry, and drama were crucial to those in camps and those after-
     wards as the world tried to make sense of such unthinkable horror. Some
     examples include: Elie Wiesel, *Night*, tr. Marion Wiesel (New York: Hill &

Wang, 2006 [1958]); Primo Levi, *Survival in Auschwitz*, tr. Stuart Woolf (New York: Simon & Schuster, 1958); Sylvia Rothchild, ed., *Voices from the Holocaust* (New York: New American Library, 1981); Nelly Sachs, *Selected Poems Including the Verse Play, Eli*, tr. Michael Hamburger (New York: Farrar Straus & Giroux, 1967); Tadeusz Borowski, *This Way for the Gas, Ladies & Gentlemen*. Ed. tr. Barbara Vedder (New York: Penguin, 1976).

18 By 'explicit' here, I mean the exact instructions on how to construct a bomb and a link to how to obtain the materials (by definition, an illegal act). The assumption is that no one would want to go through such trouble unless s/he wanted to use it. A base-like Hiroshima-type weapon can kill 200,000. More sophisticated weapons can triple or quadruple that figure depending on where it is detonated. There are also the casualties in extending concentric circles for hundreds of miles who may suffer severe radiation poisoning or potential birth defects. This is a clear and present danger.

19 I make this argument with Kevin Brown in *Genetic Engineering* (Upper Saddle River, NJ: Prentice Hall, 2002).

20 Two current books that discuss the issue of prior restraint in the context of the American judicial system are David Rudenstine, *The Day the Presses Stopped: A History of the Pentagon Papers Case* (Berkeley, CA: University of California Press, 1996) and Frank Snepp, *Irreparable Harm: A Firsthand Account of How one Agent took on the CIA in an Epic Battle over Secrecy and Free Speech* (New York: Random House, 1999).

21 Where the archetypical Joneses represent our peer group.

Index

12